The Pl
Divide

The Play Versus Story Divide in Game Studies

Critical Essays

Edited by
MATTHEW WILHELM KAPELL

McFarland & Company, Inc., Publishers
Jefferson, North Carolina

ALSO OF INTEREST AND FROM MCFARLAND

The Fantastic Made Visible: Essays on the Adaptation of Science Fiction and Fantasy from Page to Screen, edited by Matthew Wilhelm Kapell and Ace G. Pilkington (2015)

The Films of James Cameron: Critical Essays, edited by Matthew Wilhelm Kapell and Stephen McVeigh (2011)

Star Trek *as Myth: Essays on Symbol and Archetype at the Final Frontier,* edited by Matthew Wilhelm Kapell (2010)

ISBN 978-0-7864-9723-2 (softcover : acid free paper) ∞
ISBN 978-1-4766-2309-2 (ebook)

LIBRARY OF CONGRESS CATALOGUING DATA ARE AVAILABLE

British Library cataloguing data are available

Front cover illustration © 2016 Pixtawan/iStock

Printed in the United States of America

*McFarland & Company, Inc., Publishers
Box 611, Jefferson, North Carolina 28640
www.mcfarlandpub.com*

To the memory of

Boris Siddhartha Kapell
and
Nikita Nikolaievich Narovchatov.

We were on a quest together so I'm sure
we'll respawn in the same place.

Lude cum relinquere

Acknowledgments

The various contributors all aided in the making of this book, and they each deserve credit for all the good here. Robert Mejia was especially helpful with possible titles. At my most local academic library, Woodland Community College, Dena Martin and her staff tracked down a number of works used in both the introduction and conclusion. Andrew B.R. Elliott, who I previously edited a game studies book with, offered ongoing moral support from his home in Lincoln, England. Amy Kapell never once got angry when I worked weekends, and kept making spaghetti. Zoe B. Sluka-Kapell taught me about games in depth.

Ace G. Pilkington, a colleague and friend, was more helpful than he let on in this process. I'm still not going to tell him why, but thank you. John Shelton Lawrence, long-time friend and colleague, commented on early drafts of various parts of this work and his insight, as is always the case, makes me feel like an inept undergrad yet again. He has my ongoing thanks.

Contents

Introduction

The Ludic and Narrative as
Dialectic About "What Games Do"

MATTHEW WILHELM KAPELL

Scholars often cite the dictum that "academic fights are so vicious because the stakes are so low." Since the advent of postmodernism in the 1960s and 1970s those fights have shown intensity. Those of us who came of age during the rise of postmodern approaches in our own discipline—whether in the humanities or the social sciences—became used to having faculty members in our departments who would not talk to each other—no matter how closely related their specializations. Dropping the name of a French theorist at the wrong moment, or to the wrong senior professor, reputedly could derail a graduate student's progress. Conferences in literature, film, sociology, anthropology, history, and other disciplines were marked by self-segregated groups of scholars. On one side of the hotel lobby would be scholars talking of Jürgen Habermas or Jacques Derrida and on the other would be those speaking of Marvin Harris or Noam Chomsky. For a couple of decades in many departments, such schisms could only be solved by retirement.

At present in digital game studies the debate between those who focus on "play" and those who look to "story" does not conform to this "vicious" model—indeed, it is barely a debate at all. The last generation of traditionalists and the various kinds of "posties" found communication difficult. I personally witnessed one scholar throw a full teacup at another at a conference in the 1990s—the argument was about the nature of "cultural truth."

Scholars approaching video games from the perspective of story (narratologists), or of play (ludologists), mostly shared coffee or beer and casually discussed their individual paradigms. This is not always the case, of course.

1

The ludologists, especially, have been given to occasional outbursts against "narrative" in general—but they have done so with exceptionally poor understanding of that which they were attacking. As Jan Simons noted in 2007, "the issues at stake seem to have been blissfully ignored rather than resolved, as testified by the occasional outburst of anti-narratologism," and while Simons offers a rather extensive list of words used against narratologists by the best-known ludologists he is quick to also point out that this is mostly about "their efforts to carve out a niche on the already highly varied and constantly changing palette of the humanities" than it is an acrimonious attack (Simons).

So, aside from Simons' list of well-known ludologists, in digital game studies the two sides of the major debate have argued politely and listened carefully. They have tried to learn from each other's positions, and they have tried to be respectful when they disagreed. Yet, as Gerald Voorhees notes, this is nonetheless a debate that is about "an effort to define and thereby control the nature of the field" (Voorhees 9). For the ludologists the final position is rather simple: digital games are new. The cybernetic relationship between a player or players and the game program represents a new form of human activity and scholars should concentrate on game mechanics, the program/human interface, and decision trees. For narratologists digital games are merely one more stage that extends back at least to Aristotle's writing on drama if not, more generally, to the very origins of our species. Digital games are one more type of storytelling that can be traced from before Homer to current novelists and filmmakers.

The ludic approach advocates a split of game studies away from previous forms of storytelling while the narrativists see a new format of ongoing media types. This is at once an epistemological and ontological debate—and one that matters a great deal. But no tea has been hurled.

This makes the debate between the so-called "story people" and "play people" in game studies almost unique for its congeniality—and its seeming lack of concern to control the field of discourse. The congeniality also hides a problem in the conceptualization of these two perspectives. It is one this book hopes to address.

The Ludic and the Narrative: An Emergent Dichotomy and a Debate that Never Took Place

Coming, as they mostly did, from disciplines that emphasized narrative, scholars in digital game studies began with an emphasis on "story." But when new people, such as prominent ludologists Jesper Juul and Espen Aarseth entered the fray, the question of whether "story" was the correct approach to the study of digital games became central to the emerging field. Since this volume hopes to clarify the conflict between the major viewpoints they are quickly set forth here—but what comes is not intended as a comprehensive examination of the ludology/narratology divide.

Humanities scholars with backgrounds in literature or film initially answered the question of "what games do" by turning to the embedded stories. Henry Jenkins, a scholar of both pedagogy and media, offered that "games fit within a much older tradition of spatial stories, which have often taken the form of hero's odysseys, quest myths, or travel narratives" (Jenkins 119). "Narrative," after all, is a term that most English speakers know quite well. And, "narratives," in general, are something with which all members of all cultures are familiar. So, an understanding of games could be found in the stories: getting little Frogger across the road, Pitfall Harry's need to find various treasures in the deep jungle, or the saving of a princess by Mario, or Link, or ... well, that would be a long list of princess-saving games. But, with a long and detailed description of narrative paths, it was hoped, the understanding of "what games do" could be approached.

The inherent sexism of "saving princesses" aside, the examination of game stories—even when they were as simple as the moment-by-moment avoidance of asteroids or the attempt to prevent cities from falling prey to space invaders or nuclear missiles—presented a useful approach for a coherent examination of what was happening in a game.

But, as useful as such an approach is, it makes sense, even if the "final conclusions" are not all that final. It also omitted something—namely, what the player does. As ludologist Gonzalo Frasca put it in a more general context, "electronic texts can be better understood if they are analyzed as cybernetic systems" (Frasca, "Simulation" 223). What he meant, of course, is that in emphasizing only the game's story the question of what the player of the game is doing is shunted aside. Alexander R. Galloway's phrase describes it more forcefully: "video games are not just images or stories or play or games, but *actions*" (Galloway 36; original emphasis). Ignoring the player, for those interested in the ludic approach—and even for those just interested in a holistic understanding of digital games—meant ignoring a major part of the process.

These two approaches could have set the stage for a standard, and possibly acrimonious, academic debate. But it never happened. As Gonzalo Frasca could put it in 2003, it was a debate that "never took place" (Frasca, "Ludologists"). Frasca would note that, at least in part, the debate did not happen because the terms of the debate were never set. It was built on too many "misunderstandings, mistakes and prejudices" and, as a result, both sides retreated to overly general understandings of the other and claimed that no debate was necessary (*ibid.*). And, with such poorly defined terms came the issue that, as scholar Shawn Edrei notes, "not every game has a story to tell" (Edrei 97). The ludologists saw games, Steven E. Jones put it, as "cultural practices descended from go or chess rather than *Gilgamesh* or Chaucer" (Jones 4). And, of course, narratologists looked precisely to Gilgamesh, or Chaucer, or—likely far more appropriately—to using games for, as I've put it elsewhere (with Andrew B.R. Elliot), "mythic purposes" (Kapell and Elliott 363). In short, they looked to Jenkins' accounts of "hero's odysseys, quest myths, or travel narratives"—that is, "stories."

　　Perhaps because of the comparative newness of the discipline individuals on different sides of the debates decided not to debate. So, the conditions were set for a vigorous argument and paradigm-building action that did not happen. Yet, it is possible to claim, as Jesper Juul does, that

> Video game studies have so far been a jumble of disagreements and discussions with no clear outcomes, but this need not be a problem. The discussions have often taken the form of simple dichotomies, and though they are unresolved, they remain focal points in the study of games. The most important conflicts here are games versus players, rules versus fiction, games versus stories, games versus broader culture, and game ontology versus game aesthetics [Juul 11].

At the same time, however, while those dichotomies exist—especially in terms of "games versus stories"—they have never been fraught—or fought—dichotomies.

　　Yet, while narrative approaches remained popular—often more popular than ludic approaches to scholars specifically outside of game studies—the ludological methods did find a strong place. As I've (writing with Andrew B.R. Elliot, again) noted elsewhere, the "ludic nature" of games "obliges us to understand them differently ... [and] also recognizes the importance of play as a human activity" (Elliott and Kapell 3). "Ludic," as a term, has achieved popularity among scholars of digital games, but narrative approaches do translate outside the discipline better. And this insider/outsider perspective might be worth just a little time considering.

　　Perhaps it is because narrative is a more commonly understood word. Perhaps is has more to do with the fact that *ludus*, from the Latin, may mean "play," but it means the kind of spontaneous play of children suddenly breaking into a game of tag or hide-and-seek. It does not imply the planned and organized play of digital games. Or, perhaps, it is just a post-postmodern turn against "another new bit of jargon to learn." But, in other disciplines this kind of "debate-that-isn't-a-debate" has happened before and it may behoove scholars to consider how such debates turned out in the long-term when considering a similar long-term for the study of digital games.

The Division

The division between narrative and play in game studies has a precursor in other disciplines. But, all-too-often, those precursors offer a history to learn from that game studies scholars prefer to ignore when fighting for the "newness" of their field. When, for example, Edward Wesp worries that using "narrative" could lead to the "misapplication of principles taken from literary or film theory" in ways that would refuse to note the "radical departure" of games from previous media, he is arguing about a dichotomy and coming down squarely on one side of the argument—the side that implies the field is wholly new (Wesp). Yet, as Marie-Laure Ryan called for in the very first issue of *Game Studies*, such distinctions are mostly derived from a very specific definition of "narrative" almost designed to ignore the possibility of inclusion in game studies: "The inability of literary narratology to account for the experience of games does not mean that we should throw away the concept of narrative in ludology" (Ryan). However, as much as ludologists ever attempted to account for such issues, Jan Simons is correct when he notes, "Because ... ludologists sometimes seem to have lost sight of such subtle distinctions [about theory] their arguments against narrative and narratology have often been unnecessarily unconvincing" (Simons).

But, as noted at the beginning of this introduction, Simons also noted that the "debate," such as it has been, has "blissfully ignored" the issues at stake (Simons) since the middle of the oughts. It may be obvious, by this point, that while this introduction and this volume comes down on the side that narrative is important—and that the occasional ludological attacks on narrative both miss the point and are driven overly much by a desire to prove a "newness" of the field—another point is to accept what ludology brings to the study of games and ask scholars of the ludological perspective to try to learn from the mistakes of similar debates in other disciplines in the past.

In other words, it is hoped that the ludic paradigm, designed as it is to support claims of the "radical departure" of digital games and thus ignore two or more millennia of narrative theory, should at least attempt to learn from academic debates that followed a similar pattern.

The Emic/Etic Debate in Linguistics and Anthropology Applied to Game Studies

In the middle of the 1950s University of Michigan linguist Kenneth L. Pike decided to invent a new kind of terminology in an attempt to understand the relationship between the languages he studied and the cultures that employed those languages. For Pike the problem was a simple one. Listeners of a foreign language often could not determine sound variations that carried with them, to native speakers, cultural meaning. Deriving his terms from phonetics (the sounds of a language) and phonemics (the meanings of those sounds), Pike offered the notion of "etic" and "emic" units—that is, units of cultural expression that were obvious to an outsider, and units understood only from within the culture (cf. Pike, *Language* 37–45). Pike would build on both the etic and emic meanings of language and culture by reducing, as much as possible, everything to their basic syntactic units—which he would eventually call a tagmeme (Pike and Pike 8–11).

In doing so he hoped to do what game studies scholars do: find patterns of meaning. When a ludologist looks for cybernetic similarities between games, or actions within them, or a narratologists looks for equally similar translatable narrative structures, both are attempting to do what Pike offered more than half a century ago:

> No pattern can occur in isolation, autonomous from a larger kind of context or set of assumptions, and still be meaningful to human beings. Patterns require larger contexts, with relevance to more inclusive patterns, if they are themselves to be meaningful to us. The total autonomy of parts of knowledge does not exist [Pike, *Talk, Thought* 55].

It should be obvious the metaphor I hope to draw here. For Pike, the emic perspective became the "insider's" perspective, and could only be understood by direct action on the part of the user of a language. The etic perspective was the "outsider's" perspective. Pike believed both perspectives were inherently necessary for both good social science and real understanding.

In much the same way this volume offers that both ludic and narrative approaches are fully required in order to understand digital games. The "debate that never happened" (other than for the occasional ludologist's "outburst") is a debate that *needs* to happen. In ignoring the debate we are putting the utility of game studies at risk—perhaps not amongst ourselves, but certainly in the larger context of the academy and culture in general.

For Pike this was a debate he welcomed as well, and it only happened in fits and starts and then, largely, faded away. While Pike's ideas were adopted in both linguistics and anthropology, they were "debated" for three decades with seriously decreasing verve. But it is in anthropology that the terms had their greatest influence—though they were almost universally misunderstood in terms of Pike's original meaning. In anthropology the terms emic and etic were eventually dispensed with in favor of, simply, calling these the "insider's" and "outsider's" view. In much the same way, the ludic and narrative perspectives operate on similar levels. As Pike noted, there was a tendency to assume a dichotomy between the emic and etic when, in fact, they "do not constitute a rigid dichotomy of bits of data, but often present the same data from two points of view" (Pike, *Language* 41). To understand a ludic view of a game one must play it—one must be a "participant-observer" in anthropological terms. But to take a wider view it is easier to look for larger—narrative-based— cues that can be examined from game to game. Yet, in both cases, the object of study remains constant and it is only the perspective of the observer that has changed.

Pike, later in his career, offered that an "emic unit, in my view, is a physical or mental item or system treated by insiders as relevant to their system of behavior and as the same emic unit in spite of etic variability" (Pike, "Emics" 28). The classic example of what Pike meant comes from Chinese, but the American example may be somewhat more fruitful here. Where a person from Oregon might say "gah-rahge" to express the structure they park their car in, a person from Boston might pronounce the same word as "gare-ege." But all speakers of American English hear the same emic category while an external listener may have trouble in realizing they are hearing the same word pronounced in two different dialects (Kapell).

In much the same way ludic examinations excel at understanding an emic perspective of games—even multiple but similar games—while narratologists are finding data more translatable to outside understanding—that is, to non– game studies scholars, or, to etic comprehension. Pike put this point as you would expect a mid-century linguist trained by Edward Sapir:

> [E]mic units of a language must be determined during the analysis of that language; they must be discovered, not predicted.... The etic criteria may often be considered absolute, or measurable directly. Emic criteria are relative to the internal characteristics of the system, and can be usefully described or measured [only] relative to each other [Pike, *Language* 37–8].

Admittedly, I am not attempting to argue that the emic and etic units of Pike easily translate, wholesale, into the ludic and narrative units of game studies scholars. I am noting, however, that there is the possibility of deep metaphor in the system. In fact, of two deep metaphors. First, the emic and etic units first offered by Pike were useful ways to examine other language and cultures and, when adopted by other scholars, were turned into a rigid dichotomy which radically decreased their usefulness. Secondly, the debate that circled around Pike's terms followed exceptionally similar lines of argument as the debate around the ludic and narrative ideas in games studies. In the end that debate for Pike meant that the terms would be jettisoned from both linguistics and anthropology, and this book exists as a caution so that the same does not happen in games studies.

Pike's argument for his emic classification, which he called "knowledge of a local culture" similar to the act of riding a bicycle, was an attempt to understand "how to act without necessarily knowing how to analyze [one's] action." Similar to the ability to defeat a specifically difficult action within a specific game, in which stopping to think of one's actions will make success more difficult if not impossible, Pike offered that "[w]hen I act, I act as an insider; but to know, in detail, how I act (e.g., muscle movements), I must secure help from an outside disciplinary system. To use emics of ... behavior I must act like an insider; to analyze my own acts, I must look at ... material as an outsider" (Pike, "Emics" 33–4).

By now it should not be a surprise that this is how I conceptualize our debate in game studies. To understand a game one must play it, but to understand it one must also understand—when available, since not all games contain a story—its larger narrative context. Additionally, that larger narrative context tends to be the aspect of the game more easily explained to scholars outside of our field—that it, it tends to be more etically-centered and, thus, translatable.

At the same time, however, there is a reason most readers may not be wholly familiar with the terms. The debate around emic and etic became a simple dichotomy of insider and outsider, and then it faded away into near nothingness. Pike entitled a major section of his *magnum opus* on the topic, "Caution—Not a Dichotomy," but most linguists and anthropologists read it as, wholly, dichotomous (Pike, Language 41–44).

In fact only one anthropologist—borrowing Pike's terms in the early 1960s, attempted to make an actual "debate" happen. Marvin Harris, who gained some popularity in the 1970s writing popular anthropology for mass audiences, declared himself early on for "science"—and by science, he meant the etic approach. "Pike," he eventually declared,

> sees etics solely as a means of access to a participant's world of meaning ... he does not believe that it is possible or desirable for any community of observers to understand or explain human social life by attempting to strengthen and enlarge their etic preconceptions. I, on the other hand, believe that unless a community of observers is prepared to do just that ... anthropology will never achieve its scientific potential [Harris 50].

The debate between Pike and Harris would last from the early 1960s until a special section on the topic was called for at the annual American Anthropological Association meeting in 1988. However, by the time Harris and Pike meant to hash out their positions the debate was all but dead. In part this was due to their long-standing refusal to really argue out the issues. Rather, they politely disagreed, taught their students to ignore the debate, and saw it wholly swallowed in both linguistics and anthropology by postmodernism. In 1970 a student in anthropology or linguistics learned of the emic and etic views. By the middle of the 1990s this was not the case at all.

This is my fear for our debate in game studies. This book, then, is a call for a pitched argument, a more careful setting of the terms of that argument, and a recognition that the ludic and the narrative are not, in actuality, two sides of a coin, but that each offers an underlying structure of the other.

That is, the ludic and the narrative do not offer a dichotomy but, rather, a dialectic.

Emic and Etic, Ludic and Narrative, and the Dialectic

For both Pike and Harris the emic/etic debate was an important one. For Pike the interest was in uncovering exactly what the users of a language meant culturally. For Harris the tool was useful for uncovering cultural universals and thus bolstering his position that anthropology could be a real science. Neither the linguist nor the anthropologist thought of their debate as one of diametrically opposed positions, but just necessary viewpoints for an observer. Pike, specifically, labored to make his position known as non-dichotomous. For linguists and anthropologists more generally, however, the debate was initially important, then marginalized, and then reduced to a simple dichotomy. Either one was an "insider"—a person born to a culture and language tradition—or one was an "outsider"—a person trying to understand from the outside what the language and culture were all about. For two or three generations students in both fields were taught of the emic and etic as opposing perspectives. When anthropological linguist Dell H. Hymes noted that "much of their popularity [as terms], has indeed been due to their being assimilated to a dichotomy" (Hymes 120), the debate was being increasingly marginalized in both fields as postmodern paradigms engulfed it.

To put it another way, because the debate was not intensely fought it was easily reduced to simplified terms, and then marginalized, and is now largely forgotten.

But both linguistics and anthropology had decades or centuries of disciplinary history to sustain them when this particular debate evaporated. Game studies does not have that kind of institutional bedrock to rest upon.

Hymes tried to save the debate—and the terms—in the late 1980s by returning to their dialectical roots. His formulation was complex, and there is no need to revisit it here in detail. But, for Hymes, it was possible to see the emic and etic approaches in a way designed to build to new perspectives, where the "'[e]tic$_1$'—'emic'—'etic$_2$' constitute a dialectic" (Hymes 121). These two etic perspectives, drawn from Pike, allowed Hymes to see the observer's "initial frame of reference" and "reconsideration" of that frame due to emic considerations (*ibid.*).

A similar approach could easily be taken in game studies—though not, I think obviously, as a structurally complete and linear dialectic such as that espoused by both Pike and Hymes. However, each scholar in game studies (and most of the contributors here) could use the perspective of the ludic to uncover further meaning of the narrative, or the opposite and use the story to elucidate the significance of the mechanics of gameplay. As Pike declared of his own debate with Harris, though, there should be *"no sharp dividing line* between the stages" (Pike, "Pike's Reply" 62; original emphasis).

This work offers much the same idea. The dividing line between the narratological and ludological perspectives in game studies is no sharp dividing line. However, as attendance at general conferences that include sections on game studies, and conferences specific to game studies as an emergent field, continue to build upon the area's very recent history, the ludic/narrative division is stated as relatively sharp in casual conversation. Returning to Hymes, again, we can discover what may be the tragic flaw in scholars simply being able to say to each other as such conferences, "I'm doing a ludic analysis" in a way that implies a sharper division than should exist. Hymes put it this way:

> When the issues of "emic" and "etic" are treated as *passé*, they appear to me to treat the craft of anthropology [and linguistics] as *passé*.... Let me conclude by saying that these matters are not matters of anthropology and linguistics alone.... The craft of linguistic ethnography, of patient attention and discovery, of teasing out of pattern, of willingness to watch, listen, and be surprised, expressed a respect for local knowledge and local systems ... [and it must respect] the narrative structures of others, the speech act constellations of others, the historically, experientially derived values and norms of others [Hymes 125, original emphasis].

This book, then, is an attempt to make sure digital game studies does not treat the ludic and narrative approaches as *passé*. Nor does it accept that there should be a relatively simple and sharp dividing line between the approaches. It hopes to tease out patterns, but be happily surprised by the unexpected. It is designed to respect each perspective of the initial digital game studies divide, but it does not see the distance between story and play as a divide.

At the same time each contributor has been allowed to create her or his own useful approach to the dialectic of narrative$_1$—ludic—narrative$_2$ (or ludic$_1$—narrative—ludic$_2$) formulation. And, because the ludic and narrative cannot be the complete answer to "what games do" other viewpoints are offered as well.

The Decision Tree of This Volume

Each contributor to this volume, then, offers their take on using a combination of ludology and narratology in examination of a game—or, in the case of one contributor, why this division has led to other viewpoints being lost. Each contributor was asked to bring together what was needed from the study of the play of a game and the story of a game in an attempt to offer dialectic understanding rather than a simplified dichotomy.

Because of this the organization of the book follows a number of matrices. Firstly, the organization is intended to pay attention to the idea of the development of digital games over time—but this does not mean the essays present analyses of games presented in chronological order. Rather, the evolution of various kinds of gameplay are considered central to the organization.

Secondly, and perhaps of equal importance, the essays have been edited with the idea of a kind of alternate history of the field of game studies. As editor I've imagined a different decade or two in which game studies actually engaged in a spirited debate about the importance of narrative and play, and the contrasts between those viewpoints. This alternate history is organized wholly arbitrarily, but with the intent of imagining a more cohesive recent past of the field.

With the combination of these two possibilities—the development of gameplay and the development of the field of game studies—in mind, this work is designed to engage game studies as an actual discipline rather than a personality-driven area where certain "names" are known more than their ideas.

Thus, in the first essay we begin with Lindsey Joyce's ideas of the importance of play in character development in the independent game *Kentucky Route Zero*. While the game is not particularly well known, it should be—as should Joyce's use of it in understanding the ways in which ludology and narratology absolutely must interact, carefully, in any contemporary game structure.

Joyce's work sets up Andrew Wackerfuss's analysis of *State of Decay* in which he begins by creating a narrative based on his first playthrough of the game. This allows him to explore how the very act of *playing* a game requires the creation of a narrative in the mind of a player. This allows Emily Joy Bembeneck, in the next essay, on *League of Legends*, to examine the ways in which narrative is a creation of game mechanics as well. Though Bembeneck differs from Wackerfuss in that she places the origin of that narrative in the necessary storyworld that emerges as part of the game itself, rather than wholly within the mind of the player. In part this difference is a difference of games—but it is also a difference of theoretical approach between Bembeneck and Wackerfuss.

Eric W. Riddle then tries to cut this difference somewhat finer by using *Beyond: Two Souls* as a digital example of the neo–Gothic, thus emphasizing both narrative and its connection to nineteenth century literature in a narrative sense. This is both a compelling argument in its own sense and also an excellent way to set up Mark Filipowich's essay on his version of the ludic and narrative interaction in *Persona 3*. Filipowich's essay presents the interaction between play and story in a way that should have become central to game studies long ago but got lost—in much the way the emic and etic did in anthropology—far too soon.

By this time in the text it is obvious that the emergence of what will be called the "ludonarrative" is necessary. In game studies, though, the ludonarrative has largely been central to critiques against games, themselves, as Vince Locke notes by bringing the term into our alternate history, here, and by also applying the term to his mythic analysis of *Halo*. By using myth, though, Locke is able to use the term without being exclusively negative with it. This allows his analysis to be both critical and imply a general approach to game studies that too many scholars have missed—a way of considering both the ludic and the narrative by using them to see myth or other areas of import. Alexandra Orlando and Matthew Schwager offer their own version of this approach by fusing the ludic and the narrative in an analysis of what they call a "cyborg" of game studies' paradigms in *Deus Ex: Human Revolution*. This approach furthers the idea that the ludic and that narrative are so closely bound up as to be inseparable.

Tom Apperley and Justin Clemens build out from such conceptions by using, in part, Michel Foucault's biopolitics to examine the avatar of *Assassin's Creed II*. The use of Foucault allows them to see an emergence of reflexivity between the poles of story and play—a necessary step in understanding both games and the scholarship of them. That kind of reflexivity can also be found in Amy M. Green's essay on *BioShock Infinite*. For Green the necessity of repetition in gameplay is a kind of forced reflexivity between the play and the story, making *BioShock* a game that forces game studies scholarship to move forward if it is to keep current with the games themselves. In an attempt to force game studies to do exactly that, Matthew Wysocki and Betsy Brey also examine *BioShock*. They do so from a perspective that centers their work not on the repetition, as Green does, but from the perspective of player choice. While a cursory glance may suggest this makes their essay a straightforward work of ludology, their point is that player choice affects narrative and, then, narrative affects future choices. This interdependence of the ludic and the narrative is both central to their essay, and to this book as a whole.

Nicholas Ware then argues that the narrative creation of character can be seen as a driving force in gameplay, and he does so through the classic game *Street Fighter*. The idea that the ludic aspects of the game would be less enjoyable without the necessary character creation—that is, essentially, the narrative—may represent the defining metanarrative of this volume as a whole. However, since this organization is also a kind of alternate history, Robert Mejia works from a starting assumption that the debate between narratologists and ludologists has already happened leaving space for other paradigms to be considered. Thus, he turns to the considerations of a planet of rapidly diminishing resources and wonders about the ecological "footprint" of the games industry.

These essays, when combined with this Introduction and the brief Conclusion, are designed to make game scholars actually engage with their discipline in a way that is less concerned about the people writing—as it too often is—and more about the ideas under consideration. It is intended as an alternate history that recapitulated a decade or two of debate on the subject of the ludology/narratology question. The contributors approached their topics as though they were writing in a discipline that has managed to become important in departments other than those they reside in. In short, this work and the essays here assume that game studies has tried to be taken seriously enough to actually *have* debates rather than side-step them.

Having a Debate Means Having a Discipline: Let's Create an Alternate History of Game Studies

It is the hope that this book can offer some fuel to a debate that, in Frasca's phrase, "never took place." While it is not intended to lead to teacups being thrown, and it is not intended to make the fight all that intense, this work exists because the stakes for digital game studies are, actually, rather high. What Hymes hoped to offer the emic/etic debate in anthropology and linguistics this book hopes to offer to digital games studies. Hymes failed, of course, and that debate withered away. Just a few years later the anthropologist Marshall Sahlins described the outcome for his discipline distinctly, noting that anthropologists "have become the working-class of the Cultural Studies movement ... [r]elegated to the status of ethnographic proles in the academic division of labor" (Sahlins 77). There is a danger that games studies scholars will occupy a similar position in the larger world of media studies. Without a more thorough and ongoing debate among practitioners the one major paradigmatic argument that has fueled the emergence of the field may evaporate as the emic and etic debate did only a generation ago in anthropology and linguistics. And, without some debate to hang on to there will be little for scholars in other fields (our own outsiders) to see when they stop by to understand exactly what it is that digital game scholars are doing. They will find only chaos when they visit.

If that happens we will only be talking to ourselves.

Note: Quite literally everything in this Introduction is better for the comments of my friend and colleague John Shelton Lawrence. What's left that grates on the reader remains the fault of the author.

Works Cited

Edrei, Shawn. "Press Start to Continue: The Effects of Pseudo-Authorial Control on Video Game Narratives." *Ctrl-Alt-Play: Essays on Control in Video Gaming.* Ed. Matthew Wysocki. Jefferson, NC: McFarland, 2013. 96–107. Print.

Elliott, Andrew B. R., and Matthew Wilhelm Kapell. "Introduction: To Build a Past That Will 'stand the Test of Time'—Discovering Historical Facts, Assembling Historical Narratives." *Playing with the Past: Digital Games and the Simulation of History.* Eds. Matthew Wilhelm Kapell and Andrew B. R. Elliott. New York: Bloomsbury Academic, 2013. 1–30. Print.

Frasca, Gonzalo. "Ludologists Love Stories, Too: Notes from a Debate That Never Took Place." Digital Games Research Association. Utrecht. 2003.

_____. "Simulation Versus Narrative: Introduction to Ludology." *The Video Game Theory Reader.* Ed. Mark J.P. Wolf and Bernard Perron. New York: Routledge, 2003. 221–236. Print.

Galloway, Alexander R. *Gaming: Essays on Algorithmic Culture.* Minneapolis: University of Minnesota Press, 2006. Print.

Harris, Marvin. "Emics and Etics Revisited." *Emics and Etics: The Insider/Outsider Debate*. Eds. Thomas N. Headland, Kenneth L. Pike, and Marvin Harris. Newbury Park, CA: SAGE Publications, Inc., 1990. 48–61. Print.

Hymes, Dell H. "Emics, Etics, and Openess: An Ecumenical Approach." *Emics and Etics: The Insider/Outsider Debate*. Eds. Thomas N. Headland, Kenneth L. Pike, and Marvin Harris. Newbury Park, CA: SAGE Publications, Inc., 1990. 120–126. Print.

Jenkins, Henry. "Games as Narrative Architecture." *First Person: New Media as Story, Performance and Game*. Ed. Noah Wardrip-Fruin and Pat Harrigan. Cambridge, MA: MIT Press, 2004. 118–130. Print.

Jones, Steven E. *The Meaning of Video Games: Gaming and Textual Strategies*. New York: Routledge, 2008. Print.

Juul, Jesper. *Half-Real: Video Games Between Real Rules and Fictional Worlds*. Cambridge, MA: The MIT Press, 2011. Print.

Kapell, Matthew Wilhelm. Conversation with Kenneth L. Pike. 1988. Personal Conversation.

Kapell, Matthew Wilhelm, and Andrew B. R. Elliott. "Conclusion(s): Playing at True Myths, Engaging with Authentic Histories." *Playing with the Past: Digital Games and the Simulation of History*. Eds. Matthew Wilhelm Kapell and Andrew B. R. Elliott. New York: Bloomsbury Academic, 2013. 357–369. Print.

Pike, Kenneth L. "The Emics and Etics of Pike and Harris." *Emics and Etics: The Insider/Outsider Debate*. Eds. Thomas N. Headland, Kenneth L. Pike, and Marvin Harris. Newbury Park, CA: SAGE Publications, Inc., 1990. 28–47. Print.

_____. *Language in Relation to a Unified Theory of the Structure of Human Behavior*. 2d edition. The Hague: Mouton De Gruyter, 1967. Print.

_____. "Pike's Reply to Harris." *Emics and Etics: The Insider/Outsider Debate*. Eds. Thomas N. Headland, Kenneth L. Pike, and Marvin Harris. Newbury Park, CA: SAGE Publications, Inc., 1990. 62–74. Print.

_____. *Talk, Thought, and Thing: The Emic Road Toward Conscious Knowledge*. Dallas: Summer Institute of Linguistics, 1993. Print.

Pike, Kenneth L., and Evelyn G. Pike. *Text and Tagmeme*. London: Pinter, 1983. Print.

Ryan, Marie-Laure. "Beyond Myth and Metaphor*—The Case of Narrative in Digital Media." *Game Studies* 1.1 (2001): n. pag. Web.

Sahlins, Marshall. *Waiting for Foucault, Still*. Chicago: Prickly Paradigm Press, 2002. Print.

Simons, Jan. "Narrative, Games, and Theory." *Game Studies* 7.1 (2007): n. pag. Web.

Voorhees, Gerald. "Criticism and Control: Gameplay in the Space of Possibility." *Ctrl-Alt-Play: Essays on Control in Video Gaming*. Ed. Matthew Wysocki. Jefferson, NC: McFarland, 2013. 9–20. Print.

Wesp, Edward. "A Too-Coherent World: Game Studies and the Myth of 'Narrative' Media." *Game Studies* 14.2 (2014): n. pag. Web.

Kentucky Route Zero
Or, How Not to Get Lost in the Branching Narrative System

LINDSEY JOYCE

The key stumbling block in understanding and developing digital interactive narratives is not that ludic and narrative elements are incompatible—a false argument to begin with—but rather that games scholars have collectively spent too much time arguing unnecessary sides and too little time establishing a common criteria on which to assess games. In a previous article, "Creating a Collaborative Criteria for Interactive Narrative Game Analysis," I set out with the lofty (and ongoing) task to begin establishing such criteria. By cross-examining key research in the field of interactive narrative, I compiled a list of essential criteria that should be considered and included in the creation of digital interactive narratives and which attempts to better balance the relationship between story and agency. Having previously used these criteria to access agency in two highly developed and promotionally budgeted (so called AAA) games, *Mass Effect 2* and *Elder Scrolls V: Skyrim*. I now aim to test these criteria against the independently developed game by Cardboard Computer, *Kentucky Route Zero*. I have chosen *Kentucky Route Zero* not only to test the utility of the criteria outside of the AAA game space, but also to prove that the criteria can be used to test the success level of games, whether AAA or not, that attempt to push or alter boundary conventions, as *Kentucky Route Zero* does. In this way, the criteria serve not only to enable post-production analysis, but also as a means of questioning the potential success of innovative design choices against an essential criteria of consideration.

Kentucky Route Zero's non-standard approach to both character development and player perspective within a plot that is ostensibly one of small consequence makes it of particular interest for analysis. Not only do the minimal point-and-click mechanics manage to achieve a great deal, but the narrative also shows that adventure and meaning need not be derived from the high and epic stakes common to most games. The plot of *Kentucky Route Zero* can be summarized as such: Conway, a delivery truck driver in Kentucky, must deliver a package to an address he cannot find, but which he is told exists along Route Zero. On his journey to find "the zero," Conway eventually picks up additional travel companions: Shannon, a local television repairwoman whose migrant parents once worked in the coal mines in the town; Ezra, a young boy who has lost his parents; and Junebug and Johnny, two musicians who entice Conway, Shannon, and Ezra to come with them to a gig. While such a synopsis might lead the player to assume they will play as Conway, this is only partially true. Conway may arguably be the central protagonist, but there are multiple protagonists in the game and the player will take on each of their perspectives, sometimes simultaneously, throughout game play. The game switches between characters via dialogue selection menus—one of the key ludic elements of the game. In other words, players are not only presented with dialogue for Conway, as they would be in most single-protagonist or single-perspective games, but are offered dialogue for several characters throughout gameplay. This unique approach to narrative and ludic design, as well as the interfaces used to manage the drama and character development, situate the player not as a single character, *but instead as author*. It is from this position of author that the player is able to experience greater levels of agency. By using the criteria I have previously established and replicated here, I show how *Kentucky Route Zero*'s approach to player perspective and character development successfully balances both ludic and narrative agencies in a way that many single-protagonist games often fail to do.

Narrative Agency

The narrative agency in *Kentucky Route Zero* is interesting because of its multiple playable characters. The player seems to occupy two spaces in the narrative: in one space, the player acts as and through the characters and their perspectives, and in the other space, acts as the omniscient narrator or author who, despite lacking actual omniscience, orchestrates the overall story. The player's space is thus one of character development and specificity, but also one of totality: the narrative experience is crafted around many perspectives and players must keep each in mind as they move through the game. Michael Mateas and Andrew Stern note that in game narratives designed to provide agency, "the player should not have the feeling of playing a role ... [but] Rather the player should be able to be themselves as they explore the dramatic situation" ("Towards Integrating Plot" 2). *Kentucky Route Zero*'s use of multiple narrative roles and spaces for the player makes providing this agency more feasible; freed from a single character perspective, the player has more opportunity to explore and think about the dramatic situation. By elevating the player above a single-perspective experience, *Kentucky Route Zero* actually enriches the capacity for narrative agency. The player isn't confined to a single viewpoint through which to access and assess the narrative, but is present through all perspectives. In *Kentucky Route Zero*, the player is each of the characters singularly and collectively, and must not only consider choices as unique and important to a single character, but also of how those choices will impact the other characters and the narrative whole. This is not only accomplished by the way dialogue is presented, but also by the lack of feedback systems and the lack of certainty about where any dialogue choice will lead (Joyce). Many interactive narrative games incorporate feedback systems that "tell" players about their choices rather than "showing" them the effect of their choice through narrative integration. Games like Bioware's *Mass Effect* tell players if choices are good (Paragon) or bad (Renegade), while Telltale's games like *The Walking Dead* signal important choices have been made by telling players "[character name] will remember that." Choice systems focused around dialogue over-use feedback to a fault; choices become a reflection of the system's structure and authority rather than of the player's agency and *author*ity. In *Kentucky Route Zero* there is no feedback beyond the continuation of the dialogue. Players can only guess where any particular dialogue choice will take the story, but their choices nonetheless feel organic based on how they want to develop a specific character. In turn, this allows players to reflect critically upon each choice, to consider how they have been steering a character's development up to a certain point and how, given that development, the characters would react. Importantly, it also presents players with the opportunity to consider how they want the character to react in reference to how they have developed the other characters. In other words, players must negotiate each character's development within the social context of the other characters they are simultaneously developing (Archer 308). Mateas and Stern argue that a player should not feel constrained by a role in a game, but should instead be able to inhabit the space as themselves ("Integrating Plot" 2). While this is useful advice in single-protagonist games, *Kentucky Route Zero* takes a different approach to narrative agency by freeing the player from any single role at all. While one limitation of this approach may be the inability to deeply connect with a single character or "become" the protagonist, *Kentucky Route Zero*'s approach necessitates critical thinking from the level of *story*. Playing an authorial role, players must maintain consideration for the personal and interpersonal motivations of all the characters alongside consideration for how the interplay between them informs the plot as a whole. Because players inhabit the perspective of more than one playable character, they can think critically on a level not allowed by single-protagonist game systems. They think on the level of authorship rather than on the level of character.

Ludic Agency

A key function of ludic agency is the player's ability to have embodied interactions in the game space. Michael Mateas bluntly states, "Embodied interactions matter," and goes on to say that while dialogue should be significant, as it most certainly is in *Kentucky Route Zero*, it should not be the sole means of engagement ("A Preliminary Poetics" 30). Given that *Kentucky Route Zero* is a point-and-click game, the only way for players to interact with the system is to click a single button on their mouse. In this regard, there are certainly games that offer more meaningful embodied interactions with game environments. *Kentucky Route Zero*'s unique approach to narrative agency, however, lends itself to an important understanding of ludic agency. Despite not being able to move the character with the same level of freedom provided in other game types, the physicality of the characters is an important concern in how players manipulate the narrative and construct their own unique ludic experience. For instance, when Conway is hurt in an abandoned mine, players are presented with options on how to respond to the pain: they can elect to have Conway say, "I can walk on it, but it's slow," or "I can walk on it, but it's painful." Then later, when Conway visits a doctor, players not only have the opportunity to create the narrative that is constructed around Conway's injury, but also how he responds to a surgical procedure that replaces his injured leg with a holographic one. When asked about his new leg, players are given three options as a response: "This isn't my leg," "It seems better, but ... it wasn't worth it," or "It was just the heat. The shingles were cracked in the sun, and one of them slipped out under his feet." Both the players' response in the mine and the players' response about the surgery construct the ludic experience. Though players' embodied actions are restricted by the game's point-and-click mechanics, their perception of embodied action and meaning is heightened through this narrative control. Players relate to Conway's relationship with his leg not because they feel the mechanical limitations it forces on them as players (such as when a character in a game walks with a limp for a small amount of time as in *Skyrim*, impeding physical progress) but because the narrative, via the choices presented, allows them to construct a response for Conway with which they can relate and empathize.

This empathy toward characters, and the degree to which the player can embody them, is enhanced by the delivery and complexity of choices and dialogue. There are no easy choices in *Kentucky Route Zero*. Perhaps because the stakes of the narrative are so small, nuance is of more importance than opaqueness. In large games, such as the *Mass Effect* series, the stakes are high: the universe hangs in the balance. For this reason, *Mass Effect*, and games like it, often overly simplify their presentation of choices in order to make sure players, on some level, know the consequence of a choice before they've made it. The concern for players' possible frustration over an unintended outcome resulting from a misunderstood choice overrides the potential for narrative nuance and, as a result, the choices are reduced to moral challenges absolved of the weight of real ethical dilemma (Sicart 45). Players are apt to play for an outcome rather than for the experience that precedes it: save the world as the good guy, or ensure its demise as the bad guy (Smith). *Kentucky Route Zero* has no such pretense. There is no ethical dilemma and thus no need to reduce choices in the system to bifurcated moral challenges. In *Kentucky Route Zero*, although dialogue choices are still scripted, the system does not "manipulate [the dialectic]" in the same way morality-based games do (Sicart 43). In *Kentucky Route Zero*, the universe doesn't hang in the balance, and if anything does hang in the balance, players have hung it there themselves through unique construction of the narrative. For instance, the player can construct a story in which Conway is making his last delivery because his business is closing down, or a story in which he is happily retiring; the weight of the narrative and the importance of Conway's delivery are chosen by the player through this narrative choice. Additionally, the player can construct a story in which Conway focuses on his relationship with his employer's husband, or on his relationship with his employer's son, both of which offer different dramatic portrayals of Conway's past and how it may (or may not) impact his character in the present. The game, and the narrative the player constructs, is focused on the journey and the details the player is interested in pursuing more than it is interested in specific plot points that could "force the plot in a different direction" (Mateas and Stern, "Towards Integrating Plot" 1).

To this end, the narrative and ludic systems aren't focused on narrative outcomes, as many games are. In *Kentucky Route Zero*, all choices ultimately lead in one direction, and on that level all players will arrive at the same conclusion. The journey to that pre-determined conclusion differs in two important ways: in dialogue choices and how those choices map out the journey to the conclusion of the game. In other words, while the ending is the same, the choices players make in how they develop characters lead to different experiences and scenes prior to the conclusion. In this way, the choices players make are, in one capacity, futile; the plot will progress along the same string of pearls and in a very linear fashion (Costikyan). Yet, in *Kentucky Route Zero*, every narrative move is centered on character emotions, about why a character says what he or she says. Such choices, or those choices which players interpret as having consequence for the character, have been found to increase the players' perception of agency (Fendt et al. 10). In this way, *Kentucky Route Zero* is a ludic metaphor for prioritizing the journey over the destination, as the narrative is one of character development placed primarily in the players' hands.

Character Development and Interaction

Given that most games allow players to inhabit only one narrative protagonist, the demands of character development rest more heavily in the hands of the game's developers. As a result, the NPCs (Non-Player Characters) have to be made believable and real by the developers in order for the player to interact with them. In this way, the analysis of character development and interaction is more commonly about how well a game has succeeded in constructing believable agents. *Kentucky Route Zero*, however, puts character development more directly in the hands of the player. It is worth noting that, although the game offers multiple protagonists, it still dictates when players can alter their perspective between those characters. For some stretches in time, players may only be prompted with dialogue options for Conway or for Shannon, and at other times, both simultaneously. When presented with the latter scenario, players must select which character speaks. In other words, players must not only choose what will be said and by whom, but which character will be developed more deeply as a result of that choice. This navigation between characters within the system adds dimension and complexity to the characters by allowing players to develop them at their own selection. While some players may give Shannon more opportunities to talk, other players may choose to develop Conway more deeply; in either respect, their understanding of the narrative experience will be altered. Rather than being props the player cannot alter and which are used to propel the narrative forward, the protagonists in *Kentucky Route Zero* have greater capacity for complexity; players can elect when and how to flesh them out. Because players build the characters up from both sides, they are not only believable, but their dialogue carries the weight of emotional entanglement and complexity within a coherent narrative (Riedl 2).

Of course, the options for character development are still scripted by the developers—players cannot input their own dialogue. The game, however, still grants more agency by allowing players to select from emotionally rich options focused on character development over plot progression, and by allowing them to select dialogue for more than one character. Rather than reducing narrative branches to binaries such as "X responds with anger" or "X responds with sympathy," *Kentucky Route Zero* presents more cryptic and nuanced choices, the result of which is the heightened capacity for players to project their understanding and interpretation onto the narrative itself. For instance, players are presented with several different ways to develop Shannon's character, most of which offer different reflections on her life growing up as a migrant worker in a mining town. When presented with the reasons Shannon wasn't able to have a dog as a child, players can select "My folks worked alternating shifts [in the mine] for a while" or "My dad was allergic." Given the first choice, players will then be prompted to follow up with another statement from Shannon saying, "No time to care for a dog" or "And then they finally got their shifts in sync." In this interaction, players have more agency to understand the choices, and the weight of those choices, as they want rather than as the game dictates. Each selection by the player realizes Shannon's character in a different way. Shannon either becomes a child whose parent was allergic to animals (a not uncommon occurrence) or a child whose parents were always working until (and this is only implied by the narrative) they were lost in a mine collapse. The characters feel believable because players are crafting not just how a character responds in the present moment, but also what their backstory is. As *Haywire Magazine*'s editor-in-chief, Joe Köller, observes, "*Kentucky Route Zero* turns their full creative power to words, they become a tool not just for announcing future intent, but willing into existence the particulars of your backstory, moving events by casually noting them and establishing your views by expressing them." Players craft the existence of the characters across planes in time in such a way that the characters become more complex, multi-dimensional, and real. While *Mass Effect* prompts players to select a backstory for Shepard at the start of the game, the ramifications of this one-time choice are never dramatized in the narrative that follows. It feels like a hollow choice or like lip-service paid to the importance of fully realized characters. Additionally, players of the *Mass Effect* series are only ever reminded of Shepard's past deeds by NPCs. This narrative background, meant to add dimension to Shepard as the protagonist, doesn't resonate in the same way as the background stories in *Kentucky Route Zero*. Players of *Mass Effect* don't *construct* Shepard's background story; they merely *select* it once before it becomes the total experience of Shepard's past. In *Kentucky Route Zero*, character background is more malleable: the player develops it in slow fragments over the course of the game and in conjunction with the construction of the character's present experience. Thus in *Kentucky Route Zero* players not only narratively construct what the past was, but why it has bearing on the character and his/her actions in the game's present. That these actions occur simultaneously brings the multi-dimensionality of the characters directly to the foreground of the game, and makes it the ludic function by which players advance.

Drama Management

The drama management system of *Kentucky Route Zero* is perfectly hidden in the sense that players are not given any non-dialogue feedback surrounding their choices, and as a result, the story they create is smoothly mutable. Because the main mechanic of the game could arguably be called a "story" mechanic, or a truly "ludonarrative" mechanic, the system managing the story and the way players interact are inseparable from one another. As a result, the need to balance two opposing systems, one narrative and one ludic, is made null. There can be no interventions by the drama manager with the system since the system is the creation of that story. Furthermore, beyond the presentation of dialogue, the system remains invisible. No feedback is given to players other than the development of the story itself. Additionally, the story has no metric system that assesses or tracks the player's choices. The system, therefore, stays out of the way so that players feel like the story they are creating is uniquely their own. They are the author. The drawback to the invisibility of the drama manager is that, unless the game is played more than once, players may not be able to distinguish just how subtly the game alters players' experiences around their choices. In other words, without a comparative experience to gauge the differences that occur between playthroughs, players could feasibly doubt that the system is altering at all as a result of their choices. Without an awareness for how the system is tracking or responding to the players' choices, the game seriously risks damaging or erasing the potential agency it attempts to provide. This raises the question about how ideal an invisible drama manager actually is, or alternately, the question of whether players have been trained by other interactive narrative games to expect some measure of feedback that assures them the system is actually a narratively interactive one.

Narrative Experience

Despite the invisibility of the drama management system, a new story experience is constructed with each playthrough, provided that players alter their dialogue choices in subsequent playthroughs. Additionally, even if players continue to question whether the system alters the narrative trajectory based on their choices, the game's replay value also remains high (Mateas and Stern "Towards Integrating Plot" 1). By selecting different choices, the way characters are developed—and thus the players' understanding of otherwise similar events—will be different. The story changes with each playthrough because the characters within it change.

The design of *Kentucky Route Zero* and the way it invites players to interact and maintain agency through character development rather than story outcome also increases the opportunity for and importance of critical reflection (Sicart 56). Players don't have to act because they are thinking of the experience/outcome they want, but are instead free to act based on how they perceive the subtleties of characters and how such subtleties may amount to more meaningful choices. Rather than being limited to "right" and "wrong" ethical and ludic binaries, players can make choices in *Kentucky Route Zero* because, upon critical reflection, it feels right in that moment and within the context of the story experience the player is crafting. It's about the subtlety and nuance that eventually lead to deep and rich character development and story experience.

Conclusion

Overall, this analysis of *Kentucky Route Zero* shows that, despite the game's unique approach to character development through multiple protagonists (or perhaps because of it), the game provides an increased level of agency to players by treating them less as inhabitors of a single role and instead as the authors, or in the very least as co-authors, of the overall game experience. Narratively, players simultaneously think on the level of single characters and on the level of the narrative whole; how their choices affect both that character, the other characters, and their understanding of those characters within the narrative itself. Ludically, the game compensates for its minimal mechanics by focusing part of Conway's development on his body. Additionally, the ludic impetus is not on forward plot progression and momentum, but instead on character enrichment. In tandem, the ludic and narrative capacities for increased agency create a rich system that maintains the weight of choice and the importance of critical reflection. The game's system, however, is still not perfect. While the drama management system is hidden in an attempt to heighten players' immersion, its invisibility doesn't necessarily improve the overall user experience, as such players may question how and if the system is altering that experience at all.

The assessment of *Kentucky Route Zero* using the established analytical criteria also helps to cast a light on two concerns going forward: firstly, that the criteria of assessment work in the analysis of indie games, including those that take a non-standard approach to narrative and interactivity and secondly, although the criteria work against such innovative games, their application also reveal possible limitations of the criteria. For instance, the application of the criteria against *Kentucky Route Zero* reveal that, in some cases, the criteria may be too limiting, especially where it presumes the player acts through a single protagonist. In other cases, it challenges the assumption that a complete invisible drama management system is ideal; if players are completely unaware of its existence, they may question that any choice is recognized by the system at all. While some might argue this reveals drawbacks to the criteria, I view this as an essential part of the criteria growth. The criteria I have established are not meant to be static, but evolving. As games evolve so too must our understandings of how agency works within them. As game developers continue to push the boundaries of player interactivity and agency, the criteria we use to assess them must expand as well in a constant feedback loop. This back and forth is important not only for the analysis of games, but also for the grounding of game specific theories in the field. What is simultaneously at stake is the improvement of games and the theories we use to interpret, understand, and improve them. The continued growth and refinement (or ebb and flow) of these analytical criteria is essential to that improvement. The merits of the criteria and of their use continue to be lucrative not only to our understanding of how agency is provided in games, but also in the continued effort to establish critical systems for analysis in the field of game studies.

Works Cited

Archer, Margaret. *Being Human: The Problem of Agency*. Cambridge: Cambridge University Press, 2001. Print.
Bethesda Game Studios. *The Elder Scrolls V: Skyrim*. N.p., 2011. Xbox 360.
Bioware. *Mass Effect 2*. N.p., 2010. Xbox 360.
Cardboard Computer. *Kentucky Route Zero*. N.p., 2013. Microsoft Windows.
Costikyan, Greg. "Where Stories End and Games Begin." *Game Developer* 7.9 (2000): 44–53. Print.

Fendt, Matthew William, et al. "Achieving the Illusion of Agency." *Interactive Storytelling*. Berlin: Springer, 2012. 114–125. *Google Scholar*. Web. 14 Nov. 2014.

Heron, Michael James, and Pauline Helen Belford. "Do You Feel Like a Hero Yet? Externalised Morality in Video Games." *Journal of Games Criticism* 1.2 (2014): n. pag. Web. 9 Nov. 2014.

Joyce, Lindsey. "Agency in Meaning and Intent: Limitations of Morality Systems in Interactive Narrative Games." *VG6*. Oxford: Inter-Disciplinary.net, 2014. Web.

Köller, Joe. "Blank Slate." *Haywire Magazine*. N.p., 14 Apr. 2013. Web. 15 Nov. 2014.

Mateas, Michael. "A Preliminary Poetics for Interactive Drama and Games." *First Person: New Media as Story, Performance, and Game*. Eds. Noah Wardrip-Fruin and Pat Harrigan. Cambridge, MA: MIT Press, 2004. 19–34. Print.

Mateas, Michael, and Andrew Stern. "Integrating Plot, Character and Natural Language Processing in the Interactive Drama Façade." *Proceedings of the 1st International Conference on Technologies for Interactive Digital Storytelling and Entertainment (TIDSE-03)*. N.p., 2003. *Google Scholar*. Web. 9 Nov. 2014.

_____. "Towards Integrating Plot and Character for Interactive Drama." *In Working Notes of the Social Intelligent Agents: The Human in the Loop Symposium*. N.p., 2000. Print.

"Moral Decisions (Concept)—Giant Bomb." N.p., n.d. Web. 8 Nov. 2014.

Riedl, Mark O. "A Comparison of Interactive Narrative System Approaches Using Human Improvisational Actors." *Proceedings of the Intelligent Narrative Technologies III Workshop*. ACM, 2010. 16. *Google Scholar*. Web. 8 Nov. 2014.

Sicart, Miguel. *The Ethics of Computer Games*. Cambridge, MA: MIT Press, 2009. Print.

Smith, Ed. "Catherine: How Scoring Systems Kill the Mood | Medium Difficulty." *Medium Difficulty*. N.p., 13 Apr. 2012. Web. 8 Nov. 2014.

Telltale Games. *The Walking Dead*. N.p., 2012. Xbox 360.

States of Play in *State of Decay*

ANDREW WACKERFUSS

Ed's last night alive took its first bad turn not 200 yards from the compound's perimeter fence, when the pizza delivery wagon he had boosted last week inexplicably blew its front right tire. It wasn't fair—all he had done was run over one zombie. Not even a full horde. Someone else in the group must have driven the car since Ed's last supply run, dinging it up but not bothering to mention it to him. Ed knew that cars didn't really belong to anyone, not anymore, but it pissed him off all the same. If he had known, he would have planned better.

On the road ahead, Ed's headlights illuminated a new trio of shamblers, which he mowed down maliciously, mentally adding them to the kill count he kept of vehicular zombicides. "I think that last one was just asking for directions," he joked to the empty passenger seat.[1] Ed spotted a proper horde farther down the street, aligned the steering wheel, and pressed his foot to the floor. And that's when the engine caught on fire.

Ed didn't even bother slowing down; he just opened the door, tucked, and rolled. Each zombie in the horde raised its head and craned its neck, dead eyes lit red by the burning vehicle's oncoming rush. As Ed tumbled safely into a patch of brush, the car plowed through the horde's center mass, exploding, showering the area with bits of metal, bone, and brain.

As Ed stood up and brushed off his clothes, he felt more confident than ever. If there was one thing you could say about surviving several weeks through the zombie apocalypse, it really did bring out your hidden talents. Ed mused satisfactorily to himself as he sought out another car to take him back to the ranger station where, for him, this horrorshow had begun.

None of them normally would have ventured that far away from their compound, but this was a special case. Late that afternoon, as Ed was returning from a supply run, Lily had come on the radio. He was used to her frequent

28

interruptions, given her constant vigilance over their group and her continual direction of their efforts. But this time, she had a request of her own.

"Hey..." she began hesitatingly, "Do you think you could do me a favor while you're out there? I've been packing up my dad's stuff, and I found a watch box. It's from the birthday present I got him when I was 12. This stupid little plastic thing with cartoon fish on it. I don't know why he kept it, but ... it kind of made me realize I don't have anything to remember him by. So I was going to ask if you'd go up to where he died and bring me something of his."

The unexpected request threw Ed into pensive silence. Lily's father was the park ranger where Ed and his friend Marcus were camping when this whole mess broke out. Ed had been so excited to show Marcus his hometown, and the beauty of the Rockies. But it turned out ugly. It was at this ranger station that they had first seen the creatures. Ed was momentarily lost in images of those first frights, so much so that Lily took his silence for reluctance.

"No, forget it, it's stupid," she said, "it's way too risky. I'm sorry I brought it up."

But Ed assured her it was no trouble. He'd take care of it; after all he knew right where the ranger station was. Ed didn't tell her that he'd been there when her father died. That he'd seen him turn. That he had the bite marks to prove it, and that the resulting fever had almost killed him. He didn't mention any of that ... if he hadn't told her when they first joined up together, there was no point in ever revealing it.

So that's how Ed found himself driving north, up into higher elevation and toward the slopes he thought he'd probably not have reason to return to again. But Lily had given him a reason, and of everyone in the group, given all that had happened with her father, Ed felt he owed her to do it himself.

It seemed a normal trip so far—normal, a world where walking corpses populated the roadside. But as Ed neared the bridge over the canyon separating the park from the outskirts of town, he saw a strange figure off by the side of the road, standing motionless right outside the treeline. It had the dusky, dirty look of the dead, but it cast a silhouette far larger than any other rotter he'd seen. It was almost seven feet tall, with the bulk of two or even three normal ones. This must be one of those big ones the radio had warned them about.

Ed grinned. As far as he knew, he was the first of their group to actually spot one of the big guys in the wild, and Ed had recently developed a special love for hunting down the freak zombies, introducing them to the hood of his car. So he spun the wheel, lined up his shot, and gunned the engine right for the big bastard. The car hit squarely, but the thing's massive bulk offered more resistance than any previous target had posed. The car slammed to a halt like it had hit a wall. Its front bumper crunched under the impact. The big one fell to the ground but stirred, not yet fully downed. Ed frowned and tried again. As before, the impact knocked the big guy backwards and off its feet, but failed to end its unlife for good. Ed reversed slightly, realizing now that there was something wrong with the front axle, and tried yet again. Same result. Again. Same result. The car could barely accelerate now. He tried again. This was getting frustrating.

Ed now had an upsetting realization: he was much deeper in the woods than a station wagon should safely go. Each time he had hit the thing had caused it to stagger back several feet, and so each new attempt to smash it had brought the car farther and farther. He hadn't noticed because he was so fixated on the big thing. Ed now found himself firmly within the trees, with the car's tires now caught up on the uneven ground. He gunned the engine, tried reversing, and realized he was stuck. He'd have to bail before this big thing lumbered back to its feet. And of course the noise of the commotion had brought other unwelcome visitors.

Okay, not a problem, Ed thought. He'd just make his way to the station on foot and boost a car once there. There had been several in the parking lot, other campers' or even the ranger's own car, and the area hadn't been that infested when he was last there. With what he'd been learning about zombie psychology, he bet that they would have had no reason to head uphill all the way out into the sticks, when signs of life down in town would attract them. So he should be okay, Ed thought as he carefully trotted up the road to the station.

He was wrong. Ed was fast, with good reflexes and a quick sprint that usually left most zombies in the dust. He figured he'd get something from Lily's dad's things, and make it back in time for breakfast. But one look through the window at the ranger station revealed that this was no simple task. Something must have happened here, like a group had taken shelter but then got infected. It was the only way to explain how many of the bastards were stalking around. Ed heard moans behind him in the parking lot, and realized a proper horde was heading toward him. It looked like they'd come around the corner and spotted him right away. His escape paths blocked, Ed readied his hammer and started swinging. He'd taken out hordes before, and after a while he took care of this one as well. But there was a problem— well, two of them. The zombies inside the station were now alerted. And worse, the business end of his hammer had started to come loose from the handle.

Ed knew it was now time to leave. All the cars in this lot seemed burned out already, so he ran to the campground lot around the side—and straight into a second horde. Fighting his way through these finished off his hammer. As Ed crouched there with his hands on his knees, gasping for breath in a field of brown and red remains, he heard a roar he had only heard once before. The big guy was back. Ed didn't know if it was the same one, or a new version of the creature, but either way he barely had time to think before it was charging him. Ed rolled away from its first pass, flailing to keep other zombie arms off him. His chest was burning. He could hardly breathe. He needed to get his strength back but there were too many to pause. Then out of nowhere the big guy appeared again, grabbing him with both big paws.

Ed watched the scene as if outside his own body. From above, he saw the thing's muscles strain and heard it roar. A red sheen descended across the world. Ed saw himself struggle in the creature's grip, but it didn't feel like he controlled his own actions anymore. He could only watch as the thing squeezed and pulled, tension in Ed's body rising and it stretched slightly, then suddenly snapped free in two separate pieces that flew in bloody crescent arcs to collapse on the ground. Black mixed with red as Ed wondered: Would he come back?

Then Ed knew no more. Lily never got any mementos of her father. Several days later, when Ed never returned and failed to answer any radio calls, Lily said with sorrow, "I didn't really know Ed. I don't think any of us did really, except for Marcus. But I do know that he was always ready with a joke to lighten the mood—sometimes one of his cracks was the only thing that kept us from killing each other. Anyways, even if we didn't know him that well, we'll miss him. So long, Ed."

The group lost a lot of survivors before their ordeal was through, but Ed's death was the toughest. Marcus went into a depression for days. Sam stepped up to fill the gap Ed's death had left in the group, and she eventually helped Marcus pull through. But even so, the group was never the same again.

Structuring the Experience in State of Decay

This story comes from my first *State of Decay* playthrough. In a way, it is a completely unsurprising episode, one of many such character deaths that a player may experience in this or any other zombie survival game. But for some reason, Ed's death affected me. I liked him. He was funny and skilled, and my favorite character to play. And suddenly, he was the first character I lost. When I realized the controls no longer worked and I was indeed watching a death cutscene, I entered a state of helplessness and shock. As a few days passed in real life, I kept coming back to the circumstances and final moments. I told friends about it, like it was something that actually had happened that I had to get off my chest. I kept playing the game of course—if anything, I was even more obsessed with it now—but the game world seemed a bit sadder, a bit less hopeful that it would all turn out okay.

I realized that a video game had made me sad.

Not in any great way. Not in a way that compares in any meaningful sense to real life events. But still, in a very real way, Ed's death made me sad. This game had delivered an emotional impact, one that far exceeded any scripted character death that I had ever experienced, including *Final Fantasy VII*'s famous surprise fatality that often receives the title of "saddest video game death of all time" (Schreier; Ign).

So how did *State of Decay* achieve this level of emotional intensity? How did it combine scripted and unscripted elements of play to produce a spontaneous emotional experience on the level of the most tightly scripted dramatic scenes? What does this case study reveal about the debates within video game scholarship on the contrast between narrative and play? This essay examines these questions, using *State of Decay* as a case study in the interplay between scripted and ludic approaches to game design.

State of Decay is an open-world zombie survival simulator in which players take control of a group of survivors trying to outlast and escape from a zombie apocalypse in a small Rocky Mountain town. Developed by Undead Labs and published by Microsoft Studios in 2013, the game quickly became one of the year's standout titles. It sold 250,000 copies in its first two days on the Xbox live marketplace, then doubled that number by the end of its first two weeks. This made it the second-fastest selling title, behind only the cultural juggernaut *Minecraft* (Sanya "Breaking Records"). By the end of the year, it had sold more than one million copies (Matulef). By the next year, its total had reached two million (Undead Labs).

The game's success can be credited to its combination of traditional elements of third-person action-stealth gameplay with innovative features centering around not just one character, but rather a group of survivors and their compound. Over the course of the game, players will switch between different members of the group in order to establish and defend a compound, collect resources, and recruit fellow survivors. Members of the group each possess emotional states, leading to potential interpersonal conflict that must also be managed.

These features transform the game into a collective survival simulation rather than a straightforward first- or third-person adventure. They also make clear the ways in which modern games transcend the strict theoretical division between narrative and play in game design. Indeed, *State of Decay* makes for an excellent study between these theoretical positions, because its two game modes each embrace one side of the coin.

Campaign Mode

At release, *State of Decay* presented players with a traditional narrative-focused game. The story began with Marcus and Ed, two friends camping in the Rockies to escape the stress of their office jobs. They soon come under attack by zombified fellow campers, at which point the game presents players with the first quests to complete. Following the quest chain, Marcus and Ed recruit their first additional character, a useful Army veteran named Maya, and make an aborted attempt to fortify the ranger station. When Ed is bitten by the ranger, who has turned and now must be killed, they abandon this outpost in favor of hooking up with an established survivor group led by Lily. Lily, coincidentally the ranger's daughter, has gathered a group of survivors at a church in the main part of town. Upon arrival, the game enters its more permanent mode of play, in which the player switches between playable characters in order to gather resources, improve and upgrade the compound, establish outposts, and deal with plot elements as they arise.

In addition to the main quest, this stage of the game presents players with a variety of semi-scripted or spontaneous events to drive a more open storyline. This approach is now standard for open-world or "sandbox" games like *State of Decay*. While scripted plots include side quests based on specific character arcs, such as curing Ed's fever or managing relations with a local redneck clan, other spontaneous events are generated by the game's characters and the player's interaction with the environment. A depressed or angry survivor in the player's group, for instance, might start arguments with other group members, leading to injuries, waste of resources, and reckless behavior. In these cases, the game presents the player with a quest to cheer the affected survivor, by accompanying them on a short adventure to clear out a zombie nest and improve their morale. Survivors can also request assistance in supply runs, in dealing with "freak" zombies who are tougher to kill than normal ones, or in returning to base after getting lost or separated. Similarly, other groups of survivors exist who can at times request assistance. All these elements generate gameplay—even persisting while the player is away from the game. As Undead Labs' promotional materials claimed, "The open, sandbox world develops in real-time, shaped by your actions, dynamically generating content based on your choices and the ever-increasing zombie threat" (Sanya "About State of Decay").

In this way, scripted and semi-scripted events combine to lead the player through the daily and weekly routine of survival in a zombie apocalypse. Eventually, if the player pursues the main quest line to its completion, the player's survivor group will cooperate with local military elements to clear the blockade to the next town, where they will then all relocate in hopes of a less threatening situation. True to the zombie genre, which rarely ends with the outbreak fully contained, *State of Decay*'s final quest seems not to promise salvation for the characters. However, this ambiguous end still offers an ending, in that the characters' story has progressed from ominous beginning, to action-packed middle, to final achievement of the goal they had set.

Breakdown Mode

The game's first expansion, "Breakdown," has no conclusion. Undead Labs openly stated that they designed the mode in answer to what fans enjoyed in the original: "Less story, more survival. Long-term survival." In other words, while many fans did appreciate the plot and characters of the campaign mode, what made the game so unique and compelling was how it delivered on fans' desire for a long-term survival simulator.

It was this desire that lead designer Jeff Strain himself felt when he first conceived the game: to create a zombie survival simulator that was truly long term, he focused on community as an element of survival just as important as guns or ammo. With the requirement to play multiple characters, and the ever-present threat of permanent death, the game promoted long-term emotional investment in individual characters and the relationships between them (Strain). This player-driven emotional investment had the potential to become far greater than any scripted narrative could achieve.

Breakdown mode is therefore the ultimate sandbox: there is no plot to uncover and progress. There is no hope of eventual rescue or escape. Players can only build their community, defend their walls, and try to keep as many characters alive as long as possible. When local resources run out, six characters can pack up into an RV and leave the area—but the engine soon breaks, stranding them again with the same problems they had before. In game terms, each trip on the RV progresses the player to the next level of Breakdown, respawning the world at a higher difficulty level where resources become scarcer and infestations more intense. The only plot, therefore, is raw survival.

Ed's Last Day: A Balance of Narrative and Play

The existence of these two game modes makes *State of Decay* a useful case study in the theoretical distinction between narrative and play. Each mode displays traits of both approaches, but each also shifts the balance point in opposite directions.

The campaign mode, in addition to its formal narrative elements, also features play-driven storylines generated by game features of resource limitations, survivor emotional states, group interactions, and above all the injuries and fatalities inflicted by the ever-increasing zombies. These elements actually outweigh the formal elements in the time a player will spend interacting with them.

Conversely, while the breakdown mode excises most formal narrative in favor of highlighting the spontaneous elements, it still retains the short quests that the game spontaneously generates during play. These include the missions to cheer up survivors, help hunt down freak zombies, and interact with other groups. Gameplay in this wide-open world therefore at times does progress through scripted scenes as well as purely spontaneous play.

To illustrate the balance the campaign mode achieves between narrative and play, we can return to the story of Ed's disastrous final quest. This story emerged through an interaction between a formal quest and the challenges that arose through spontaneous play. These included:

Formal narrative elements:
- Ed's joking and generally flippant attitude come from his scripted personality: he is designed as a wisecracking sidekick to Marcus, the first character the player controls and the closest thing to a protagonist.
- Lily's quest to obtain something of her father's is a standard quest generated once the player progresses to a certain point in the game. Lily assigns it over the radio to whichever character the player happens to control at the time. The dialogue proceeds as scripted, with a second conversation taking place while the character chosen drives up toward the ranger station.
- The surprisingly high number of zombies at the ranger station seems scripted by the designers: many players have reported more intense infestations surrounding this quest. The designers apparently meant the quest to be difficult to complete.
- The fact that I chose Ed for this quest came from earlier scripted elements. He was one of three characters present for the father's

death, and had himself been bitten by the man after he turned. Therefore, though the game allowed me to attempt the quest with any character, other scripted elements prompted me to use Ed.

- Lily's kind words after Ed's death represented a unique variation on her standard death speech. As I later learned, after a character dies, the player returns to the compound in control of one of the other survivors. This survivor is listening to Lily give a short speech on their loss. While most other characters receive the same generic eulogy, Ed's death prompts a more specific invocation.
- Similarly, while the death of a survivor always carries the potential to affect the emotional states of others in the group, Ed's death will automatically inflict "depression" on his friend Marcus. The two begin the game together, and are scripted to be close friends. Marcus' depression is therefore automatic if Ed dies. It will eventually generate a follow-up quest for one of the other survivors to take Marcus on an emotionally fortifying zombie hunt, one of the periodic mood maintenance missions. This element shows how scripted and semi-scripted elements overlap.

Semi-scripted/mechanical elements:
- Ed's habit of running down zombies with his car came from an achievement for running over 250 zombies with a vehicle. My attempt for "Vehicular Zombicide" cost Ed his first car, because I had been running down so many zombies to get the achievement to pop.
- Ed's obsession with killing the juggernaut zombie with his car stemmed from another achievement—"Get Outta My Dreams," earned by killing each type of special zombies with a car. If not for this achievement, I would probably have ignored the beast altogether, and not lost Ed's car before reaching the station. That loss made escape far more difficult from the surprising situation at the station.
- The fact that fellow survivor Sam increased her role in the group after Ed's death came from the fact that she was my only other survivor with the reflexes skill. This key skill is incredibly useful in combat, and is another reason why I had been so overconfident with Ed in the first place. Game mechanics

therefore shape player choices in which characters to use based on the need to possess needed skills—whether combat skills like reflex, or skills related to maximizing facility use in the group's home base. Players must balance using their best characters so as to increase their stamina and other survivability skills, versus keeping them out of danger so that they provide maximum collective benefit.

- A second character mechanic encourages—in fact, mandates— players to switch frequently between survivors. Any survivor away from the base for a significant amount of time becomes tired, reducing their maximum stamina and eroding their effectiveness. While several items or character skills can mitigate these penalties, over time no survivor will withstand constant use. Players must therefore approach the game as a collective survival simulator, rather than a traditional narrative filtered through the eyes of a sole protagonist. Although the game begins with Marcus, and although his skill set is among the game's most useful combinations, mechanical elements prevent him from ever becoming the sole protagonist. At times, he will inevitably—as he was during Ed's final journey—become unable to contribute until he has sufficient rest to recover from his exertions. Survival thus becomes a group endeavor, a task that can only be accomplished collectively. That lesson in fact becomes one of the game's overall meta-narratives, which the designers impose mechanically far more than they assert through dialogue or script.
- A final mechanical element may be presumed, but should still be mentioned: the design choice for "permadeath," and the parallel choice not to allow any backup saves, gave stakes to this story that otherwise could have just been immediately reset. Without that option, my mistakes created permanent consequences for Ed and his group.

Spontaneous elements:
- Other than the influence of achievements guiding my play, the loss of both cars was purely spontaneous. The first car had been damaged through use by another character, while the second was rendered useless by my ineffectual attempts to run over the only zombie in the game who can withstand a direct hit from a vehicle. Having not yet learned how to approach these beasts, my first attempts literally drove Ed to disaster.

- Ed's hammer breaking reflected a similar dynamic that can emerge through play: the loss of a weapon through repeated use.
- Ed had the bad luck of his player planning poorly. Resource-based dilemmas can be made worse when, as in this case, an overconfident player pays less attention to them than is appropriate. I had grown overconfident with Ed: his character level and rare skill set had made him a seemingly unstoppable character, and I therefore neglected to adequately prepare for what turned out to be a difficult quest. This overconfidence cost Ed his life.

The early video game theorist Gonzalo Frasca wrote that games provide a way of structuring simulation, just as narrative offers structure to representation. Furthermore, he wrote, the element of play adds to the emotional content of a story in the same way that those who watch a sporting event feel the experience differently than those who actually live the game on the pitch ("the feeling of playing a soccer match cannot be compared to the one of watching a match") (Frasca). Other scholars have used concepts from the science of emotions to describe how video games draw out emotional experiences by adding agency to events, prompting players to feel a story more deeply than if they had passively experienced it without being able to affect its outcome (Järvinen).

We can expand on these ideas using this example from *State of Decay*: Only through combining the three elements of script, mechanics, and spontaneous play could a story emerge that affected me as much as Ed's death did. If his demise had come through purely scripted events, such a fatalistic approach would have undermined the pathos. I would have possibly felt somewhat sad, but not as much knowing that there was nothing I could have done to prevent it. Scripted elements did, however, contribute to the drama in an essential way: it seemed cosmically unfair to me that Ed would die trying to do a favor for Lily, a gesture that would also tie up a loose end from his own past. Finally, the spontaneous elements added a key emotional element of shame and blame: It was my fault Ed died. I had killed him, not the writers. His death was not scripted; it could have been prevented, had I planned better or played better. But I did not. Ed paid the price.

Ed's story, and my experience in *State of Decay*'s two game modes, shows how narrative and play elements do not represent the dichotomous states that early game design theory first explored. To be sure, the campaign mode includes scripted plot developments, which if followed through will end the game. But players will, in practice, spend the majority of their playtime in unscripted or semi-scripted encounters generated by the game's mechanics rather than its writers. The game's basic appeal rests on its open-endedness, its sandbox nature, and its ability to offer players a world to explore and overcome. A purely scripted experience would play entirely differently—as can be seen with a comparison to a contemporary success in zombie gaming, Telltale Studio's "interactive drama" take on *The Walking Dead* franchise.

Conversely, the fact that *State of Decay*'s breakdown mode eliminates scripted plot does not mean that the game lacks plot. In fact, the game retains a meta-plot in the same way that other genres' conventions and mechanics impart narrative and even political meanings to otherwise spontaneous gaming experiences (Wackerfuss). In *State of Decay: Breakdown*, this meta-plot generates through the player's repeated establishment, maintenance, and then abandonment of a series of survivor compounds, each of them becoming more difficult to maintain in the face of dwindling resources. The continual recurrence of the same dynamic thus creates a plot without direct intervention from scripted dialogue. This plot is simple: this situation is hopeless as a long-term proposition. Nothing will end this zombie apocalypse. Those enduring it must simply do that—endure—and in the meantime, cultivate human relationships as best they can, in order to keep themselves sane and alive for as long as possible. But not forever.

This admittedly bleak scenario matches well with *State of Decay*'s main plotline, which suggests that the survivors' quest to escape the infected valley has proven fruitless. Upon breaching the wall that had blocked them from exit, they discover that the next town is the same as the last: a desolate landscape, burned out cars, and corpses beginning to rise. The infection has already spread, and nowhere is safe.

Such an ending stays true to the zombie genre from its earliest origins. As in George Romero's founding trilogy of films, zombie stories often eschew a final triumph. There is no final zombie to kill; any potential cure to stop the outbreak proves illusory; any attempt to establish new societies or places of protection break down under the weight of human failings; any escape from these degenerating situations will only start the cycle over again.

Given these dynamics, it becomes clear that even though *State of Decay*'s two game modes seemingly highlight the differences between narrative and play in game design, each in the end resolve into the same basic narrative and play style. Neither mode is purely scripted, or purely sandbox. Both combine elements in order to generate meaningful, emotional player experiences that have the potential to surpass those achievable by either of these approaches alone. *State of Decay* thus reveals how game design can turn the dials between narrative and play, combining both approaches in order to generate different user experiences and emotional interactions.

Note

1. All quoted game dialogue from Undead Labs, *State of Decay*, published by Microsoft Studios, 2013.

Works Cited

Frasca, Gonzalo. "Simulation Versus Narrative: Introduction to Ludology." *Video Game Theory Reader*. Ed. Mark J.P. Wolf and Bernard Perron. New York: Routledge. 2003.

Ign. "Top 100 Video Game Moments: #1: Aerith's Death." *Ign.com*. Web. 15 February 2015.

Järvinen, Avi. "Understanding Video Games as Emotional Experiences." *Video Game Theory Reader 2*. Eds. Mark J.P. Wolf and Bernard Perron. New York: Routledge. 2009.

Matulef, Jeffery. "State of Decay Sells One Million Copies." *Eurogamer.net*. October 2013. Web. 15 February 2015.

Sanya. "About State of Decay." *Undeadlabs.com*. 2 October 2014. Web. 15 February 2015.

Sanya. "Breaking Records." *Undeadlabs.com*. October 2013. Web. 15 February 2015.

Schreier, Jason. "The Real Reason Aeris's Death Made You Cry." *Kotaku.com*. 27 April 2013. Web. 15 February 2015.

Strain, Jeff. "State of Decay: Year One." *Undeadlabs.com*. 5 June 2014. Web. 15 February 2015.

Undead Labs. *State of Decay*. Published by Microsoft Studios. 2013.

Undead Labs. "TWO. Million. Sold." *Undeadlabs.com*. Web. 15 February 2015.

Wackerfuss, Andrew. "'This Game of Sudden Death': Simulating Air Combat in the First World War." *Playing with the Past: Digital Games and the Simulation of History*. Eds. Matthew Wilhelm Kapell and Andrew B.R. Elliott. New York: Bloomsbury. 2013.

Game, Narrative and Storyworld in *League of Legends*

EMILY JOY BEMBENECK

Historically, game studies has often been concerned with the relationship between game and narrative. Even long after the great debate of the early 2000s, we still encounter questions related to just how exactly games tell stories, and whether they actually tell them at all (Aarseth; Eskelinen; Frasca; Murray). *League of Legends* is a strong example of a case where game and narrative are actually quite separate, but still in a complicated relationship. We will attempt to understand how the dissonance between game and narrative in *League of Legends* is problematic by looking at four factors of its characters: believability, rigidity, interaction, and distance. After defining the problems apparent in this relationship, I offer an understanding of storyworld that may help us better see the possibilities of story in what may appear to be a game of pure mechanics.

Overview of League of Legends

League of Legends, developed by Riot Games, is one of the premier e-sports games at the time of this writing, with over 67 million players each month and revenue of over one billion dollars in 2014 ("Our Games"; Grubb). Not only is the game one of the most-played in the world, but it is also watched online by millions of interested fans. The 2013 annual Championship earned the record of the most watched e-sports event in history at the time, with over 32 million viewers having tuned in, and over 8.5 million watching concurrently. *League of Legends* is a Massive Online Battle Arena (MOBA) game, in which two teams of five players each compete against each other to gain control of a map.

In a typical MOBA, each player of a team controls a single avatar, known as a Champion in *League of Legends*, each of which has a unique set of abilities and statistics. The players move their avatars on a pre-determined map that has each team's base located in opposite corners of the square map. The object of the game is to destroy the opposite team's base (in *League*, this base is called a "nexus"). While seemingly simplistic, MOBAs are extraordinarily complex.

At the time of this writing, *League of Legends* had a roster of 119 Champions from which a player can choose. Champions work better in some roles during the game and have synergies with and against other Champions that are not immediately clear to the player, but rather discerned from practice or from study outside of the game on various websites and forums. Further, *League of Legends* has two systems that players can use to further define their Champions. Each player has a set of masteries that take the appearance of a skill tree, and ask players to make a series of quick choices to provide their Champions with bonuses around the three major areas of offense, defense, and support. Players are also able to slot runes into their Champion that provide additional bonuses on top of masteries. While these choices take place before a match officially begins, additional choices must be made throughout the match. Champions earn gold by defeating other Champions, computer-controlled entities, and map objectives. This gold can then purchase items that provide additional bonuses and ability modifiers. Due to Champions' unique innate characteristics, some item choices will be substantially better than others. The game does try to suggest wise choices, but the player has full responsibility and control over this process.

This amount of complexity leads to a great opportunity for mastery. There are various ranks players can earn from winning matches against similarly skilled opponents. As noted previously, *League* has a very active professional scene that results each year in a world Championship. While similar in many ways to a traditional sport, *League of Legends* differs in its reliance on fictionality to provide a narrative framework for play. In most professional sports, we are quite comfortable playing and watching a purely abstract game. In basketball for example, we watch players interact with a ball, a net, and arbitrary lines drawn on a floor, with no fictional underpinning for the existence of these elements. The game is only its set of rules that restrict actions individuals may take in reality, but offers no fictional basis for why those rules exist as they are. *League of Legends*, on the other hand, does involve game pieces and rules, but the rules are grounded in a fictional logic, and the game pieces are characters and objects that exist in a fictional world.

The Narrative Framework of League of Legends

I call the narrative of *League of Legends* a "framework" because games in the MOBA genre emphasize the skills of the players as related to the ever-evolving mathematical meta-game, but treat the game's story as only extra information unrelated to gameplay, or a "narrative wrapper" (Dansky). Websites created by fans of the game are devoted to Champion usage statistics and player rankings. They highlight the dramatic nature of the meta-game surrounding *League of Legends* as players and Champions rise and fall with each patch to the game. Narrative, however, plays no role in the shifts made to the meta-game, and fan websites place no emphasis on Champion backstories or the game's narrative in general. In such a game, it may seem surprising that story and narrative would exist at all. As the developers at Riot Games themselves state, the story is the story, and the game is the game (RiotRunaan).

However, there is a story and it does impact the game in many ways due to this very separation. The narrative that frames play, as quoted below, explains both the role of the player within the game (a "Summoner" is a player) and the function of various objects on the game map. It also places the game map (the "Field of Justice") into a geographical and political context, and provides a rationalization for the diverse set of possible Champions that a player/Summoner can choose to play at the start of a match. The story then goes like this:

> Until only twenty years ago, [the world of] Runeterra was on a collision course with disaster. As quickly as Runeterra's denizens would band together in ancient times as tribes, opposing tribes would war to settle their disputes. No matter the era, the preferred choice of warfare has always been magical. Armies would be enhanced or decimated by spell and rune alike. Champions made the most of magical items forged for them as they led or supported armies. Summoners—often the *de facto* leaders of [the continent of] Valoran's political forces—would unleash mighty magical powers directly against foes and their holdings with little regard for consequence. With such an abundance of raw magical power at their disposal, there was little motivation for summoners to explore more environmentally-friendly forms of warfare.
>
> Within the last two hundred years, however, the dangers of unchecked magical warfare began to expose the fragility of Runeterra to everyone residing in Valoran. The last two Rune Wars drastically altered the geophysical landscape of Valoran, even after magical energy was focused on restoring it. Violent earthquakes and horrific magically-fueled storms made life on Valoran

challenging, even before factoring in the horror of warfare on the populace. It was theorized that another unchecked Rune War would tear the world asunder.

As a direct response to the world's growing physical and political instability, Valoran's key magicians—including many powerful summoners—came to the conclusion that conflicts needed to be resolved in a controllable and systematic way. They formed an organization called the League of Legends, whose purpose was to oversee the orderly resolution of political conflict in Valoran. Housed in the Institute of War, the League would be given the authority by Valoran's political entities to govern the outcomes of the organized conflict they would administer.

The League resolved that all major political conflict would be settled through the use of specially prepared arenas strategically located throughout Valoran. Summoners representing a particular political allegiance would each call forth a Champion; the Champions, leading mindless minions generated by novice summoners manipulating a nexus, would fight to achieve the objective of the arena they were in. The most common victory condition of a battle arena would be to destroy the opposing faction's nexus. These arenas are collectively referred to as the Fields of Justice" ["Institute of War," qtd. with permission].

This story created the fictional world within which the game exists and the group of characters that give the game its name. And yet, despite, or perhaps because of, this close relationship between fictional world and game elements, the narrative plays no role in actual gameplay. As we will look at in more detail later on, players control their chosen Champions, not through the guise of a "powerful summoner," but directly through hundreds of mouse clicks. A match in *League of Legends* is instantiated not by any political unrest or calling of the Institute, but by the willful click of a player on a button labeled "Play." The narrative framework of this game scaffolds an unnecessary rationalization for game elements, and in the process damages the very creations intended to provide the game with its meaning—the Champions themselves.

Four Factors of Dissonance

Let us look at how this dissonant relationship between narrative and game limits the meaning-making potential of Champions via four primary angles, though this is not necessarily an exhaustive list. We will look at (a) **Believability:** how the story challenges the ontological status of Champions through its extreme focus on explaining mechanics; (b) **Rigidity:** how this strict narrative rationalization does not allow for coherent character/Champion development or expression during play (c) **Interaction:** how the game does not allow Champions to react to other Champions or events in a meaningful way despite narrative expectations of this happening; and (d) **Distance**: how the narrative limits the direct relationship a player can form with his or her chosen Champion during play.

First then, let us turn to the topic of **Believability**. As we have seen, the game's narrative tries very hard to rationalize components of the gameplay itself, but its failure to be exhaustive differentiates those elements not described by the narrative as jarring abstractions with no basis in either reality or fiction. The narrative mostly succeeds in providing a world in which gameplay could be happening, but it overreaches its bounds and tries to give a narrative reason for various buildings on the map and many of the mechanics that occur during play. Under these strict narrative demands, any element without a narrative component strains the player's suspension of disbelief to the extent that the narrative is no longer a meaningful or even accurate description of the world. While the narrative explains at a simplistic level why Champions are fighting at all and names elements on the map, it does not explain why Champions provide gold when killed or how Champions respawn after death and the varied time with which this occurs. It does not explain why Champions need to gain levels every time they enter the map, and why their abilities get stronger as they level rather than being appropriately matched to their gladiatorial experience. Now, there can be rationalizations made for all of these presumably, but the very effort of doing so challenges the ability of players to buy-in to the narrative context of the game.[1]

Before the match even begins, the game already subverts its narrative underpinning and challenges the basic assumptions about what a Champion *is*. For example, a specific Champion in *League*, supposedly a member of the League of Legends and occasionally called on to fight in the Field of Justice, can be chosen by two different players in the same match, as long as the players are on opposite teams. This means that Team A may have chosen Lux (a priest-like Champion) as one of its Champions, but Team B can also choose Lux as one of its Champions. The game does not limit a team's choices based on the Champions chosen by the other team. Thus, when the players enter the map and begin the match, Lux is fighting against herself.[2]

This calls into question the ontological status within the fiction of the Champions themselves. Are the Champions merely clones of themselves? Are they images fighting an unreal battle? What exactly is happening? One can attempt many rationalizations, but the narrative simply does not allow Champions to fight each other, though the game itself does. Thus, the story fails in its primary intent to explain or rationalize game mechanics and damages the believability of all of its aspects beyond just character ontology. Since

Champions are the most important part of *League of Legends*—they are eponymous, for one, and the only consistent feature of the game across maps, modes, and events—damaging their believability cripples the narrative as a whole.

Champions are the name given to the play-pieces of the game, true, but this identity lingers beyond any single match. The visual identity of Champions litters the meta-game space. Players use portraits of Champions on the official game forums. Websites dedicated to the game display Champion statistics via the visual representation of individual Champions. Players speak of Champions by their names and typically play one or two Champions far more often than any others. The game is even entirely monetized through Champions, as each individual Champion costs a certain amount to unlock and various visual extensions to the Champion cost an additional amount. During a match, members of a team are identified on the map as their Champion, and they are denoted in chat by both their chosen Summoner name and their Champion name. As you can see, the game *is about* Champions and relies on them for financial sustenance and visual coherence. It is named after them, after all.

In such an environment, it should be unsurprising that damaging the believability of Champions damages the potential for players to buy-in to the fictional setting of the game at all. The narrative is not only insufficient to explain the game, but it is also apparently wrong. Champions cannot be what we were told they were, or what we see before us could not happen. Therefore, it becomes painfully obvious that we are in a game, a mathematical construct, *not a story*, or at least not the one we were told.

Second, let us look at the problem of **Rigidity**. Each Champion in *League of Legends* has a backstory that explains where the Champion comes from, what motivations led him or her to the League, and what relationships he or she shares with other Champions. Unfortunately, while these backstories provide the possibility of character expansion and development, the game itself does not allow this to happen in a coherent or believable way.

Let us look at a recent example involving the Champion Darius. Darius comes from the country of Noxus, where he served in the military from a young age and was known for acts of extreme bravery and leadership on the battlefield. He played a key role in the support of Noxus' recent leadership change and has a strong loyalty to his country. He carries a large axe, and his abilities involve thematically relevant acts of decimation and decapitation. Darius is a serious force of might and not someone an opponent should take lightly.

Riot recently released a new skin, a set of visual adjustments to the Champion, for Darius that gives him the title of Dunkmaster. The skin shows him wearing basketball shorts and a jersey with Noxus colors and with "Noxus" written on the front. Instead of an axe, he carries a basketball pole and headboard, and dribbles a basketball in his other hand. The skin also adds a prolific number of voiced quotes to his repertoire. If a player chooses Darius and equips the Dunkmaster skin, Darius will now say thematically relevant comments when using specific abilities, buying certain items, and encountering specific heroes. The extent to which this skin expands his vocal repertoire is unusual and helps to further develop his personality and character as not just a warrior on the battlefield, but one on the court as well. In short, the skin develops and expands his character in a playful but coherent way. He is still a champion of Noxus and a force of might within his sphere of influence—in this case, basketball.

The problem is that *League*'s narrative dictates that Darius' appearance on the game map equals his appearance on a field of battle at national scale. Coming to work dressed for a basketball game when your work is gladiatorial team combat will likely not result in favorable outcomes for your team. However, *League* the game allows for this event to take place, even though the narrative does not. Because the narrative places such a restrictive bound on the purpose of Champions on the field, it leads us to expect that Darius as a member of the League of Legends would only appear in battle dressed appropriately. In effect, the game-narrative relationship imposes restrictions on the possible development of these characters due to its problematic focus on using narrative solely to frame ludic elements. When these restrictions are relaxed, the game-narrative relationship forces the dissolution of credulity. On their own, both the game and the narrative allow for interesting developments to happen to characters; together, they force characters into a static rigidity that interrupts their potential and strains their believability.

Third, the story/game relationship is problematic due to the lack of **Interaction** between Champions. Regardless of which Champions are chosen by the players in a match, abilities perform the same, item availability does not change, and Champions act no differently depending on other Champions in the match. They are frozen in time, cookie-cutter figures with the backstory of a personality, but no personality in practice. Although we saw an interesting example of Champion personality in Darius as the Dunkmaster, there are other elements of his history and identity that are never depicted in the game despite their closer relation to the game itself than his skill at basketball. For example, his close relationship with Swain (another Champion), the Grand General of Noxus, has no impact on gameplay, even when he is allied with Swain on a team or playing against him, as the League dictates. One may perhaps expect that the two Champions would acquire a bonus when fighting together, or a penalty when fighting against each other, but in fact no change occurs at all.

I have previously noted that the game allows two copies of the same Champion to participate in the same game. On the opposite side of the problem, if two different Champions with relationships to each other participate in the same game, there is no consequence. While Darius and Swain have a positive relationship, other Champions are rivals like Morgana and her sister Kayle. Yet, they can play as allies on the same team without any penalty or consequence. Now, the League may dictate that Champions simply fight as they are summoned, but as Morgana's stated goal was to join the League only to kill her sister, it is rather difficult to believe that she would play nicely on the same team. The game and these narratives simply do not match. The narrative expects players to believe that in the same instance of the world in which Morgana hates Kayle, she also plays well with her. This is difficult to believe, especially without any support from the game to ease our acceptance of this event. The game does not allow for any narrative interaction between these two Champions to take place, and actually subverts the narrative of their personalities through its insistence on rationalizing the game map and the events that play out there.[3] Not only is the game-narrative relationship too *rigid* to allow for character development, it is too strict even to allow the representation of the characters as they already are. Without any possible interactions between characters, they are simply static points in narrative space-time, with no past and no future.

Lastly, let us look at the game-narrative relationship's problem with regard to the **Distance** it imposes between player and Champion. As seen in the story text above, the identity of the player during a match is not actually the Champion he or she has chosen, but rather that of a Summoner that exists outside of the game map and controls the actions of the Champion. When a player first creates an account to play the game, they must choose a "Summoner name" by which they are known to other players. While the entire nature of a Summoner and their relationship to Champions is never explicitly communicated to the player, there are elements of play that do manifest the relationship. For example, at the start of a match, a player does make choices about how a Champion will appear in the game (what skin they will equip) and what stats and bonuses the Champion will benefit from during the match (masteries and runes). Further, the player is able to choose two extra abilities known as "Summoner Skills" which are added to the Champion's ability kit and are available for use throughout the match. In addition, a player earns levels and bonuses that persist from match to match in contrast to the way a Champion starts fresh at level 1 in every different match.

While it is quite common in a video game to choose an avatar to play as during one's session and also to build that avatar as one wishes, it is unusual and unexpected to be identified as a separate fictional entity from the fictional avatar one has chosen to play once the game actually starts. In *League*, the player is given the odd position of being a human in charge of a Summoner in charge of a Champion, a role that is never clearly communicated to the player and thus has little hope of being a catalyst for meaningful experience. The Summoner itself is never visually depicted, has no interaction with other Summoners on the level of the game world, and has no backstory or narrative of its own. It is only an empty shell that serves to distance the player from the avatar that she is playing during any particular match. It does provide an identity that spans matches, but one that is devoid of any meaning and thus questionable at best, and distracting at its worst. Riot recently noted the inherent problems in this narrative design, and stated "the very idea of all-powerful Summoners made Champions little more than puppets manipulated by god-like powers" (Gnox).

The gameplay also does not fully support the notion that Summoners are controlling Champions. To buy a Champion an item during the game, the Champion himself has to travel to the shop located on the game map and purchase an item. One would think that an "all-powerful Summoner" would be able to simply provide a Champion with an item without the shop middle-step. Further, when a Champion dies, the player must simply wait until their respawn timer expires and they come back to life. There is no action that a Summoner takes to make this happen, and they are powerless to adjust the time between lives. The idea of a Summoner is really only a rationalization of there being a player at all. Otherwise, in the narrative of *League*, Champions would just fight each other on the field of battle, resolve their political conflicts, and go about their day. The game would not need to be played at all. The end effect of the Summoner notion then is to make the player an afterthought, when without the player, we would not have a game (or narrative) at all.

These four factors of the game-narrative relationship damage the notion of Champions to such an extent that it reveals the underlying truth of their ontology. They are, in fact, *not* characters, but only play pieces. The game-narrative relationship strips their identity of anything beyond their game function. The drama of the game is between players, not characters, and the relationship even goes so far as to subvert that. The narrative framework of the game, at this point, seems mostly irrelevant.

A New Hope

Riot gradually became aware of these various problems and decided to rewrite the story of *League,* apparently sensing the same narrative irrelevance I have just described. While this change had been happening over time through character revamps and world events, it was only in September of 2014 that Riot announced they were moving toward a narrative in which the eponymous League of Legends as a fictional group would no longer exist.[4]

> At a very broad level, we've decided to push League's story beyond its original focus on explaining in-game action and forge a new narrative path for Runeterra—a *world* in which the factions and Champions we all know and love have full freedom to grow, travel, and kick ass on a *world*wide scale. From Champion interactions to bios to events (and beyond), we aim to expand the scope of League's story and pursue a more dynamic and wide-ranging *world* fit for the outsized capabilities and personalities of our Champions. [...] [T]his new approach is focused on opening up *possibilities* and unlocking a wider, more fully-fledged *world*" [Gnox, emphasis added].

As one may expect, this announcement resulted in a variety of reactions within the game's community. While some were vehemently opposed to the rewrite, and many were nervous about its implications for both the game and its narrative, others were happy to see the change and excited about the future. We can draw one firm conclusion from this: players of a competitive, team-based, mathematically-driven game are open to and excited about story developments surrounding the game that they play. This further implies that despite the problematic narrative surrounding the game, the fictional world of the game held meaning, however nebulous, and attempts to develop and sustain that world are welcome and appreciated, regardless of how those story changes and developments are related to game mechanics.

Note Riot's use of language in this announcement though. I have emphasized the words "world" and "possibility" especially because I want us to think about a new kind of relationship for game and narrative in *League of Legends*—one that emphasizes a storyworld over a narrative, and possibility over rationalization. This new relationship may offer some solutions to the stated problems and provide a framework for realizing the potential of story elements in a game that does not rely on or even allow a narrative to create gameplay value.

Story and Storyworld

I have noted that Riot says that the *League of Legends* story is separate from the game, but we have not yet investigated the term "story" to really understand what is being communicated. In this final section, we look at differences between story and narrative and meet the related concept of storyworld. Through this discussion, I hope we can come to an understanding of storyworlds as possibilities of narrative and as forces that serve to ground experience within a game, despite the lack of pure narratives within actual gameplay.

The lay public typically associates the word "story" with "narrative," and we see this happening in Riot's declaration of story-game separation as well. What they are calling a "story" is a chain of events that occurs between specific characters in a fictional place and/or time, a common understanding of a "narrative." In *League*, the chain of events we were familiar with was that leading up to the inception of the League of Legends and the individual backstories of how each Champion came to join the League. In an actual match of gameplay, however, both of those narratives or narrative groups have occurred in the fictional past.

As I have said earlier, Champions as understood under the strict game-narrative framework are static; they are frozen in narrative space-time.[5] The particular Champions in any match have no narrative reason for being there aside from being summoned, and the actions players take through their Champions have no narrative component at the story level. Rather, we can tell engaging narratives about the team play that occurs during a match, but those are stories of human competition facilitated by game pieces and a game map— it is not a story of how Champions in Runeterra encounter difficulty and overcome it through the strength of their various personalities and characters.[6] In essence, the Champion only brands a set of abilities and offers a gamepiece with which a player may interact with other players on the game board or map. Under this simplistic understanding of "story," Riot is correct then that, for the most part, the "story" or narratives of *League* are separate from the gameplay of individual matches, as we have seen.

However, we are left with the obvious fact that players are still playing specific Champions with specific ability kits and specific appearances on a map where locations are specifically labeled with currency that can buy specific items with specific names. If story were truly absent from the game, players would be manipulating generic blue cubes on a generic grey plane, using abilities with generic names and upgrading their cubes with generic increases.[7] Every name of every element, and essentially, every choice made by the creators to not use the abstract is a choice to inject story into the game.[8] Though no narrative on the level of the fictional world may result, story is apparent at every turn and every moment during a match of *League of Legends*. But then, one may ask, if the story is not telling a narrative, how is it a story at all?

The elements of story I have described here are not being combined to form a narrative, true, yet they are clearly not abstract and certainly fictional. The difference between Riot's understanding of story as narrative and our discussion of story as diverse elements in the fictional world is important. We are speaking not about *a* story, but about *story* in a broader sense. More precisely, the elements of story in the game are representations of various characteristics and entities within the storyworld. In Herman's work, a storyworld is a "mental model of who did what to and with whom, when, where, why, and in what fashion in the world to which recipients relocate as they work to comprehend a narrative" (Herman 9–10).

My understanding of storyworld is slightly different. Rather than being a collection of the events, inhabitants, and motivations that happen within narrative's fictional universe, a storyworld, particularly in video games, is rather the possibility of those events, inhabitants, and motivations. To rephrase Herman's definition then, I would say that:

> A **storyworld** is a mental model of who *may do* what to and with whom, when, where, why, and in what fashion in the fictional universe to which recipients (readers, players, viewers, etc.) recenter (to borrow Marie-Laure Ryan's term) as they work to comprehend and create the connections between the situations and characters inhabiting it [Ryan 21–3].

When we realign the definition of storyworld with one of possibility, we are better able to account for the evolution of storyworlds in such elements as fan fiction and reboots, regardless of declarations of canon or fictional truth.[9]

Let us unpack this definition a bit by using the current game under discussion as an example. The storyworld of *League* is that which contains all the various possibilities of narrative that can result in the fictional universe. This includes the narratives of the (now-former) League of Legends, its history, the former biographies of now-revamped Champions, the biographies of yet-to-be-designed Champions, fan fiction, and other examples of both developer and player authorial action. But beyond just possibilities of narrative, it contains the raw elements of story before any narrative is formed. It is the characters and their personalities. It is the names of various countries in Runeterra. It is the choice to have a nexus as opposed to a throne or a base or a fortress. The storyworld is everything fictional about *League*, both in the game and beyond it. Whether a meaningful narrative results from those elements during the course of play is mostly irrelevant. The storyworld is active even without narrative as it grounds the action of the game in a single, fictional universe, and as it allows players the ability to play with various story elements, particularly Champions.

Building on Carey's understanding of journalism or other forms of communication as culture, a storyworld also communicates a culture of possibility within which play can happen, both play with narrative elements and play with game pieces and other players. The restrictions imposed by *League's* original narrative is a factor of storyworld potential not being realized. A game does not need to be explained by a narrative, nor does it even need a narrative to result during play to still tell a story, when we understand story as a broad set of narrative elements with cultural commonality. The storyworld communicates itself through that diverse set of elements, not through a coherent linear narrative. This means we can see Darius on the game map dressed in his Dunkmaster costume and still be very aware that we are in the world of *League*, even though there is no logical or coherent reason for that to be happening. It does not need to be logical or coherent in terms of a linear narrative; the fact that it is an element of the same storyworld (as communicated through names, colors, and actions) is coherent and logical enough. The fictional reality that a player finds herself in is one "brought into existence, [and] produced, by communication," which in *League of Legends*, is primarily the communication of characters' personalities and identities through visual representation (Carey 25).

In a game-storyworld relationship, characters do not require linear narrative development. They do not need a single biography.[10] Darius can be both a solider of war and an amazing dunkmaster *simultaneously*. Instead of focusing on the actions that players take on game elements, the storyworld focuses on the possible identities of its characters. The map becomes a place where players can play with different identities of Champions, not in order to fulfill a narrative requirement or construct a linear narrative around them, but simply to engage with the character as an interesting personality that has aspects to discover and appreciate. Story impacts every element of play, because the Champion is the central element of the storyworld. Despite the fact that the dramatic narratives resulting from *League of Legends* gameplay focus on competitive outcomes, the experience of play is one deeply colored by the Champion a player has chosen to play. A storyworld allows a player to experience a world simply in being, rather than one in action, purely through the virtue of their chosen Champion's being a fictional entity within *League's* storyworld.

Conclusion

Understanding the game-narrative relationship as one instead between game and storyworld allows us to see more fully the complex interactions that occur in terms of communication between the game and its player. Further, it removes the chains of narrative coherence that plagued the early development of *League*'s story and undermined the possible experiences players could have with the storyworld. It would be interesting to further study the particular modes in which storyworlds are communicated beyond simple linear narratives, but also through the environment as Carson hinted at, and various other aspects of and beyond the games themselves.

Despite an apparent separation in *League of Legends* between game and story, we have discussed a different understanding of the relationship between the game and the communication of its storyworld that provides opportunity for meaningful story experience without the necessary requirement of a coherent linear narrative. Future evolutions of *League*'s story are likely to rely more heavily on this understanding of the possible game-story relationship in order to solve several of the problems currently apparent in the game-story relationship within League. Further, as game developers work to innovate and capitalize on the emotional potential of story and games, we are likely to see more interesting modes of storyworld representation and integration.

Notes

1. As Murray noted, players not only need to suspend disbelief to engage in narrative play—they need to actively create the imaginary world into which the narrative invites them (110).

2. A similar discontinuity occurs in *DOTA 2*, in which heroes may only be chosen by one team in a match, but they may be chosen by either team's faction, despite their narrative connection to only one or the other faction.

3. Riot is making some progress in this regard, but it is in reaction to the problems I am describing. The recent rewrite of Shurima and its associated Champions provided Nasus with voiced lines that are only triggered when his mad brother Renekton is in the game.

4. In mid–2011, Skribbles gave warning of some imminent changes to lore. In early 2012, RiotRaven noted that the game's current process of story progression would be ending, and later in 2012 Kitae announced changes in the writing team as well as the plans to update Champion lore. As of this writing, the latest update was in September of 2014 when Gnox announced the reboot of *League*'s narrative.

5. I speak here of the game modes as defined and allowed by Riot themselves. There is a player-created game mode known as League of Legend Factions that is heavily engaged with lore and story progression. In the current storyline season at this writing, there were 4,061 (including duplicates) players. In comparison, *League*'s current statistics declare that over 7.5 million players play the game concurrently during daily peak time every day ("Our Games"). The existence of League Factions shows that the storyworld is capable of evolution beyond League, but it is only confirms the assessment that *League* does not support in-storyworld emergent narrative within the official game. As Sylph's

post makes clear, there is also an active role-playing community on the forums, but again, this is confirmation that the storyworld allows for many interpretations and evolutions, but that the game itself does not.

6. Theorists have attempted to label various levels of narrative that occur during gameplay, whether linear, scripted narratives or as emergent narratives that rely heavily on the player as co-author, and of course, many gradations of these categories. For initial discussion of "emergent narratives," see Aylett, expanded in Louchart et al. For a recent discussion focused more broadly on games and levels of narrative engagement, see Calleja. The narrative I describe here is akin to his description of "ludic narrative involvement," as MOBA narratives of gameplay typically have little to no elements of immersion. They exist in the world of reality, and focus on player manipulation of game pieces and choices on the game map purely for the objective of winning, not for any narrative purpose or outcome. This topic deserves further study.

7. As has been discussed many times, Tetris provides a good example of an abstract game with no story that can yet be understood via narrative. See Murray for the classic discussion.

8. I think a good example of this is the *DOTA 2—Character Art Guide*. Intended for community-creators, it highlights how to make sure each character is "immediately and uniquely identifiable," not just as a game object, but as a particular Hero.

9. I include the term "create" in my definition, because I agree with Sicart that play "is an act of appropriation of the game by its players," but also that more broadly, a recipient is required for meaning to exist at all, and that meaning is always dependent on the particular context of that recipient. See Bogost and Brathwaithe and Sharp for different understandings of meaning-creation in games.

10. We can look at a character from classical literature to see a similar phenomenon. Burgess attempted to write a biography of Achilles through the *Iliad*, but this endeavor encountered problems. Achilles is a character within a storyworld that allows for many understandings of his character. Medea is another classical character that comes to mind with varied possibilities. In effect, we understand these characters not as single threads through time, but as all the possible choices they could coherently make.

Works Cited

Aarseth, Espen. *Cybertext: Perspectives on Ergodic Literature*. Baltimore: Johns Hopkins University Press, 1997.

_____. "A Narrative Theory of Games." *Proceedings of the International Conference on the Foundations of Digital Games*. New York: ACM, 2012. 129–133.

Aylett, Ruth. "Narrative in Virtual Environments—Towards Emergent Narrative." *Proceedings of the AAAI Fall Symposium on Narrative Intelligence*. n.p., 1999. 83–86.

Bogost, Ian. *Persuasive Games*. Cambridge, MA: MIT Press, 2007. Print.

Brathwaite, Brenda, and John Sharp. "The Mechanic Is the Message: A Post Mortem in Progress." *Ethics and Game Design: Teaching Values Through Play*. Ed. Karen Schrier. Hershey, PA: ISR, 2010. 311–329.

Burgess, Jonathan S. *The Death and Afterlife of Achilles*. Baltimore: Johns Hopkins University Press, 2011.

Calleja, Gordon. "Narrative Involvement in Digital Games." *Conference Proceedings from Foundations of Digital Games.* Chania, Crete, Greece: FDG, 2013.

Carey, James W. *Communication as Culture, Revised Edition: Essays on Media and Society.* New York: Routledge, 2008.

Carson, Don. "Environmental Storytelling: Creating Immersive 3D Worlds Using Lessons Learned from the Theme Park Industry" *Gamasutra.* UBM Tech. 1 Mar. 2000. Web. 4 Feb. 2015.

Dansky, Richard. "Screw Narrative Wrappers." *Dansky Macabre.* Tumblr. Web. 22 Jun. 2014.http://media.steampowered.com/apps/dota2/workshop/Dota2CharacterArt-Guide.pdf

Eskelinen, Markku. "The Gaming Situation." *Game Studies* 1.1 (2001): 68.

FACTIONS. *League of Legends Factions.* n.d. Web. 28 Oct. 2014. http://leaguefactions. net.

Frasca, Gonzalo. "Simulation Versus Narrative." *The Video Game Theory Reader.* Eds. M. Wolf and B. Perron. New York: Routledge, 2003. 221–235.

Gnox, Tommy. "Dev Blog: Exploring Runeterra." *League of Legends.* Riot Games, Inc., n.d. Web. 30 Oct. 2014. http://na.leagueoflegends.com/en/creative-spotlight/dev-blog- exploring-runeterra

Grubb, Jeff. "*Hearthstone, Dota 2* Can't Compete with *League of Legends* in Terms of Player Spending." *VentureBeat.* VentureBeat. 23 Oct. 2014. Web. 28 Oct. 2014.

Herman, David. *Story Logic: Problems and Possibilities of Narrative.* Lincoln: University of Nebraska Press, 2004.

"Institute of War." *League of Legends Wiki.* Wikia, n.d. Web. 28 Oct. 2014. http:// leagueoflegends.wikia.com/wiki/Institute_of_War.

Kitae. "Champion Bio Updates." *League of Legends Official Forums.* Riot Games. 31 Jul. 2012. Web. 30 Oct. 2014.

Louchart, Sandy, et al. "Purposeful Authoring for Emergent Narrative." *Interactive Storytelling.* Berlin Heidelberg: Springer, 2008. 273–284.

Murray, Janet. *Hamlet on the Holodeck.* Cambridge, MA: MIT Press, 1998. Print.

"Our Games." *Riot Games.* Riot Games, Inc., n.d. Web. 28 Oct. 2014. http://www. riotgames.com/our-games

Riot Games. *League of Legends.* 2009. Video Game.

RiotRaven. "A Message to Lore Fans: Where Our Lore Is Going" *League of Legends Official Forums.* Riot Games. 6 Jan. 2012. Web. 30 Oct. 2014.

RiotRunaan. "Riot, Destroy the League, Don't Erase It." *League of Legends Official Forums.* Riot Games. 7 Sept. 2014. Web. 28 Oct. 2014.

Ryan, Marie-Laure. *Possible Worlds, Artificial Intelligence, and Narrative Theory.* Bloomington: Indiana University Press, 1991.

Sicart, Miguel Angel. "Against Procedurality." *Game Studies* 11.3 (2011).

Skribbles. "Reinforcements, Reconsiderations, Retcons—Oh My!" *League of Legends Official Forums.* Riot Games. 24 Jun. 2011. Web. 28 Oct. 2014.

Sylph. "Institute of War: The Chamber of Antiquity—(Lore Archives & Other Literary Works)." *League of Legends Official Forums.* Riot Games. 20 Sept. 2010. Web. 28 Oct. 2014. http://forums.na.leagueoflegends.com/board/showthread.php?t=256575.

Valve Corporation. *DOTA 2.* 2013. Video Game.

Valve Corporation. *DOTA 2—Character Art Guide.* n.d. Web. 15 Jul. 2014.

Narrative-Heavy Games as Neo-Gothic Literature

Beyond: Two Souls *and the Player/Viewer in Contemporary Cultural Anxieties*

Eric W. Riddle

Tom Bissel's essay "Extra Lives: Why Video Games Matter" argues that, while on the surface movies and video games appear similar in their narrative structure, they are in fact quite different: "In terms of storytelling, they could not be more different. Films favor a compressed type of storytelling ... because they have someone deciding where to point the camera" (359). Continuing, Bissel argues that storytelling in games is immense and virtually limitless, that games "contain more than most gamers can ever hope to see, and the person deciding where to point the camera is, in many cases, you" (359–360). Movies and television offer purely passive experiences. Viewers sit and see what the director has chosen to show them. Literature, while more engaging with the mind and imagination, still offers little by way of choice to the reader. Video games allow for active and interactive experiences to the player. Thus, games do not require a rich storyline for players to enjoy them.

Tetris, for example, has no obvious storyline. The blocks fall and the player organizes them into rows and columns. *Tetris* is wholly a ludic artifact. It is meant to be played. *Tron* has somewhat more player interaction due to its multiplayer element, but the narrative only exists in the movie world. Without the film, the video game narrative is virtually non-existent. Even games like *Space Invaders* or *Galaxian* have minimal storylines, though it is understood that aliens are coming to earth and attempting to do something that the player's avatar disagrees with. Thus, players must protect one object from other objects. Not much else is known about the story or why the aliens are invading, but that story is not relevant to the game as a whole. However, video games only truly become their own genre when ludic and narrative elements come together.

Contemporary academics discuss the validity of video games in academia through two major aspects of the video games: the narrative and ludic. Narrative refers to the storyline and plot of the game. Ludic refers to the way the game is played: the controls, the buttons, how the character moves, and the interface through which players interact with their avatars. Ludic, in academic discourse, also reminds readers to consider that "games are not designed as artifacts only to be looked at or understood narratively like films or television, but to be played" (Kapell and Elliot 3). It is the combination of the two elements that make video games unique.

With the numerous advancements in video game technologies and gaming capabilities, many modern games are opting for narrative-heavy games with complex story arcs and multiple narrative threads woven together. These games typically have a lessened ludic element. Narrative-heavy games use cut scenes (mini-movies) to move the story along. Oftentimes, during these cut scenes, the player must be ready to push a button to react in real time to the events taking place on the screen. Thus, contemporary, narrative-heavy games require players to be much more active and involved in the story than a movie with a similar narrative might. It is for this reason that blending heavy narrative with a real-time ludic interface can take an engaging plotline, one that would make an excellent film, and make the story so much more powerful to the player/viewer. Video games are evolving, and one evolution occurring is the transition from story to interactive Gothic literature.

In Kyle Bishop's book *American Zombie Gothic*, Bishop quotes Steve Bruhm's explanation of what Gothic does: Gothic functions as "a barometer of the anxieties plaguing a certain culture at a particular moment in history" (Bishop 26). Bishop also quotes Fred Botting: "Gothic Narratives 'retain a double function in simultaneously assuaging and intensifying the anxieties with which they engage'" (Bishop 26). This idea of social anxiety will come up multiple times in discussions of Gothic. Games that opt for a highly narrative structure, especially ones with cinematics and cut scenes, often follow a somewhat Gothic feel. It is then not outside the realm of possibilities that these games are engaging players more than a film or novel could to assuage certain social anxieties that are more common to gaming demographics than others.

Looking mainly at game developer Quantic Dream and their most recent games, 2013's *Two Souls* and 2010's *Heavy Rain,* this essay looks at how the

narrative and ludic elements combine to create what could be the next evolution of Gothic literature; that is to say, an interactive Gothic text that contains the same elements of traditional Gothic literature but allows "readers"
to immerse themselves fully into the game and participate in not only the
events of the story but also the outcome. Sean Hollister, a reviewer for *The
Verge*, noted that *Beyond: Two Souls* has crossed "the blurry line between
movies and game." Hollister calls *Beyond: Two Souls* an "interactive movie"
and a "Choose Your Own Adventure book writ at large." Hollister, along with
many others, does not have the words to describe *Beyond: Two Souls* as anything other than a playable movie or a book come to life, where decisions and
story are as important as playing the game.

Beyond: Two Souls (*BTS*) has a fairly engaging storyline. It follows the
life of Jodie, voiced by Ellen Page, and her constant companion, a disembodied entity from another realm called Aiden. The story jumps around in time
in true Gothic fashion. In one chapter of the game Jodie is a young girl of
five or six. In another she is an awkward teenage girl going to a party, and
later she is in her early twenties. As the story jumps around, the game forces
players to piece the story together little by little. Looking at *BTS* chronologically, Jodie's childhood was traumatic. Her parents become afraid after other
entities from this unknown world start harassing Jodie. They drop her off at
a research facility where Nathan Dawkins, voiced by Willem Dafoe, takes care
of her. Jodie grows up and is recruited by a government agency. She also finds
herself on the lam and homeless at times, making friends with other homeless
people who take her in and shelter her. However, the game does not play out
chronologically which makes her life seem more disjointed and unpredictable
than merely rough. This narrative back and forth is typical of classic Gothic
narratives. One Gothic narrative that has a similar narrative disjointedness is
Strange Case of Dr. Jekyll and Mr. Hyde (*Jekyll/Hyde*) by Robert Louis Stevenson. *Jekyll/Hyde* employs these narrative switches to establish and maintain
the suspense plot, though it does something unique. *Jekyll/Hyde* begins with
Misters Utterson and Enfield out for an evening stroll. Utterson becomes the
main focus for most of the story, but we get parts of the narrative from Dr.
Lanyon in letters, and Dr. Jekyll himself offers some pieces. It is not until the
very end of the novel that the reader is told that Hyde, the clear villain of the
story, is, in fact, Dr. Henry Jekyll. Modern readers have been stripped of the
experience of this classic literary twist due to the popularity of the narrative
and its popular culture significance (C. King 158), but readers at the time
Jekyll/Hyde came out would have had no idea that Jekyll and Hyde were one
in the same. These little vignette-like stories all come together to give readers
the whole story, piece by piece, until the moment when Dr. Lanyon reveals

to Utterson by a posthumous letter that Jekyll is Hyde, but readers are left to get the explanation of how that is possible for Jekyll in the chapter "Henry Jekyll's Full Statement of the Case" (Garrett 105). And while some critics question the veracity of Jekyll's full statement (Linehan xii), Jekyll's full statement supposedly "gathers up the threads of the preceding episodes ... and joins them in a continuous, intelligible series" (Garrett 107). The story unfolds not just through multiple people, but in multiple timeframes. Enfield begins "The Story of a Door" telling Utterson about something that happened. Utterson then tells a story in a different timeline from Enfield's story. The stories unfold slowly until Jekyll's story returns to the very beginning and tells his piece of the tale, taking readers back to a previously unknown set of events. These time-jumps keep readers guessing about what is happening in the main storyline and how the pieces all fit together.

Quantic Dream, the developer behind *BTS*, is no stranger to narrative-heavy games. Their 2010 breakout hit, *Heavy Rain*, was similar to *BTS* in that it is also very narrative driven. Both *BTS* and *Heavy Rain* have numerous cutscenes and cinematics. *Heavy Rain*, however, includes an element that is unique to video games, one that movies simply cannot allow. *Heavy Rain* has multiple potential endings, each one depending on how the player plays the game. During the narration of the story, players make decisions that affect the outcome of the story. If players decide to let certain characters die, the ending will reflect those decisions. Thus, there are as many as fifteen to twenty different possible endings. This interactive decision-making engages players and makes them consider the outcomes of their actions more than they would in a game that followed a more linear plot. *BTS* also has elements of decision-making. In a scene where Jodie goes to a birthday party as a teenager, she, through the player/viewer, must make decisions about whether or not to engage in underage drinking, kissing, dancing, and many other issues facing teens. When Jodie becomes homeless later on in the game, players are given the option to cause "self-harm" to their avatar when Jodie finds a large knife in a moment of desperation.

While these decisions may not make the ending of *BTS* so drastically different as those of *Heavy Rain*, players still must consider the outcomes of their decisions and think through the consequences. This ludic element of decision making, each button a different choice, allows players a more intimate gaming experience than other games. Players must decide what Jodie says but also must accept the consequences of their actions. The action and fighting sequences are similar. If the fight scene requires the player to duck but the player presses the jump button, Jodie will take damage and the player may feel as though he or she let Jodie down. The player must protect and guide

Jodie, much like Aiden does in-game. Sean Hollister mentions in his game review how the controls for Jodie are very intuitive and natural and how the choices, though sometimes forced on the player, do not affect the enjoyability of the game.

You're not *controlling* Jodie so much as guiding her and protecting her, something that the game tries to drive home early on. It perhaps manifests itself most prominently in the game's action sequences. In a clever design choice that also makes for a far more intuitive control scheme than *Heavy Rain*, Jodie is always already throwing punches and dodging out of the way by the time you press a button—you simply mirror the motions she's already begun, driven by her natural instincts, to make sure she succeeds. Or fails, as the case may be: some of the game's most intriguing possibilities occur when Jodie doesn't get her way. There's no such thing as a "Game Over" screen in *Beyond,* and the plot will move along no matter what. Even waiting can occasionally be a choice. Just because there's no game over doesn't mean there aren't consequences for your actions, though. People can die, lives can be ruined, and Jodie can wind up with emotional scars.

Some players, however, may become bored with the repetitious nature of the action scenes: "The novelty wore off—hard. These [action] scenarios influence how the story unfolds, but they turn into filler, a detriment and distraction rather than a means of immersion" (Carmichael). When the ludic elements of the game distract from or prevent immersion into the game, something may need to be done to fix them. If players get bored with the gameplay or the controls that maneuver the character around, they are much less likely to keep playing. Thus we can see how important it is to find a balance between clever ludic designs and repetitious gameplay. Without a balance, players may not be willing to finish the game. Carmichael, in spite of this, states, "The controls and gameplay are tiresome, and they can be difficult to manage (or boring), but they're of little consequence compared to the well-written story, the depth of the characters, and the empathy you feel toward them." It seems that Carmichael is willing to overlook a shortcoming of the physical playing of the game when the emotional playing is so strong and powerful. However, without the ludic elements, the game would merely be a film that could not have the same level of emotional impact. Even with the repetition and "tiresome" gameplay, the narrative and ludic elements combine to make an enjoyable and powerful experience.

Returning to Bishop's descriptions of Gothic literature as a means of dealing with societal pressures, *BTS*'s story offers some unique catharsis to modern players. As noted above, a young, successful government agent finds herself running from the law and homeless. The game, released in late 2013, offers players the chance to deal with their own fears of economic turmoil and recession. People once well-off were finding themselves homeless or without the same level of stability they previously knew. The economic crash of 2008 affected many people directly and many more indirectly due to the ripple-effects of the various industries affected by the recession (Falcão Vieira and Falcão Vieira 138). It comes as no surprise, then, that a modern Gothic narrative would include a fall from grace and depression caused by the sudden loss of everything once known. Further, player choices affect the outcome of the story. It is possible to make a decision that will negatively impact the gameplay, thus making each decision real. Just as in real life, it is not always easy to see what the right choice is and only upon reflection can we see how our choices have affected our outcome.

One other scene already discussed, the teenage birthday party, involves societal stresses about appropriate behavior in social situations, especially among youth. Jodie has a constant, for all intents and purposes, imaginary friend who follows her around and to whom she regularly speaks. She feels comforted when she can feel its presence and the opposite when she cannot. She does not know how to behave as other children do because of Aiden, and often fears letting her peers get to know the real her. This game could be commenting on one of two acceptable social behaviors. The first may be that letting people know who we truly are, know our special gifts, can be intimidating and lead them to ridicule us. It is not unheard of for children to be bullied because they are passionate about a topic that other students do not understand or agree with. In one powerful scene, Jodie, through a decision of the player/viewer, must decide whether to lie or tell the truth about her gift. Players/viewers are forced to consider the implications of lying to a benevolent person or what could happen if they tell the truth. Another issue the game could be addressing may be how we interact with and understand behavioral disorders, especially as the number of youth diagnosed with behavioral disorders continues to rise significantly. According to CDC data, the number of diagnosed autism cases has risen from 1 in 150 children in the year 2000 to 1 in 68 in the year 2010. Jodie could easily be placed on the autism spectrum due to her inability/lack of desire to be social and her living with a constant disconnect to reality. Again, the social anxieties of the era influence Gothic narratives.

One of the largest and most prevalent concerns in Gothic literature is that of natural evil—the idea that evil exists in the world and is hard to discern or recognize. Stated another way, seemingly good people can commit heinous acts without warning. To emphasize this schism between good and evil, and partly as a measure to assuage concerns of the people, "Gothic novels present no restful human shades of grey: the characters are mostly either endowed with somber, diabolical villainy or pure, angelic virtue" (Varma 19). Victorian England was very much dominated by an aristocracy who could easily turn from upstanding citizens to evil-doers. Much of this evil stems from disobeying not only the laws of the land but also those of the dominant religion. In 1886, Robert Louis Stevenson penned *Strange Case of Dr. Jekyll and Mr. Hyde* (*Jekyll/Hyde*), which has become synonymous with the struggle between good and evil. The novel is so popular that many people who have never read it are familiar with some of its major themes: "Most Americans and Europeans who have never read the original story could summarize its plot, or at least explain its central premise" (C. King 158). Oscar Wilde wrote *The Picture of Dorian Gray* in 1890, which has a similar theme. Both of these narratives involve a divided protagonist who is struggling with the desires of behaving contrarily to how society would have him behave.

When it comes to the struggle between good and evil, many contemporary people might argue little has changed in the last two centuries—that good and evil still abound and the anxieties derived from that belief still fuel cultural behavior. *BTS* follows a very similar pattern as *Strange Case of Dr. Jekyll and Mr. Hyde.* Jodie, a young woman, is seemingly good at heart and wants to do what is right. Aiden is emotional and jealous: "Even without discernible language or a physical body, he demonstrates an amazing range of emotions. He's prone to angry fits of violence. He can be jealous. He throws tantrums" (Carmichael). Aiden is the Hyde to Jodie's Jekyll, though Jodie has less natural evil in her than Jekyll does.

Traditionally, Gothic literature is mainly characterized by a blending of supernatural and natural events. J. M. S. Tompkins, in the introduction to Devendra P. Varma's *Gothic Flame*, also addresses this element of Gothic. Qualities of the Gothic include "the sentiment of the past (highly anachronistic in detail), the development of the intricate plot of suspense, and the conflict of the imagination and rationalism in the explained supernatural" (qtd. in Varma xi). The Gothic takes otherwise unexceptional people and makes them act and react in extraordinary situations. Readers, then, must attempt to discern what is imagination and what is real. The Gothic finds a way to discuss societal concerns or fears in a supernatural and thus unthreatening way. Admittedly, Jodie is not an "unexceptional person." She has Aiden. This idea still applies, however, in that Jodie is not a physically large or particularly powerful person. She is often confused, concerned, and seeking validation. She is us. She is the player/viewer. She is a normal person who happens to be tied to an unidentifiable entity. As for the extraordinary circumstances, she passes that Gothic requirement with flying colors.

Late in the game but near the beginning of its internal chronology, Jodie finds herself walking through a research building in which scientists have built and subsequently opened a portal to Aiden's dimension. Entities similar to Aiden, though not nearly as nice as he is, come out of the portal and kill everyone inside, turning some in to zombie-esque beings, using their bodies to wreak havoc. Jodie is called in to investigate and shut down the portal even though she has no formal scientific training or real combat experience yet. Outside the building, protecting the entrance as she arrives are myriad police officers in riot gear. She, unarmed and unarmored, passes the guards and enters. She has to fight her way with only Aiden to protect her.

Another characteristic of Gothic literature present in many modern video games is a deep reliance on setting as an important element of the narrative. The Gothic of the 18th and 19th centuries "aimed at a medieval atmosphere by the use of medieval background—haunted castles, dungeons, and lonely towers..." (Varma 13). This can be seen in *Dracula*, *Castle of Otranto*, and *Frankenstein*, all of which include castles, forests, and the ruins of society. On the other hand, some Gothic narratives, *Strange Case of Dr. Jekyll and Mr. Hyde* and *The Picture of Dorian Gray*, for example, forgo the physical castles and towers with modernistic representations: decrepit laboratories and surgical theaters, dank alleys, and other ruined locations. Again, *BTS* meets this requirement in the Gothic literature checklist easily.

Much of *BTS* takes place at night, in rain and snowstorms, on the dirty and dank streets, or in laboratories. An early scene has Jodie, roughly 8 years old at the time, going into her dark garage to get some cooking oil for her mom. A dark garage can be just as menacing and terrorizing as a haunted castle or a scientific laboratory, and in *BTS*, the garage is a Gothic setting. As Jodie enters the garage, the lights flicker, and a menacing red light glows. Shadows dance around Jodie, and the low-light garage seems haunted. Another of the opening scenes has Jodie on the run from the police. It is nighttime, and she is hiding on a train. When the train stops and police enter the train car to search for her, she exits to the roof of the speeding train. Rain is pouring down, and players must fight their way past police and find a safe way to dismount the train. She jumps off and runs through dark, foreboding woods. Players must focus on dodging uprooted trees, low-hanging branches, and weaving in and out of the woods. Police send attack dogs to track her down, so she must avoid those as well. The setting, the woods at night in a rainstorm, is about as clichéd as it gets as far as dramatic chases go, but the interactivity of the game keeps players engaged even if the setting is less than unique. Again, it is the proper blending of ludic and narrative elements that make video games such a unique experience.

One crucial element in Gothic literature is "the development of the intricate plot of suspense" (qtd. in Varma xi). When a story's focus changes between characters, "we may be given a good picture of the origins of a conflict. We are shown how differently the various characters view the same facts" (Bal 148). In many classic Gothic novels, the point-of-view shifts between multiple parties in an attempt to paint a complete picture of the events. Peter Garrett extends this idea more, writing specifically of *Frankenstein*: "As we have seen, presenting or projecting multiple versions is the main way Gothic fiction reflects on narrative; here, by endowing the creature with speech, *Frankenstein* reflexively heightens its formal drama, lodging at the center of the novel an account whose perspective forcefully contests the authority of the one that frames it" (85). In Shelley's *Frankenstein*, we get to see the captain's point of view as well as that of Frankenstein and the creature. These various points of view come in the form of letters and word-of-mouth narratives. The various points of view provide a clear, mostly complete narrative for the events that unfolded. At the end of the novel, Dr. Frankenstein dies and his story is finished by the ship's captain, who sees the creature mourning over Frankenstein's body. According to Peter Garrett, "the most remarkable feature of Mary Shelley's monster story, and what most distinguishes it from its nineteenth-century successors, is that it includes the monster's story" (85). This inclusion of the monster's narrative allows readers to think a little more deeply about who is the evil one. Readers at the time would have been more influenced by these multiple narrative points-of-view because of the novelty and originality of the narrative. Garrett continues, "But for modern readers, whose reception of *Frankenstein* is inevitably mediated through the many popular versions of its story, the surprise of this moment is much greater" (85). Mieke Bal addresses this issue of multiple points of view skewing a reader's view or providing doubts about a character: "This technique can result in neutrality towards all the characters. Nevertheless, there is usually not a doubt in our minds which character should receive most attention and sympathy" (148). In most fiction the protagonist is easy to identify, but sometimes a novel can make readers question. True, the creature murdered innocents and is aware (Shelly 210), but he also shows remorse. The creator abhorred his creation and left him to fend for himself in a world dark and sickly, and Frankenstein showed no remorse even in death. In *BTS*, players/viewers are only given glimpses in to Aiden's story, and even then only at the end in one of Jodie's visions, but they do get to control and act as Aiden at various points in the story. They are able to choose what actions Aiden undertakes and give him a voice. So while *BTS* does not include the monster's story to the same extent as *Frankenstein*, players/viewers do build a strong connection to and even a sympathy for this disembodied entity.

Neutrality toward characters and the inclusion of multiple points of view, while somewhat weak in *BTS*, is very present in *Heavy Rain*. *Heavy Rain* tells the story of the origami killer, a kidnapper/murderer who leaves little pieces of origami at his crime scenes. The gameplay jumps back and forth between four main protagonists: Scott Shelby, a former policeman and private investigator; Norman Jaden, an FBI profiler; Madison Paige, a journalist; and Ethan Mars, father to the kidnapped boy. Each chapter has the player controlling a different character through a different part of the story. The puzzle pieces slowly fall in to place as the story progresses, allowing players to figure out what is going on in the quest to find the murderer. Each character has its own set of skills, talents, etc. Players must learn to control and navigate the world through each different character. As for gameplay, it is very similar to *BTS*. Button-pushes interrupt the numerous cut scenes. The action is fairly passive, but the decisions made in-game have a large impact on the outcomes of the game. These points-of-view truly affect the gameplay as killing off a character, or allowing one to die, removes their story from the narrative and changes the ending of the game. Not only is the narrative itself complicated, but the suspense grows through player-chosen scenarios. There is virtually no way to predict what will happen in any given moment.

BTS has a similar, though smaller, narrative-switch, though the player only ever plays as Jodie or Aiden. Each has his or her own game mechanics and controls, but the story focuses only on their tales. What makes *BTS* an excellent example of this Gothic-esque point-of-view is that its viewpoint switches more in time than in person, even more so than *Jekyll/Hyde* and *Frankenstein*. Jodie's story, as mentioned above, jumps through time in a disorganized and unpredictable way. In one chapter Jodie is 8 years old, living in a research facility and testing/proving her abilities. In the next she is in her early 20s and working for the CIA. Then she is 16 and going to a party. If the story were told in a chronological or linear manner, players would start out as a young Jodie and work their way through young adulthood. As it is, the story keeps the player/viewer guessing. Also, decisions made in one time affect the gameplay in later times. Thus, it can be hard to see a causal relationship between decision and consequence, but making a "wrong" decision as a teenager will affect how Jodie reacts to adult situations, even so much as altering the ending the player will see. Not only does this keep players engaged and interested in finding out how the story will end, it is also a unique and exciting ploy to keep players playing the game. When players beat *Heavy Rain* or *BTS* and find out there are multiple endings, many people will play the game again, making different decisions to find out how else the story might end.

Video game developers are trying new and unique elements, both ludic and narrative, to get gamers interested in games again, and academics are taking note of some of these new methods. A major debate that is taking place among academic gamers is which is more important when discussing video games: the ludic or narrative elements. I believe that the two cannot be separated when it comes to modern video games. Without a narrative element, games are unsophisticated and unengaging—or at the very least, will be perceived as "simple" and "old-fashioned." Without a unique ludic element or any ludic elements at all, the game becomes a movie. It is the blending of the ludic and narrative aspects of modern video games that make them a genre all their own and something that can be studied. That said, when a game is narrative-heavy with a complex and intricate plot, the ludic can take a backseat to the story and turn the game into an interactive movie and a neo–Gothic narrative. This neo–Gothic narrative allows for players to assuage modern societal fears and concerns in a safe and unthreatening environment while still experiencing some new and exciting gameplay.

Works Cited

Bal, Mieke. *Narratology: Introduction to the Theory of Narrative.* Toronto: University of Toronto Press, 1985. Print.

Bishop, Kyle William. *American Zombie Gothic.* Jefferson, NC: McFarland. 2010. Print.

Carmichael, Stephanie. "*Beyond: Two Souls* Deepens Our Human Connection to Video Game Characters (Review)." VentureBeat.com. VentureBeat. 8 Oct. 2013. Web. 10 Sept. 2014

Falcão Vieira, Euripedes, and Marcelo Milano Falcão Vieira. "The Economy in Crisis and Global Imbalance: An Essay on Structural Causes." *Pensamento & Realidade* 26.1 (2011): 133–152. *Academic Search Premier.* Web. 12 Sept. 2014.

Garrett, Peter. *Gothic Reflections.* Ithaca, NY: Cornell University Press, 2003. Print.

Hollister, Sean. "'*Beyond: Two Souls'* Review: Crossing the Blurry Line Between Movies and Video Games." *TheVerge.com.* Vox Media, Inc. 8 Oct. 2014. Web. 11 Sept. 2014.

Linehan, Katherine, ed. *Strange Case of Dr. Jekyll and Mr. Hyde.* By Robert Louis Stevenson. 1886. New York: Norton, 2003. Print

Kapell, Matthew Wilhelm, and Andrew B.R. Elliot, eds. *Playing With the Past: Digital Games and the Simulation of History.* New York: Bloomsbury. 2013. Print.

King, Charles. "Themes and Variations." *Strange Case of Dr. Jekyll and Mr. Hyde.* By Robert Louis Stevenson. New York: Norton, 2003. 157–163. Print.

Quantic Dream. *Beyond: Two Souls*. 2013. Video Game.

Quantic Dream. *Heavy Rain*. 2010. Video Game.

Shelley, Mary. *Frankenstein by Mary Shelley, Dracula by Bram Stoker, Dr. Jekyll and Mr. Hyde by Robert Louis Stevenson*. New York: Penguin, 1978. Print.

Stevenson, Robert Louis. *Strange Case of Dr. Jekyll and Mr. Hyde*. 1886. Ed. Katherine Linehan. New York: Norton, 2003. Print.

United States. Center for Disease Control. *Autism Spectrum Disorder: Data & Statistics*. 24 March 2014. Web. 17 Sept. 2014.

Varma, Devendra P. *The Gothic Flame*. London: Arthur Barker, LTD., 1957. Print.

"Thou Art I"

The Interaction of Play and Narrative in Persona 3

MARK FILIPOWICH

As videogames transitioned from a few enthusiasts' hobby projects in the mid-twentieth century into a medium with increasing cultural presence, players began to consider whether they belonged in museums and universities alongside classical works of art (Stalker 91). However, the question of "are games art?" is inextricably attached to "what is art?" a question with a long history and a myriad of perspectives, all of which seem incapable of yielding a satisfactory answer. What constitutes art and whether or not games qualify distracts from how players experience them and, ironically, in trying to define art, one loses sight of how games function in an artistic way. So rather than try to create a top-down definition of games as a global human experience, scholars—both popular and academic—have instead moved the more rigorous questions about what effects games are capable of communicating as independent texts. Videogames are composed of elements from other art forms— they include textual, visual, cinematic, and sonic elements of design—and so use the literary, cinematic, musical, and theatrical languages of other story-telling forms (Lavallée). However, games add the unique ingredient of player interactivity that demands its own kind of analytical competence from a would-be critic.

A life-long player might be able to intuitively understand a game's rules after a few moments of play and a literature or film aficionado might be able to appreciate the use of dialogue or the cinematographic use of space, but neither is an apt critic until they approach the cross-section of both elements. When a system dictates player behavior, what does that say within the context of the fiction? When a game focalizes on a character or an event in a particular light, how do those feelings then dictate how the player acts in the game's rules? Most importantly, how do the rules of play and the flow of narrative compose the game's theme: what does a game say simply by existing and how can a player understand that message? *Shin Megami Tensei: Persona 3* (Atlas; hereafter, *Persona 3*) is a game that effectively enmeshes all elements of design to achieve its artistic purpose. This essay discusses how the rules that guide play, the progression of story, and the outside cultural references referred to by both, are crafted to reinforce *Persona 3*'s theme of maturity and identity formation. *Persona 3*'s themes are enforced by tarot card symbolism and Jungian psychoanalysis both in their relation to the events of the plot, but also in how each are systematized through play. The underlying mythology of the tarot and the structure of Jung's theories not only shape meaning by interacting with the plot but in how each are the model for different but interwoven mechanics. It is through the marriage of plot and system that meaning is created and theme is expressed; *Persona 3* provides an excellent case study of how it is the consonance between systems and aesthetics that makes understanding a game through criticism possible. Before discussing how, though, it is important to understand the history behind both play-based and narrative-based criticism and how the limitations of each prompted a richer critical approach to videogames. Finally, this essay summarizes the mechanics and plot of *Persona 3* before analyzing how elements of play and narrative contribute to forming its central themes.

Ludology vs. Narratology—Round 1: FIGHT!

Early videogames were simple rulesets expressed in rudimentary shapes and sounds, many of which required reflex movements and pattern recognition to master (Barton and Loguidice) and told only the most basic stories. Over time, more inventive mechanics led to more complicated systems and more nuanced experiences; arcade and early console games became more sophisticated and many writers sought to understand how they worked as games, without trying to impose meaning on its still-limited content (Eskelinen). However, even in these early days videogame developers, critics and players were able to impose a narrative onto the ever-complicating mechanics. A well-known and divisive interpretation of a mechanically based game comes from Janet Murray's book, *Hamlet on the Holodeck*, where she interprets *Tetris* (Pajitnov and Pokhilko) as "a perfect enactment of the over tasked lives of Americans in the 1990s." (143). For Murray, the increasing pace and desperation to organize an endless bombardment of abstract shapes creates an aesthetic resembling the overworked American in the burgeoning technological age. Murray's interpretation, though not universally accepted, shows that even the most abstract games can be "read" as a story. As games evolved and some developed a more overt interest in storytelling, the norms of game design shifted. Eventually critics began to question which design elements were more necessary to a videogame: play or storytelling.

At the dawn of the 21st century, videogame criticism was marked by a rhetorical battle between two academic camps: ludologists from computer science and mathematics backgrounds viewed games as interlocking systems of rules, while narratologists educated in the humanities and social sciences understood games as storytelling texts resembling film, literature and theatre (Goodwin, "Part 1"). The first discussions were limited to peer-reviewed journals between these two factions of scholars. However, as games like *Dear Esther* (The Chinese Room), *Loved* (Ocias) and *Train* (Brathwaite) garnered mainstream attention, they brought the ludology/narratology debate with them (Goodwin, "Part 2"). During this time, the critical community of videogames on blogs and online publications began to flourish, inviting writing from a wide background of players who complicated the conversation and elevated the standard of discourse (Abraham). Meanwhile, reporters for large videogame press sites, YouTube personalities and popular audiences took the ludology/narratology debate to its furthest extreme and started to wonder what made a game a game. Many refused to acknowledge the so-called "art games" with little or no player input on games at all (Goodwin, "Part 3").

As the debate spun on, the limitations of both theories became more glaring. The focus on traditional mechanics of play became an excuse to marginalize voices interested in politics and self-expression (Anthropy) and the problems of defining games by a set of criteria actively limited the scope and methods with which games could express ideas (Portnow "What"). Ultimately, old loyalties faded—though not completely—and critics developed a more comprehensive approach. Critics such as Dan Pinchbeck argued that focusing on either a game's rules or its stories could not provide a complete reading; rather, the critic must translate the point of intersection between play and narrative. In his doctoral dissertation, Pinchbeck posits that mechanics and narrative express ideas in harmony, not in competition: "when gameplay is understood as a network of affordances, and story as a network of proto narrative units ... not only is an understanding of the gameplay function of story evident, but this analysis yields a deeper level of understanding about the nature of ... games and gameplay than has previously been available" (5). Although—perhaps ironically—Pinchbeck's participation in developing *Dear Esther* would bring the ludology/narratology debate into mainstream consciousness, his 2009 dissertation is just one of several writings working toward a holistic approach to game criticism.

Criticism Beyond Ludology and Narratology

Joel Goodwin's three-part overview of the ludology/narratology debate details how paradigms shifted away from privileging one side of the binary. Goodwin, a former ludologist, began to see the ways that storytelling techniques like writing and cinematography could alter the impact of even the most familiar and anesthetized mechanics, "After twenty dull platformers that do nothing for the brain, it's the twenty-first that fucks you up." Goodwin writes, admitting, "I could no longer ignore that storytelling alone could transform tired mechanics into something that could engage" ("Part 2"). For Goodwin, and many other critics, no analysis was complete until it understood how a videogame functioned as both a set of rules and interactions and as a work of fictive art. *Loved* is a significantly different experience from *Super Mario Bros.* (Nintendo) even though the "if-then" statements that make up their rules are virtually identical. *Loved* is different because its aesthetic considerations mark it with a particular identity and theme that would be unrecognizable in *Super Mario Bros.* or any of its derivatives. Narrative provides a context for the player's behavior and thus alters the tone and meaning of those behaviors.

Understanding a videogame is not a matter of paring it down to its basest parts, rather a videogame is composed of the mathematics that make up its rules, the aesthetics that dictate its story, the culture surrounding its development and the player's response to the resultant text (Keogh). The search for a universal theory of videogames is not just frustrating; it ignores the nuanced interplay between mechanics and narrative. As Brendan Keogh argues,

> There does exist a videogame text that the videogame critic is able to analyse.... The significance, however, is that this text belongs to neither the virtual nor the actual world but to the cybernetic ebb and flow between the player's body, the videogame hardware, and audiovisual and haptic representation. It is in this circuit where the player has a phenomenological engagement with the videogame that the critic must ground the analysis.

Understanding videogames requires a phenomenological approach that appreciates the subtle interplay of all factors of composition on a text-by-text basis. In fact, to arbitrarily divide criticism by mechanics and narrative is ultimately futile because they are too deeply enmeshed in one another. To privilege or ghettoize one is to prevent a full understanding of the other.

For example, *Missile Command* (Sega), an arcade game released in 1980, weaves its mechanical and storytelling design elements to compose a theme about Cold War anxieties. *Missile Command* gives the player three armed military bases to defend five unarmed cities against an endless onslaught of missiles. Each base is able to fire anti-missile ballistics and the longer the player holds their cities the more points they earn; the game ends when all five of their cities are destroyed. The reading argued by Portnow ("Narrative") suggests that *Missile Command* imposes a constant moral choice over two separate but constant choices. Firstly, the player must choose between defending one city easily by dooming the rest or defending all of them by balancing more numerable and unpredictable variables. The second moral conflict in *Missile Command* is the choice between allowing soldiers to fail in their duty to prevent losing points or to protect military power instead of civilians to prevent losing their only method of defense; essentially the player must assign value to both the lives of their volunteer army and their defenseless populations. Moreover, the player must negotiate the sense of hopelessness that comes with knowing they can never win. The player is never audience to a scripted plot but there are carefully placed cues to codify the game's systems and player behaviors into a narrative. Readings such as Portnow's illustrate that analyzing either aesthetics or play without the context of the other limit the ability for a game to produce meaning; a game like *Missile Command* can only argue its complex theme through the unity of its simple mechanics and plot.

Information is cognitively organized as narratives and the closer they resemble established interpretations the less time and effort it takes to digest them (Young and Saver 75). Human memory is organized as a series of narratives and reality is codified into language and slotted into a place in a story. Furthermore, language is broader than simply words; the mechanisms that work to comprehend words are also used to comprehend and interpret images, sounds, and other signs that represent meaning; in turn these meanings become more stably understood and serve to integrate later, similar information. As Babuts explains, "On the one hand, language in reading and conversation can function as a coded trigger to evoke ideas, images, and other phenomena; on the other hand, perceptual material from the visible world can prepare the way to language, verbal expression, and written texts" (180). In order to make sense of reality, one must be able to understand it as language; language then paves the way to new knowledge. Similarly, the mechanics of a game are codified into language and ultimately arrange into a coherent story.

However, mechanical story is colored by each game's narrative context: slaying an enemy in a stealth-based war game like *Metal Gear* (Konami) holds different meaning than it does in *The Legend of Zelda* (Nintendo), even though they share numerous ludic similarities. Again, the context arranges the player's behavior in a different kind of story; the Hollywood-inspired espionage of the former carries different connotations than the high-fantasy adventure of the latter. When approaching a videogame, the mechanics intrinsically alter how its plot can be understood; likewise, aesthetic information from the plot, setting, tone and mood are capable of altering—even dictating—player behavior (Filipowich "Tighten"). Most important, however, is not that the connections between ludic and narrative design elements are composed to reach a theme. Intentionally or not, a videogame inevitably carries meaning beyond its content and it is at this crux that deeper meanings are formed.

Among the most influential early critical writings to incorporate both sides of the ludology/narratology debate was Clint Hocking's critique of *Bioshock* (2K Games). *Bioshock* guides the player through the ruined wastes of the city of Rapture after a popular uprising deposes an objectivist government. The game offers a critique against the "rational self-interest" of philosopher Ayn Rand (Cox). By exploring the city and learning its history, the player learns how the ruling class used Rand's philosophy to justify their exploitation of laboring classes and how the laboring classes, in turn, revolted and destroyed the city. The theme, then, appears to be that rational self-interest is a veil for exploitation and, like Rapture, those who own that philosophy are doomed to destroy themselves. However, as Hocking argues, the internal systems of *Bioshock* reward self-interest. The player encounters several young girls with magic powers whom they can either liberate for a small power-up, or kill for a larger one. Furthermore, the plot of the game begins with the player-character helping the mysterious Atlas until they are betrayed; thus the player is forced to be altruistic to a stranger and is inevitably punished for doing so. Both the mechanics and narrative imply that one should be self-interested even though at its surface the game argues that a society is doomed without altruism.

Game criticism seeks to interpret meaning composed by resonant design elements (Brice). Though *Bioshock* states outright that objectivism and self-interest are bad, the most efficient route to success is marked by self-interested, predatory behavior. Hocking's critique illustrates how systems create narrative: *Bioshock*'s so-called "ludonarrative dissonance," while currently a nebulously defined term in games studies (Franklin), composes a meaning directly opposite *Bioshock*'s stated artistic purpose. Hocking's analysis indicates how meaning is subtly formed in the (in this case, conflicted) marriage between content and formal composition. With that in mind, let us turn to *Persona 3* as a game that illustrates how the intersection of play and storytelling can construct and uphold themes.

A Summary of Persona 3

Persona 3 begins with the Player-Character (PC) arriving at the dorm of Gekkoukan High School, the private school they will be attending for the coming year. During several segments of daytime, the PC attends classes, joins clubs and builds relationships with people in the suburbs of the fictional Iwatodai City. Moreover, there are three daytime skills the player can improve by conducting various activities around town; these skills broaden whom the player is able to befriend. Every day, when the clock strikes midnight, the town is overcome by the "dark hour," a mysterious shift in reality that warps the city and its buildings into dangerous parodies of themselves. During this time, citizens of the town transmogrify into standing coffins, where they are vulnerable to creatures known as shadows. During the dark hour, shadows feed on townspeople's minds and leave them in a zombie-like trance. In the dark hour, the PC and their dorm-mates—keepers of the rare power of persona that allows them to combat shadows—protect the people around town and explore the shadow's nesting grounds, a tower called Tartarus. The goal of the game is to balance the PC's waking duties as a high school student with their nocturnal duties as a shadow-hunter.

Each phase plays considerably differently—in the waking world the player selects an activity for each portion of the day to either build their stats or relationships with classmates or other townspeople. Alternatively, the PC can shop for weapons and items that are necessary during their excursions into the dark hour. These segments are inspired by life simulators such as those used in *The Sims* (EA) and dating simulators such as those employed in *Sister Princess* (MediaWorks). The ludic goal in daytime is to maximize stats and relationship growth as efficiently as possible while plans are frequently interrupted by scripted and random events such as exams, class trips, club duties and so on. The challenge is to adapt to these interruptions while also managing time and growth in both day and night worlds effectively. During the dark hour, the game shifts genre entirely to an exploration and combat-based Role-Playing Game (RPG) like *Final Fantasy* (Square-Enix) and *Diablo* (Blizzard). The PC and a party of three other selected dorm-mates comb through the dungeon-like tower of Tartarus to scavenge for weapons, money and other useful items and improve their combat powers by battling shadows.

An Analysis of Persona 3

Persona 3 straddles lines between multiple genres and conventions. Many videogames are made of the same storytelling ingredients as epic literature and theatre (Travis "*Halo: Reach*"; Rodning; Bills) but this is more true for RPGs (Valdes; Travis "Bioware"), especially those developed by Japanese studios or those inspired by Japanese RPGs from the late 90s (Goodden; Filipowich "Scrapping"). Much of the *Megami Tensei* series (Atlas) is in line with this tradition, weaving speculative fables of magic, post-apocalypse and urban horror. Yet the *Persona* series deviates markedly from its primordial series by taking place in a modern-day Japan almost entirely unmarked by supernatural phenomena. Furthermore, while it keeps the turn-based combat and statistical abstractions of player fighting abilities from *Dungeons and Dragons* (Gygax and Arneson) and its countless progeny, most of *Persona 3* involves keeping routines, developing friendships and achieving academic success in an unremarkable world. Initially, *Persona 3* is a cacophony of influences, ranging from ancient myths from across the globe, anime, Jungian psychoanalysis, gothic horror and urban fantasy. However, the game gradually draws these influences together and through its unusual blend of tropes and its web of mechanics; it composes its central arguments about maturation, identity formation and community.

Like many RPGs and the epics they are inspired by, *Persona 3* begins *in medias res*, with the not-yet named player-character arriving at the dorm as it is attacked by a large shadow, which then chases the PC through the dorm. *Persona 3* begins with a desperate retreat and then a battle with the world's supernatural force, yet for the next several hours the player is very slowly introduced to the high school and the rules for the waking world. The rapid shift from surreal action to slow, mundane world-building in *Persona 3* irritated players more attuned to traditional RPGs (Noe) but this stark paceshifting is the earliest instance of the game rupturing its own identity to create a baseline for the PC's later growth and identity-building.

Early into *Persona 3* the game is deliberately difficult to identify as a player; this difficulty reflects the PC's own difficulty forming their own identity in the plot's onset. The game's controls and interface are suited to exploration and movement, but when the player reaches the rooftop they enter a turn-based form of combat reminiscent of *Final Fantasy* and other Japanese RPGs. Afterward, the player's ludic behavior comes closer to a life or dating sim as new locations in town are unlocked, new students and important Non-Playable Characters (NPCs) are introduced, and finally metrics for gauging the PC's aptitudes and relationships are established. Note, however, that the moment the rules of play shift is precisely when the narrative drops the PC into a new context. The game reframes the narrative in a new tone just as it expects new ludic behavior from the player, indicating that these shifts serve a purpose. The initial hours are intentionally jarring to reflect the confusion and lack of identity in the PC. Indeed, over time these breaks become less jarring and the relationship between daytime life sim and dark hour RPG becomes clearer to the player at the same pace the PC finds a place in the world. The gradual change from incoherent systems/aesthetics to complex unity reflects the PC's growth from a confused teenager with no place into a mature adult in a community. *Persona 3*'s narrative aesthetics and mechanics interrupt and reinvent themselves regularly in the beginning because at this point the PC has no identity; he is a late adolescent searching for a place in the world without yet having the cognitive tools to understand it.

As the game progresses, the player develops a routine and becomes more adept at balancing the conflicting demands of the supernatural force haunting the town (the RPG) with the demands of school and the demands of friendship (the life sim). Over time, the player develops the in-game ludic tools to manage all of the material *Persona 3* initially inundates the player with while also practicing their own mental shortcuts for balancing the game's various demands. Again, we see formal elements resonate with one another for a purpose. Just as the player enters a confusing and inconsistent game in the first few hours, the PC is thrust into an unfamiliar and intimidating new setting. Also like the player, the PC becomes more capable as he grows up, becoming an adult at the same pace that the player learns the game. The game's mechanics and content are crafted to instill a feeling of panic and discomfort in the first hours to align the player's feelings with the feelings of the protagonist. As the player adapts to the game, this adaptation is properly abstracted as the PC's personal growth over the course of *Persona 3*'s plot.

The theme of development is not just instilled by the player's pace of learning the game; it is repeatedly expressed by both narrative symbolism and the ludic abstraction of those symbols. When the clock strikes midnight and shadows pour into the streets to feed on townspeople's minds, the struggle for identity becomes literal. *Persona 3*'s central conflict deals directly with the formation and establishment of identity: the greatest threat the PC and their fellow citizens face is a literal loss of identity. More importantly, though, is that *Persona 3* expresses identity as a duality: the mundane, life-simulator of the waking world operates under one identity while during the dark hour the game becomes a more traditional RPG. However, beyond the ludic duality of identity, *Persona 3* expresses identity as a duality in aesthetics as well. The dark hour is characterized by numerous urban horror motifs (Peterson): environments shift to a darker color palate, people are replaced with standing coffins, walls bleed and shadows adopt the shapes of warped objects and everyday items. In contrast, the waking Iwatodai is a bright, populous, safe and chic coastal city; by twisting such a pleasant setting into a place of horror, *Persona 3* is establishing a second, darker identity beneath Iwatodai. The game's plot follows the PC's group in trying to eliminate the dark hour and therefore choosing the more pleasant identity of the waking Iwatodai. The game's central theme, identity formation, is reflected in the aesthetics bisected by the mundane everyday world and the mysterious and dangerous dark hour.

By dividing identity so sharply between two worlds, *Persona 3* establishes different contexts for characters to grow or regress. During the waking hours, most of the player's time is spent at school. The player is required to spend their weekday mornings in classes while afternoons are mostly preoccupied by other activities somehow connected to the role of high school student. Gekkoukhan High School demands almost all of the player's time and it's the anchor of the player's new world. During the dark hour, when the townspeople freeze and the city becomes a horror version of itself, the high school transforms into Tartarus, a massive tower and the source of the shadows. The layout of Tartarus is procedurally generated, each floor is unique but the aesthetics of each section are identical. Every time the player climbs the tower, it is a new tower with the same walls, floors and monsters; only the specifics of the ascent are impermanent. Checkpoints mark incremental points of progress but otherwise the player must meander through endless neon corridors while shadows bubble out of the floor looking to kill them. Tartarus, that is, the nightmare version of high school, is simultaneously unchanging and unmappable, reflecting the PC's initially established identity as a lost teenager, fearing both maturity and the high school where it is supposed to take place.

During the day the player is trapped in school by time and at night is trapped in the nightmare version of school by space. Tartarus is the ancient Greek word for the underworld, so in *Persona 3*, high school becomes hell. But like Greece's Tartarus, no matter how terrible the trials, it can be overcome (Bernstein 82). Progress is marked by tiny increments that can only be understood after the experience is finished. Whether it's completing an exam in the waking world or clearing new floors in Tartarus, one recognizes the change, not the changing. Only after the PC's friendships grow deeper or higher skill levels are earned, does all the effort seem to pay off. These incremental improvements mark the player's growth out of the charmless, slacker the PC is seen to be in the opening scene and into a mature and capable young adult. High school might be hell, but enough rote repetition of activities marks a change in the student, just as grinding levels in the RPG of Tartarus marks an improvement in the digital adventurer (McCarter).

While the waking and dark hours provide narrative foils, they also influence one another's systems in significant ways. The player builds the character's power in two ways: in the waking world they develop their three life-sim abilities and make friends with NPCs, while in the dark hour they level up by gaining experience points from defeated enemies, unearth money and equipment and practice new spells against shadows. These different paths appear to have little overlap at first but they eventually converge and directly influence one another. Many relationships can only develop when a player has achieved a certain level in their waking stats. For instance, Mamoru, the PC's athletic rival from another school, will only befriend the PC if they have a high enough courage level. What's more, relationships are pivotal to developing combat abilities during the dark hour. In combat, the player makes use of several personas; each persona is tied to one of twenty-one arcana. Meanwhile, in the waking world, every arcana is represented by an NPC. When the player develops a relationship with the representative of an arcana in the waking world, every persona attached to that arcana in the dark hour becomes stronger. Every time the player improves their relationship with what the game calls a "social link," they improve the power of all personas belonging to that social link's arcana. Moreover, when the player holds the power of personas belonging to a given social link's arcana, that social link will develop more quickly.

Competence in both worlds is engineered to snowball in harmony. As the player learns to draw together the disparate elements of *Persona 3*, they become unilaterally stronger and both of the PC's identities, waking student and dark hour warrior, progress concurrently. By unlocking higher-level personas the player becomes stronger and better equipped to survive the dark hour while mastering the waking world stats opens more relationship arcs with social links in the waking world. The circle is completed in the player's relationships to others, deeper friendships strengthen personas and stronger personas improve friendships. Here *Persona 3* mechanically encourages players to mature into a good friend with a place in the community, just as the plot follows the maturation of the cast of high school students. Resonating ludic and narrative data is responsible for emphasizing and arguing *Persona 3*'s themes.

As mentioned, *Persona 3* draws on several different traditional symbols, and while these seem random and deliberately confusing early on, they develop a consistent meaning the longer the player plays the game. Tarot symbolism plays an important role in reinforcing the themes of *Persona 3*. The cards in the Tarot form a story, beginning with the numberless fool card and ending in the number twenty card, judgment. The stages in between represent stories or conflicts that take place in a lifetime. In *Persona 3*, each of the social links represent a major arcana in the tarot story and embody the conflict associated with that stage in the tarot story. For example, in *Persona 3*, Bebe, as his classmates call him, is the social link tied to the Temperance card, which represents balance and stability. Temperance is a suitable emblem for the personal conflict the PC helps Bebe deal with. Bebe is a French exchange student, and even though he has few friends in Japan, he develops a deep fondness for the country. As his relationship with the player progresses, his aunt becomes ill and he is called to return home. Bebe's conflicts are tied to reconciling the various forces pulling him in opposite directions. He has few friends, but he loves his new home; he befriends the player, only to be called away; he must be present for his family, but Japan represents a rare opportunity for him personally and scholastically. The player's goal is to help Bebe make peace with his circumstances and balance his familial responsibilities with his own aspirations. Bebe lacks a sense of balance in his life until the player resolves his subplot, which is fitting given the arcana Bebe represents. Furthermore, the usable personas of the Temperance arcana are balanced evenly between physical attacking, support spells and offensive spells of every element. Personas belonging to the Temperance arcana don't consist of any major strengths or weaknesses—they're well-rounded and adequately suited for most threats without being especially designed to meet any one of them. Again, this reflects the concept of balance central to the Temperance card's meaning in the tarot. Both the narrative and the mechanics are engineered to reinforce the card's main idea. In a game about maturation and identity formation, it's significant that the primary symbolism it draws on deals with specific conflicts of identity out of which each character must mature.

Again, the reason the player's party is combating the shadows in the first place is because they hollow out their victim's identities. The threat the party protects the world from isn't open destruction; it's a manifested impulse that destroys people's identities. At the end of each month, a larger, more powerful monster escapes from Tartarus and attacks the city. When the larger shadows are defeated, the cases of "apathy syndrome" (the name the waking world gives to victims of shadows) abate and the sufferers return to normal. Therefore, shadows represent a literalized fear of losing one's identity. On a deeper level, they embody the shadow archetype of Carl Jung's psychoanalytic theories. The shadow, according to Jung, is an antagonistic reflection of the self, often characterized in fiction as the villainous reflection of the central character. It's appropriate, then, that the antagonistic forces in *Persona 3* are called shadows and that they represent an animalistic craving for waking people's identities. Moreover, overcoming the shadows restores the towns-people's selves and protects them from for another month. This is reflective of Jung's psychoanalysis. Jung believed that the human life, like a story, is composed of a series of phases and conflicts that must be overcome to achieve mental health. These conflicts take place in different stages of life like the arcana in the tarot deck narrate a lifetime of conflicts. Moreover, the shad-ows redouble in importance in *Persona 3*'s theme of maturation, as they threaten Jungian mental health. The shadows arrest the tarot story and they siphon out their victim's identities, symbolically they are the constant threat of undoing identity, of sinister human impulses and fears that must be kept in check.

The various personas take on the names and imagery of Greco-Roman, Norse, Mesopotamian and Japanese legend, all of which are categorized by major arcana in the tarot story. These resembling figures similarly exist in Jung's collective unconsciousness, the pool of stories and mythologies that individuals draw upon in forming their own identities. For instance, Thor is a persona belonging to the Chariot arcana; the Chariot arcana represents mobility and strength; the social link who represents Chariot in *Persona 3* is Kazushi—a teammate in whatever athletic club the player signs up for—who hides a knee injury from the coach in order to participate in an upcoming competition. During this subplot, Kazushi exhibits conflicts related to the characteristics of the Chariot card; he defines himself largely by his abilities and potential as an athlete, and his conflict deals with his sudden loss of mobility, resolved when the player convinces him to seek physiotherapy. Where Kazushi's more "Chariot-like" aspects were a source of conflict—his pride, his ambition to move ahead of others—they eventually become righted and he is able to mature beyond that phase of his development. Kazushi nar-ratively mimics the conflicts of the Chariot card in the tarot story while also exemplifying a Jungian complex that stifles maturity.

The associations between Jung's theories and the tarot's mythology are also reflected in play. Returning to the Chariot arcana, the personas belonging to the Chariot all emphasize physical strength and power. Many also include lightning- and fire-based attack magic. The personas belonging to the Chariot are especially engineered to reflect direct power, either by smiting enemies with force or with the more fearsome forces of nature. This again reflects the Chariot as an emblem of strength and conquest. Moreover, Chariot personas usually adopted mythical figures of masculinity and power such as Ares, the Greek god of war, and Zouchoten, a guardian of heaven in Buddhist faith. Compare this with the Hierophant arcana, represented by the couple that owns the local bookstore. Hierophant personas typically hold skills that heal allies or reduce incoming damage, which is more suiting to the gentle nature of the old couple whom embody Hierophant in the waking world. The abilities of a persona reflect concepts attached to arcana they belong to by both referencing concepts established in classical mythology and by demanding certain styles of play.

Conclusion

The player's purpose, in both worlds, is to help others overcome some conflict arresting them in their current stage of maturation. In doing so, the protagonist works through those conflicts themselves, the player masters the interlocking systems in the game's world and the PC matures into a socially competent figure in the mythology (Filipowich "I"). The player's activities in the rules and the narrative aesthetics cooperate to communicate an overall theme unified by Jungian symbolism. Whether it's the player's confusion mirroring the protagonist's confusion, the former's learning the ame abstracted as the latter's maturation, or the appropriate mechanical and narrative expression of *Persona 3* symbolism, every fragment of play works to emphasize the importance of developing an independent, adult identity.

Persona 3 thus illustrates the importance of cooperation between play and aesthetics, not the dominance of one over the other. Meaning is composed and expressed between these traditions, even if experts in one or the other argue for pre-eminence. Though there are ludologists and narratologists continuing to bicker for design primacy, games like *Persona 3* are too deeply rooted in the marriage between these elements for either approach to successfully encompass the complicated ways they express their ideas. Criticism of all games, be they pioneers like *Loved*, traditional like *Super Mario Bros.*, commercial like *Bioshock*, classical like *Missile Command*, narratively dense like *Dear Esther* or systematically driven like *Tetris*, they demand a nuanced, integrated approach to properly understand them; games produce meaning through the interplay of these seemingly disparate design elements. Indeed, it is often games designed with this interplay in mind, such as *Persona 3*, that are most satisfying to play as objects of amusement and unpack as artistic accomplishments. Therefore it behooves the critic to approach the medium with an appreciation not only of ludology or narratology, but with a competence in how the relationship between the two produces meaning.

Works Cited

Abraham, Ben. "An Oral History of Videogame Blogging." Critical Proximity. San Francisco. Moscone Center. 16 Mar. 2014. Lecture. Web. 9 Sept. 2014. http://critical-proximity.com/2014/03/16/an-oral-history-of-videogame-blogging/

Anthropy, Anna. "Rise of the Videogame Zinesters." *The Escapist*. 5 Aug. 2008. Web. 15 Aug. 2014. http://www.escapistmagazine.com/articles/view/video-games/issues/issue_161/5109-Rise-of-the-Videogame-Zinesters

Atlas. *Megami Tensei*. 1987–2014. Various.

Atlas. *Shin Megami Tensei: Persona 3*. 2007. PlayStation 2.

Babuts, Nicolae. "Signs and Reality: The Tiger Effect." *Symposium: A Quarterly Journal in Modern Literature* 56.4 (2003): 179–95. Web 17 Aug. 2014. http://resolver.scholarsportal.info/resolve/00397709/v56i0004/179_sartte.xml

Barton, Matt, and Bill Loguidice. "The History of *Pong*: Avoid Missing Game to Start Industry." *Gamasutra*, 9 Jan. 2009. Web. 8 Sept. 2014. http://www.gamasutra.com/view/feature/132293/the_history_of_pong_avoid_missing_.php

Bernstein, Alan. "Thinking About Hell." *The Wilson Quarterly* 10. 3 (1986): 78–89. Web. 16 Sept. 2014. http://www.jstor.org/stable/40257027

Bills, Paul. "*Journey* and the Epic." *Complicate the Narrative*. Paul Bills, 30 Nov. 2013. Web. 18 Aug. 2014. http://complicatethenarrative.blogspot.ca/2013/11/journey-and-epic.html

Blizzard. *Diablo*. Sierra Entertainment: 1996–2014.

Brathwaite, Brenda. *Train*. 2009. Board game.

Brice, Mattie. "Ludonarrative Resonance." *Alternate Ending*. Mattie Brice, 15 Sept. 2011. Web. 17 Aug. 2014. http://www.mattiebrice.com/ludonarrative-resonance/

The Chinese Room. *Dear Esther*. 2008.

Cox, Harrison. "Video Games from a Critical Distance—An Evaluation of *Bioshock*'s Criticism of Ayn Rand's Philosophy of Objectivism." *Gamasutra*, 8 Sept. 2011. Web. 16 Sept. 2014. http://www.gamasutra.com/blogs/HarrisonCox/20110908/90171/Video_Games_From_a_Critical_Distance__An_Evaluation_of_Bioshocks_Criticism_of_Ayn_Rands_Philosophy_of_Objectivism.php

Eskelinen, Markku. "The Gaming Situation." *Game Studies* 1.1 (2001): n. pag. Web. 8 Sept. 2014. http://www.gamestudies.org/0101/eskelinen/

Filipowich, Mark. "I Am Many: Multiple Identities in *Persona 3*." *Medium Difficulty*, 18 Jun. 2013. Web. 16 Sept. 2014. http://www.mediumdifficulty.com/2013/06/18/i-am-many-multiple-identities-in-persona-3/

Filipowich, Mark. "Scrapping the Underdog Narrative." *bigtallwords*. Mark Filipowich, 12 Nov. 2013. Web. 18 Aug. 2014. http://big-tall-words.com/2013/11/12/scrapping-the-underdog-narrative/

Filipowich, Mark. "Tighten Up the Narrative in Level 3: The Grammar of Videogames." *Medium Difficulty*, 21 Sept. 2013. Web. 15 Aug. 2014. http://www.mediumdifficulty.com/2013/09/21/tighten-up-the-narrative-in-level-3-the-grammar-of-videogames/

Franklin, Chris. "Ludonarrative Dissonance & Game Vocabulary Criticism." *Errant Signal*. Chris Franklin, 16 Sept. 2013. Web. 15 Aug. 2014. http://www.errantsignal.com/blog/?p=543

Goodden, Mary. Interviewed by Mark Bridle. "The Story Mechanic Part Five: Mark and Mary Talk JRPGs." *God Is a Geek*. 31 Aug. 2012. Web. 18 Aug. 2014. http://www.godisageek.com/2012/08/story-mechanic-part-five-mark-mary-talk-jrpgs/

Goodwin, Joel. "A Theoretical War, Part 1." *Electron Dance*. Joel Goodwin, 24 Apr. 2012. Web. 14 Aug. 2014. http://www.electrondance.com/a-theoretical-war-part-1/

Goodwin, Joel. "A Theoretical War, Part 2." *Electron Dance*. Joel Goodwin, 1 May 2012. Web 14 Aug. 2014. http://www.electrondance.com/a-theoretical-war-part-2/

Goodwin, Joel. "A Theoretical War, Part 3." *Electron Dance*. Joel Goodwin, 8 May 2012. Web 13 Aug. 2014. http://www.electrondance.com/a-theoretical-war-part-3/

Gygax, Gary, and Dave Arneson. *Dungeons and Dragons*. TSR, Inc: 1974

Jenkins, Henry. "Game Design as Narrative Architecture." *Electronic Book Review*. Web. 7 Aug. 2014. http://www.electronicbookreview.com/thread/firstperson/lazzi-fair

Hocking, Clint. "Ludonarrative Dissonance: The Problem of What the Game Is About." *Click Nothing*. Clint Hocking, 7 Oct. 2007. Web. 15 Aug. 2014. http://clicknothing.typepad.com/click_nothing/2007/10/ludonarrative-d.html

Keogh, Brendan. "Across Worlds and Bodies." *Journal of Games Criticism* 1.1 (2014): n. pag. Web. 16 Aug. 2014. http://gamescriticism.org/articles/keogh-1–1/

Konami. *Metal Gear*. 1987. NES

Lavallée, Sylvain. "For Impure Video Games: In Defense of Cinematic Storytelling." *Postcards from the Uncanny Valley*. Sylvain Lavallée, 21 Sept. 2013. Web. 9 Sept. 2014. http://uncannypostcards.blogspot.ca/2013/09/for-impure-video-games-in-defense-of.html

Maxis. *The Sims*. Electronic Arts: 2000–2013.

McCarter, Reid. "Developing a Persona Part 2: The Daily Grind." *Digital Love Child*. Reid McCarter, 3 May 2012. Web. 27 Sept. 2014. http://digitallovechild.com/2012/05/03/developing-a-persona-part-2-the-daily-grind/

MediaWorks. *Sister Princess*. 2001. PlayStation.

Murray, Janet. *Hamlet on the Holodeck*. New York: The Free Press, 1997.

Namco. *Pac-Man*. Midway, 1980. Arcade.

Nintendo. *The Legend of Zelda*. 1986. NES.

Nintendo. *Super Mario Bros.* 1985. NES.

Noe, Greg. "How *Persona 3* Destroyed My Love for Japanese RPGs." *The First Hour*. Greg Noe, 15 Apr. 2010. Web. 18 Aug. 2014. http://firsthour.net/full-review/how-persona-3-destroyed-my-love-for-japanese-rpgs

Ocias, Alexander. *Loved*. 2010. Browser.

Pajitnov, Alexey, and Vladimir Pokhilko. *Tetris*. 1984. Sega System 16.

Peterson, Michael. "*Persona 3* and Free Will." *Project Ballad*, 31 Jan. 2012. Web. 22 Aug. 2014. http://www.projectballad.com/2012/01/31/persona-3-and-free-will/

Pinchbeck, Dan. "Story as a Function of Gameplay in First Person Games and an Analysis of FPS Diegetic Content, 1998–2007." Ph.D. diss. University of Portsmouth. 2009.

Portnow, James. "What Is a Game—How This Question Limits Our Medium." Video. *Extra Credits*, 27 Nov. 2013. Web. 15 Aug. 2014. https://www.youtube.com/watch?v=blj91KLOvZQ

Portnow, James. "Narrative Mechanics." Video. *Extra Credits*, 19 Mar. 2012. Web. 8 Sept. 2014

Rodnig, Kirsten. "*Shadow of the Colossus* as an Example of Post-Modern Literature." Kirsten Rodnig, 7 Feb. 2013. Web. 18 Aug. 2014. http://videogameliterature.blogspot.ca/2013/02/shadow-of-colossus-as-example-of-post.html

Sega. *Missile Command*. Atari: 1980. Arcade.

Sontag, Susan. "Against Interpretation." *Against Interpretation and Other Essays*. London: Penguin, 1964. 3–14

Square. *Final Fantasy*. Square-Enix: 1987–2014. Various.

Stalker, Philipa. "Gaming in Art: A Case Study of Two Examples of the Artistic Appropriation of Computer Games and the Mapping of Historical Trajectories of 'Art Games' Versus Mainstream Computer Games." MA thesis. TS. University of the Witwatersrand, Johannesburg, 2006. Web. 8 Sept. 2014. http://wiredspace.wits.ac.za/handle/10539/1749

Travis, Roger. "*Halo: Reach* as Epic." *Living Epic: Video Games in the Ancient World*. Roger Travis, 10 Sep. 2010. Web. 18 Aug. 2014. http://livingepic.blogspot.ca/2010/09/halo-reach-as-epic.html

Travis, Roger. "The Bioware Style (Sketch 1)." *Living Epic: Video Games in the Ancient World*. Roger Travis, 8 Nov. 2010. Web. 18 Aug. 2014. http://livingepic.blogspot.ca/2010/11/bioware-style-sketch-1.html

2K Games. *Bioshock*. 2007.

Valdes, Valerie. "Epic Conventions in *Mass Effect*." *Medium Difficulty*, 20 Mar. 2012. Web. 18 Aug. 2014. http://www.mediumdifficulty.com/2012/03/20/epic-conventions-in-mass-effect/

Young, Kay, and Jeffery L. Saver. "The Neurology of Narrative." *SubStance* 30.1/2 (2001): 72–84. Web. 10 Aug. 2014. http://www.jstor.org/stable/3685505

The Power of Ludonarrativity

Halo *as Participatory Myth*

Vince Locke

Can games teach you to be a better person? Veteran voice actor Troy Baker, who has been featured in some of the most highly regarded video games of all time, including *Bioshock Infinite, Infamous: Second Son* and *The Last of Us*, thinks so. He participated in an AMA (Ask Me Anything) on the website *Reddit* in January of 2015, during which a fan explained that playing *Second Son* helped her cope with the sudden death of her mother. She asked Baker if he believes that games have the power to change people's mindsets. Here is Baker's response:

> You are the proof that they can, and that they *are*. They are doing just that. And you are a shining example of the fact that these are not just games, but these experiences help us cope, help us comfort, can guide us and teach us as well as just be an escape. But yes, you are proof they can do much greater things than just entertain.
>
> And I think they already are. I see the conversations that were sparked by BIOSHOCK, Infamous, Last of us [sic], that touched on very relevant, serious, grounded issues like homosexuality, loss, racism, nationalism, and the conversations that were had were not over how to defeat this boss or this level but it's what it means to us as people, as a culture. And those are the conversations that spearhead true change [Baker].

As Baker points out, the best games spark debate and discussion, just as the best books and films do, and, as this woman's anecdote indicates, games can be a coping mechanism for people. There is a website devoted to such personal stories called *How Games Saved My Life* and there is some academic research that supports Baker's assertion that games can be a force for personal and social change (Fish, Russoniello and O'Brien; Grizzard et al.). So the question is not *can* games make you better, it is *how* do they do so?

Consider this famous passage from the classic text-based adventure game

Zork: "You have moved into a dark place. It is pitch black. You are likely to be eaten by a grue." This passage illustrates one of the most defining characteristics of games: ludonarrativity. Ludonarrativity is the ability to tell stories through play, stories that are participatory in nature and feature *you* as the protagonist. But ludonarrativity is more than simply "choosing your own adventure" in which you imagine yourself as a character in the story and help determine the events of the story and the way the story unfolds. Ludonarratives are experiential; you *are* the protagonist of the story and the events are happening *to* you. Although you are experiencing virtual events, you are still *experiencing* them and they do have an impact on you.

Many researchers have examined the physical and psychological effects of playing games and still others have looked into the educational merits of games.[1] But few scholars have yet to consider the way game design affects players, despite the fact that the makers of the most celebrated games, like those featuring Troy Baker, deliberately design their games to have profound effects on the player's psyches. To borrow a phrase from game design teacher James Portnow, these designers use "mechanics as metaphor" to allow you to experience the messages of their games in personal ways (Portnow). A commonly used definition of game mechanics comes from Raph Koster: "Game mechanics are rule based systems/simulations that facilitate and encourage a user to explore and learn the properties of their possibility space through the use of feedback mechanisms" (qtd. in Cook). In other words, the mechanics are ways game designers allow you to play the games; they are the rules that determine the ways games work. A simple example of game mechanic as metaphor that Portnow cites is the fog in the *Silent Hill* games. The environmental design of the early entries in the series was hampered by the limitations of the hardware of the time to render the environments. The designers' solution was to use fog to disguise the games' short draw distances and low graphical resolutions. But this solution served more than just a practical purpose—it served a metaphorical one as well. The games' environments represented the characters' clouded psychological states, whose "fogginess" you were thereby able to experience for yourself.

It is just this use of mechanic as metaphor that makes games such powerful works of literature. Because of their participatory nature, games possess the unique ability to blend ludic elements with more traditional narrative devices to create stories that allow you to inhabit them in personal and individualistic ways that other narrative forms cannot accomplish, making the characters' experiences become your experiences. This essay looks at the *Halo* series of games and, as we shall see, the resulting ludonarrative in which you merge with the character means that games such as these are the perfect vehicle for the sharing of myths.

The Function of Mythology in Ludonarrativity

"Myth" is a term that is commonly misunderstood. Our society tends to think of myths as false beliefs that need to be debunked. In fact, there is a popular television program devoted to "busting" such myths as that ducks' quacks do not echo and that it is impossible to water ski behind a cruise ship. As these examples show, we regard belief in myths as a sign of ignorance or lack of education. But those beliefs are not actually myths, they are unexamined assumptions that people hold about the world.

So what is a myth? At its most basic level, a myth is a story. In fact, the word "myth" comes from the Greek *mythos*, which literally means "story." For the Ancient Greeks, all stories were myths; that is, the Greeks didn't distinguish between stories that were rooted in actual experience and those that we would consider as fictional. All stories counted equally in this mindset. *The Iliad*, with all its gods and heroes, was perceived as a legitimate retelling of the Trojan War. And lest we fall into the trap of thinking that this perception is wrong-headed or unsophisticated, we need to remember that we still practice this kind of mythmaking today. Consider the story of American history that we teach our children: America was discovered by Christopher Columbus and later settled by pilgrims who were escaping religious persecution and then along came George Washington who chopped down a cherry tree and could not tell a lie about it and so forth. Now, none of this narrative is actually supported by historical fact and is therefore "untrue." But as Karen Armstrong puts it, "A myth ... is true because it is effective, not because it gives us factual information.... A myth is essentially a guide; it tells us what we must do in order to live more richly" (Armstrong 10). The lack of historical accuracy to our story of history does not matter because the point of the story is not to present the facts; the point of it is to illustrate to our children the professed values of American society: honesty, personal freedom, manifest destiny and exceptionalism.

In his seminal work *The Hero with a Thousand Faces*, Joseph Campbell explains that mythology serves a ritual purpose to connect people to their larger communities. "Rites of initiation and installation ... teach the lesson of the essential oneness of the individual and the group" (384). Just as we use that narrative of American history to indoctrinate our children into our society, so does every society use their own narratives to a similar end. But even though the particulars of the stories might be different, Campbell believed that the structures of the stories are fundamentally the same. The multiple stories are really variations of the same stories—monomyths that are central to the development of humanity.

Campbell derived the concept of the monomyth from James Joyce, who wrote, "The monomyth is an everlasting reiteration of unchanging principles and events inflected in [a] particular and unique way" (581). This means that monomyths are stories that can be broken down into a small group of recurring archetypes or universal symbols that resonate across cultural lines. Common character archetypes, for example, are heroes and villains, parents and children, teachers and students, damsels and rescuers and so forth. When a variety of stories from different cultures are broken down in this way and compared, shared storytelling patterns emerge. These patterns, or paradigms, are the monomyths, the central narratives that form the basis of the various retellings of them; in essence, there is only one story, but a thousand different versions of it.

In his book, Campbell focuses on the monomyth of the Hero's Journey, which is comprised of three basic stages or acts: the Departure, the Initiation and the Return.[2] As Campbell describes it, "A hero ventures forth from the world of common day into a region of supernatural wonder: fabulous forces are there encountered and a decisive victory is won: the hero comes back from this mysterious adventure with the power to bestow boons on his fellow man" (30). To elaborate on this description, in the Departure stage the hero, who is often a common, unremarkable person, receives a "call to adventure" which requires him/her to leave home. We see it in *Star Wars* when Luke's family is killed; we see it in the Harry Potter series when Harry receives his letter from Hogwarts; we see it in *The Hunger Games* when Katniss volunteers to take her sister's place as tribute. This call changes those common peoples' lives by putting them on their paths to becoming heroes. The Departure is followed by the Initiation stage in which the heroes undergo training and trials in order to prepare themselves for the coming ordeal; Luke must learn the ways of the Force to restore freedom to the galaxy, Harry must learn magic to fight Lord Voldemort and save the wizarding world and Katniss must learn leadership skills to lead a revolution against the oppressive government of the Capitol. Finally, in the Return stage, the heroes return to their homes and families after surviving their ordeals and their return brings new life and light to the world.[3]

Since the purpose of mythology is to connect the individual to the larger community through the teaching of a shared set of values and stories and the construction of a common history, the Hero's Journey monomyth serves as a rite of passage for the individual. The story replicates and enshrines the experience of moving from childhood to adulthood and thus into becoming a productive member of the whole. However, Armstrong states, "If we do not apply it to our own situation and make the myth a reality in our own lives, it will remain as incomprehensible and remote as the rules of a board game, which often seem confusing and boring until we start to play" (Armstrong

10). In other words, we must actively engage with the myth in order for the myth to be effective.

So in what way does all of this relate to games? To begin with, there is little doubt that games can and do function as a narrative form. Games such as *Bioshock* and *The Last of Us* often win praise and awards for their writing and voice acting. And as noted above, the ludic elements of games make them more immersive (for lack of a better term) than other narrative forms. Thus, in theory, the ludonarrative aspect of games gives them the potential to be powerful tools for mythmaking. As Jamin Warren, the host of the online PBS series *Game/Show*, points out, the Hero's Journey monomyth has been used often to establish such classic game characters as Mario, Link and Sonic. "And these early video games provided a new way for us to interact with the monomyth. For the first time, *we* got to be the heroes" (Warren, "Will Mario, Link and Sonic Last Forever?").

To test our theory, let's examine the way designers employ mythology in their ludonarratives more closely by considering the Hero's Journey paradigm as it appears in the main trilogy of the *Halo* series.[4] *Halo* is classified as a First Person Shooter (FPS) because its dominant mechanic is that it is played from a first person visual perspective.[5] This perspective arguably allows you to more fully inhabit the game environment because it removes the potentially alienating barrier of a third person visual representation of you that appears onscreen. The use of the first person perspective therefore results in a more personalized story experience in which you become the hero and the hero's journey becomes your journey.

The Ludonarrative of Halo

The series is set in the twenty-sixth century and its premise is that a galactic war is being fought between humans and a collective of alien races called the Covenant. Whereas humanity is governed as a democracy under the United Nations Space Command (UNSC), the Covenant is a theocracy ruled by a race of religious zealots called Prophets. As humanity ventured out into space, it began colonizing planets that were once inhabited by a technologically advanced but long extinct race called Forerunners. The Covenant worships this precursor race as gods and views humanity's presence on these planets as blasphemous. The Prophets declare humans to be infidels and the Covenant embarks on a holy war to wipe out the human race.

The structure of the trilogy corresponds nicely to the three-act structure of Campbell's paradigm: the original *Halo: Combat Evolved* functions as the

Departure, *Halo 2* is the Initiation and *Halo 3* works as the Return. The call to adventure occurs immediately in the first game. The human starship, the *Pillar of Autumn*, has escaped from the colony planet of Reach as it was being conquered by the Covenant by making a blind jump into deep space. The ship emerges in the orbit of a mysterious ring-shaped world the Covenant calls Halo. Unfortunately, the Covenant are present and they attack the ship as the game begins. You take control of a cybernetically-enhanced space marine called Master Chief and are immediately tasked with taking the ship's AI, Cortana, and escaping to Halo's surface.

Most of this backstory, however, is not revealed in the game itself; it is presented in the game's original instruction manual (which was omitted when the game was re-released on its tenth anniversary) and in the series' extended fiction. Similar to the beginning of the original *Star Wars* film, the attack on the *Pillar of Autumn* is already underway when you begin the game. You take control of Master Chief as the character is being awakened from cryogenic sleep and just as Master Chief does not know what is happening, so too are you thrust into the story *in medias res* and must find your way with limited knowledge. This fog of war confusion is the first use of mechanic as metaphor in the game, literally putting you into Master Chief's boots.

The character of Master Chief is essentially a blank slate. Although the character does have an extensive backstory that is explored in the series' extended fiction, in the games themselves Master Chief is laconic and faceless. This blankness is a common trope for FPS games; designers deliberately create player-characters in this way so as to allow the players to "imprint" themselves onto those characters and more easily imagine themselves in the games. This blankness of character has led Warren to state that Master Chief, unlike Mario, Link or Sonic, will not be a character that survives the test of time because unlike those heroes, Master Chief's journey does not enable growth in his character (Warren, "Will Mario, Link and Sonic Last Forever?"). Warren makes a valid point that Master Chief is not innately memorable in himself, but he overlooks the fact that the journey in which Master Chief takes part is not Master Chief's journey. It is your journey. The call to adventure is not for Master Chief, it is for you; Master Chief does not save humanity, you do. You are the hero of the story and it is your experiences along the way through Master Chief that makes the character and story memorable.

The journey continues on the surface of Halo, which you come to learn is really a doomsday weapon constructed by the Forerunners to eradicate a parasitic organism called the Flood. The Flood threatens the entire galaxy by birthing creatures similar to the face-huggers from the *Alien* films that infect other lifeforms and transform them into mindless soldiers of the Flood. The

Forerunners designed Halo to kill all life in the galaxy capable of sustaining the Flood. The Covenant mistakenly believes that Halo is a weapon they can use against humanity and while they attempt to unlock its power they accidentally release Flood specimens that had been contained in the ring. These specimens promptly take over both the Covenant and humans present and it is up to you as Master Chief to destroy Halo and prevent the Flood from leaving and infecting other worlds. You must therefore assume the mantle of the hero in order to work for the larger good.

Whereas the original game functions as the Departure, putting the player on an alien world and awakening you to Master Chief's role in the larger narrative, *Halo 2* begins not long after the events of the first game and represents the Initiation stage of the Hero's Journey. In this stage, you undergo trials to prepare you for the final ordeal.

Halo 2 begins closer to home with Master Chief aboard a space station orbiting Earth when a Covenant fleet appears and attacks the planet. By now, you know the backstory and are prepared to control Master Chief in repelling the invaders. The designers made some minor tweaks to the game mechanics, such as allowing you to dual-wield weapons and to highjack enemy vehicles, and they added some new Covenant races, but on the whole the gameplay is familiar to you. The sense of familiarity carries over into the game's setting; once the Covenant are driven off, you follow them to a new Halo ring where the game continues. All of these ludic and narrative elements serve the purpose of letting you transfer your skills from the first game into this one, thus making you feel comfortable and competent at playing the game.

But this installment introduces three major ludonarrative elements to the series that befit its place in the Hero's Journey paradigm. First, you are given a new player-character in addition to Master Chief. This is the Arbiter, Master Chief's Covenant counterpart, a disgraced leader of the Covenant race called Elites. The Arbiter led the Covenant forces in the first game and is held responsible by the Covenant's ruling Prophets for the destruction of the original Halo. You control the Arbiter as he completes missions for the Prophets in order to gain redemption for his failure. The Arbiter's role in the game teaches you to see the story from the other side of the conflict, to realize that the story is more complicated than was previously thought and to understand that the Arbiter is not that different from Master Chief. The trials of the Arbiter initiates you into taking a larger worldview beyond the simplistic dogmatic perspective of human versus alien that you previously held.

The second major addition to the story is the introduction of the Prophets, notably the Prophet of Truth. Truth grows to become a major antagonist in the story. His designation as the Prophet of Truth is somewhat ironic since he is one of the few characters that knows the truth of the Forerunners and the Halo installations, but relies on falsehoods to control the Covenant. He leads the Covenant to believe that activating the Halos will turn them into gods and uses this lie to give them the fervor to fight the "demon" Master Chief as a holy mission. The lesson you take from dealing with the Prophet of Truth is that the concept of truth is not an absolute and that some people in power will bend the truth to serve their own ends. You thus learn the value of questioning your own beliefs and learn the necessity of questioning those in power.

The final addition to the game is the introduction of the Shadow archetype, the main foe that must be confronted and defeated.[6] In the previous game—and the majority of this game as well—you fight against many enemies and seemingly insurmountable odds that stand in both Master Chief's and the Arbiter's paths. These enemies, however, are merely threshold guardians, to use a term of Campbell's. They are there to challenge the hero and try to prevent the hero from proceeding. In overcoming these guardians, the hero increases in skill and "levels up" in preparation of confronting the Shadow, which appears in *Halo* in the form of the Gravemind. The Gravemind is a massive plant-like creature that acts as the overseeing intelligence of the Flood. By the Flood's assimilation of Covenant soldiers, the Gravemind learns of the Prophet of Truth's plan to activate the Halos, which would naturally destroy the Flood. The Gravemind captures Master Chief and the Arbiter and forges a temporary alliance with them to stop the Prophet. Although both Master Chief and the Arbiter know the Gravemind is the ultimate enemy, they agree to work together to save their peoples.

The Gravemind plays a relatively small role in *Halo 2*, but it is important to the overall story because as the Shadow it plays a much larger role in the final stage of the Hero's Journey. It is from meeting the Shadow that you learn that the conflicts that occur between individuals like Master Chief and the Arbiter or between governments like the UNSC and the Covenant pale in comparison to threats people have in common. You learn that it is necessary to put aside ideological differences and cooperate for the greater good.

Finally, we come to *Halo 3* and the Return stage of the paradigm. In this stage, the hero has gained all of the knowledge, skills and experience needed to defeat the Shadow and restore life to the world. The hero returns to where he or she began with the wisdom to be a better person. *Halo 3* depicts not only a figurative return, but a literal one as well; the final chapters of the game take place on a reconstruction of the original Halo installation from the first game and the ending of *Halo 3* parallels the ending of the first one. You as the hero literally come full circle in your journey, but this time you are not alone. Master Chief is joined by the Arbiter and other allies met along the way and together they fight to destroy the Flood and end the war between the Covenant and humanity.

Once the game ends, you return to your home, family and community with the wisdom to be a better person and a valuable member of society. It is by experiencing the events of the *Halo* myth firsthand in the safe environment of virtual reality that this transformation is made possible. And this transformation is not just conjecture, but is the result of what we can call the "Superhero Effect" after a recent study that shows people who are given superpowers to play with in a game display increased empathy and are more likely to help others outside the game (Rosenberg, Baughman and Bailenson).

Mythology, Truth and Reality

It can be argued, however, that game experiences are virtual and therefore not "real." Yet, the argument may go, it seems that virtual experiences can affect behavior in the short term, but *playing* a hero does not *make* one a hero. After all, hero myths have been around forever, but not everyone exposed to them behaves heroically afterward. There are three main responses to this objection. First, as Campbell discusses, the Hero's Journey is a metaphor for rites of passage, giving meaning to our life experiences and making them sacred. One does not have to behave heroically in order to be a good person and live a meaningful life. Secondly, many studies have shown that play is extremely important to our development as people (Brown and Patte 66). In fact, play is so important that the United Nations declared it to be a basic human right because, as former British Prime Minister David Lloyd George said, "The right to play is the child's first claim on the community. Play is nature's training for life" (qtd. in Brown and Patte 145). Play allows us to practice our roles in society and what we want to be, therefore playing as a hero makes us more inclined to be heroic when we need to be. Finally, virtual experiences can be as impactful as non-virtual ones since we are actively participating in the experience. As Warren puts it, "What's weird is that I remember these moments [in games] as lived experiences, not as played ones…. When you recall a scene from a movie or book, it doesn't feel personal. It doesn't feel like *I* did it" (Warren, "Are Game Memories Real?"). Cognitively, the memories we forge while playing games are created in the same way as memories we make from physical activities. We live the roles of heroes in games, not just view them. We *are* Master Chief.

As noted earlier, the lack of historical accuracy to myth is not the point of these stories. The point is to illustrate the values of our society. So what values are illustrated by *Halo*? The first game in the series was released on November 15, 2001, just two months after the events of 9/11. Although the game was in development for several years before that tragic day and was not directly influenced by it, the parallels between the games and the War on Terror are inescapable. The games capture the zeitgeist of the early twenty-first century and help us deal with the pressures and uncertainty of our time. By playing these games and participating in their myth, we become better able to face the challenges of our world and find our places in it. As Armstrong says,

> Human beings are unique in retaining the capacity for play.... In art liberated from the constraints of reason and logic, we conceive and combine new forms that enrich our lives, and which we believe tell us something important and profoundly "true." In mythology too, we entertain a hypothesis, bring it to life by means of ritual, act upon it, contemplate its effect upon our lives, and discover that we have achieved new insight into the disturbing puzzle of our world [9–10].

So Troy Baker is right, games can do more than just entertain. They prompt debate and discussion on some of the most pressing concerns of contemporary life and they do so in ways that other forms of storytelling cannot. The participatory nature of these ludonarratives means that we experience those concerns in socially and physically safe ways and are made better for it. Games make us heroes.

Notes

1. The PBS series *Game/Show* episode "23 Ways Gaming Makes You a Better Person" presents a good summation of research that has been conducted into these benefits of gaming and provides links to the research. It can be viewed online at http://youtu.be/ FsF68eEyyXs.

2. Each of the stages that Campbell identifies is comprised of several sub-stages. For example, the Departure stage encompasses the Call to Adventure, Refusal of the Call, Supernatural Aid, the Crossing of the First Threshold and the Belly of the Whale sub-stages, all of which are present in *Halo: Combat Evolved*. This essay, however, is meant only to give an overview of the paradigm as it is applied to games, not be an exhaustive analysis, and so it borrows a simplified form of the paradigm from Lee Sheldon's *Character Development and Storytelling for Games*.

3. For a more thorough analysis of the Hero's Journey as it is used in science fiction films, see Donald Palumbo's *The Monomyth in American Science Fiction Films: 28 Visions of the Hero's Journey* (Jefferson, NC: McFarland, 2014).

4. This essay focuses on the original *Halo* trilogy of *Halo: Combat Evolved*, *Halo 2* and *Halo 3*. It should be noted, though, that as of this writing there are five other games in the *Halo* franchise with two others yet to be released. Most of these games are spin-

offs of the main series, however, and tell separate stories. *Halo 4* and 5 are direct sequels to the trilogy, but they also tell a separate story called the "Reclaimer Saga."

5. Note that the games do shift to the third-person perspective when the player takes control of a vehicle. However, these sequences are brief and mostly optional. They are included primarily for the purpose of making it faster to travel through the environments and, with few exceptions, do not impact the story.

6. The archetype of the Shadow is derived from Carl Jung's *Man and His Symbols*. In Jungian psychoanalysis the Shadow represents repressed unconscious desires, the dark side of one's self; in mythology, the Shadow takes form as the alien Other, a force of darkness that stands opposed to the hero.

Works Cited

Armstrong, Karen. *A Short History of Myth*. Toronto: Vintage Canada-Random House, 2006. Print.

Baker, Troy. "I Am Troy Baker." *Reddit*. Reddit, 5 Jan. 2015. Web. 10 Jan. 2015.

Brown, Fraser, and Michael Patte. *Rethinking Children's Play*. London: Bloomsbury Academic, 2013. Print. New Childhoods Series.

Campbell, Joseph. *The Hero with a Thousand Faces*. 2d Ed. Princeton: Princeton University Press, 1968. Print. Bollingen Ser. 17.

Cook, Daniel. "What Are Game Mechanics?" *Lostgarden*. N.p., 23 Oct. 2006. Web. 17 Jan. 2015.

Fish, Matthew T., Carmen V. Russoniello, and Kevin O'Brien. "The Efficacy of Prescribed Casual Videogame Play in Reducing Symptoms of Anxiety: A Randomized Controlled Study." *Games for Health Journal*. Liebert Publishers, 10 July 2014. Web. 3 Feb. 2015.

Grizzard, Matthew, et al. "Being Bad in a Video Game Can Make Us Morally Sensitive." *Cyberpsychology, Behavior, and Social Networking*. Liebert Publishers, 20 June 2014. Web. 3 Feb. 2015.

Joyce, James. *Finnegan's Wake*. New York: Viking Press, 1939. Print.

Microsoft Game Studios. *Halo: Combat Evolved*. Xbox vers. Washington, 2001. DVD-ROM.

Microsoft Game Studios. *Halo 2*. Xbox vers. Washington, 2004. DVD-ROM.

Microsoft Game Studios. *Halo 3*. Xbox 360 vers. Washington, 2007. DVD-ROM.

Portnow, James. "Mechanics as Metaphor, Part I." *Extra Credits*. The EC Network. Web. 10 Jan. 2015.

Rosenberg, Robin S., Shawnee L. Baughman, and Jeremy N. Bailenson. "Virtual Superheroes: Using Superpowers in Virtual Reality to Encourage Prosocial Behavior." *Plos ONE*. Public Library of Science, 30 Jan. 2013. Web. 25 Jan. 2015.

Warren, Jamin. "Are Game Memories Real?" *Game/Show*. YouTube, 13 Jan. 2015. Web. 25 Jan. 2015.

_____. "Will Mario, Link and Sonic Last Forever?" *Game/Show*. YouTube, 27 Aug. 2013. Web. 10 Jan. 2015.

Zork. PC vers. *Infocom-if.org*. Infocom, 1980. Web. 25 Jan. 2015.

The Cyborg Game
Narrative/Ludic Fusion in
Deus Ex: Human Revolution

ALEXANDRA ORLANDO *and*
MATTHEW SCHWAGER

The original *Deus Ex* game is widely praised for offering gameplay options, an engaging story and the three unique endings chosen by the player (cf. IGN Top 100, Gamasutra, PC Gamer). The game was born into an era of PC gaming where lengthy campaigns spanning up to 40 hours of gameplay were not limited to Japanese role-playing games and industry-standard genres of 3-D gaming were still being developed. Along with 1999's *System Shock 2*, *Deus Ex* marked the end of the cyberpunk golden age, offering questions about the relationship between humans and machines in tandem with the release of new gaming technologies. Almost a decade later, Eidos Montreal released the highly-anticipated prequel *Deus Ex: Human Revolution,* resembling the characteristics of the modern 10–15 hour AAA blockbuster title, yet was fully evocative of the original's multitude of genres and themes in the iconic cyberpunk world. You play as Adam Jensen, a cybernetically-augmented security officer and a face of the ever-changing relationship humans have with mechanical enhancements. Adam is an agent of change in the game world and a hybrid of meat and machine, bureaucracy and individuality and chaos and peace. The *Deus Ex* series itself represents a multiplicity of options and genre combinations that makes it difficult to place within one category alone. *Human Revolution* challenges genre conventions reinforced by the standard of the AAA games industry—that is, the notion that a game that takes a first-person perspective will almost always primarily involve gunplay and massive casualties. *Human Revolution* turns this industry standard into an optional entry into the game; not only does the player not have to fire a gun but they are also able to explore multi-faceted elements of the game world. This essay focuses on the fusion of the ludic and narrative elements of *Deus Ex: Human Revolution* in the context of the prolific ludology/narratology debate with the case study showing exactly how the game does not differentiate between the two through the cinematics and the gameplay. The game is generically, mechanically and narratively a cyborg of the games industry.

Likewise, cyborg approaches to video games are relatively new with the history of game studies slow to adopt cross-disciplinary or blended approaches to theory. The original concept was that the video game needed a critical space all its own—ludology, or the study of play within games, whatever those games may be. We can observe that ludology has become intimately tied to the video game as an illustration of new media methodology. Espen Aarseth's *Cybertext: Perspectives on Ergodic Literature* offered that hypothesis that "to claim that there is no difference between games and narratives is to ignore essential qualities of both categories," a stance ostensibly challenged by Murray's *Hamlet on the Holodeck: The Future of Narrative in Cyberspace*, which took video games as objects comfortably open to interpretation through a storytelling, narrative, or "cyberdrama" framework (Aarseth 5). These two figures, though not the only ones in their respective corners, provided a structure for the ensuing "ludology/narratology debates," which sought to define what methods were appropriate for the study of games.

The video game has been more or less accepted as a formal object of study, relieving the initial anxiety of the game being "'reduced' to media, film or literary studies," which concomitantly has relieved some of the anxiety that separated video games from narrative (Wesp). Game studies have now included comparative theories outside the ludology/narratology binary that include positions regarding game ontology and game rhetoric (see Bogost, Ruggill and McAllister). These positions may not refer to games as structure, but portray video games as broader examples of social action, cinematography, ethnic representation, challenge, disability study, and modification culture, among others (see especially Frasca, Walther, Sisler, Iverson, Carr and Targett, Verlysdonk, Hamilton, Hepting). The inevitable cross-disciplinary research, it seems, has worked to broaden the narrowness of the initial critical spectrum.

It is within this methodological milieu that we present a case study of *Deus Ex: Human Revolution*, a study that offers a bridge leading from notions of storytelling or rule-based experiences to broader ideas of interactivity and visuals. Our analysis of *Deus Ex* invests in Björk and Juul's conception of the "zero-player game." The zero-player game exists not as a literal construct, but as an exploratory concept meant to develop the function of the "player" within a game design paradigm—in short, it is a conceptual proposition addressing "what can we learn from studying 'games' for which no human involvement is required," namely, what we replace when we replace the player (Björk and Juul). In citing designed instances of the zero-player game, whether it be a game operated by AI players, a "solved" game whose most efficient play strategies are systematically mapped, or a game-like document providing critical or artistic commentary on general game playing, Björk and Juul describe the multiple ways a game signifies to players, as well as the multiple demands the game places on the player in terms of interactivity. Their general conclusion is that intentionality is ascribed to players—from a design perspective, one takes "intentional stances" toward players to anticipate future actions based on previous goal-motivated behavior. From a design perspective, it is not important whether players have specific goals in mind, but simply that they act as though they have those intentions: to win rather than lose, to collect rather than wander, to engage rather than ignore, etc.

We posit that game elements can be described similarly, as being open to the inscription of intentionality based on appearance and action; such elements can appear to follow physical rules, designed or mechanistic rules, or goal-motivated behavior, and this paradigm still holds no matter if a portion of the game experience is cinematic and quasi-interactive or carefully programmed for interaction. What matters are the intentional stances a player can take toward these elements, as well as the concomitant decisions players make in interacting with these elements. In this essay, we present diegetic email, social boss battles, cinematics, and reward systems as extending and confusing these intentional stances; with experience, the player may learn to ascribe design intentions to something that one would intuitively assume to be a decorative and purely physical part of the video game's environment, or ascribe goal-motivated behavior to elements that would otherwise follow the conventions of the non-interactive, the non-playable, and the purely designed.

Though this approach may seem to be ignoring the ludic elements of the game in favor of an overall narrative description, we are cognizant of games existing as both "designed artifact" and "play[ed] out in a concrete ... instance" (Björk and Juul). Our argument is that to code game elements along these lines is to complicate notions of play—to take seriously the player's reception of the game is to afford access to those interstices in which the differentiation between reading and playing becomes invisible.

Modern video games carry on traditions of separating interaction and narrative events, creating particular moments of "hands on" and "hands off" notions of play. While it is highly important to discuss cinema's direct relationship to games, as in Geoff King and Tanya Krzywinska's *ScreenPlay: Cin-*

ema/Videogames/Interfaces, or how Gretchen Papazian and Joseph Michael Sommers in *Game on, Hollywood!* make connections to filmic genres and adaptation, we are more interested in how games use filmic techniques in combination with game mechanics to create a narrative, even during the most action-oriented parts of the game. Commenting on how video games are perceived in the context of the ludology/narratology debate, Ian Bogost states that "the reality of a game is a construction of player perception, but that construction exists more fundamentally, at some level of depth that corresponds with mechanics" (*Video Games Are a Mess*). A game as a creation of a development team is its own entity, but to study games is to study the user input required to display the intended experience.

It is important to examine *Human Revolution* as an AAA industry First-Person Shooter (FPS) because it follows a model of success and profit-making that can be seen in most games made by the largest modern developers, but also as a game which subverts the genre. Traditional cinematic elements of blockbuster games under-emphasize the need for the player to be involved in the construction of the narrative. *Human Revolution* remedies this by utilizing cut scenes, and the social boss fights in the game to accommodate and reflect player choice. The game also implements narrative signs directly into the combat portions of the game that works to consistently sustain the story. Ultimately, *Human Revolution* makes cinematics a playable experience shaped by the player, showing that narrative can be a game just as much as a firefight. The hybridity of the narrative and ludic elements of the game world maintains high levels of participation with the player. We can also think about how the narrative is shaped to make the story a fully interactive experience.

Building the World On-Screen: Hacking and Cinematic Text

Hacking is a *Deus Ex* gameplay mainstay; the skill gives the power to interrogate most of the digital spaces in the game world, as well as disrupt narrative and genre conventions. Mastering Adam's hacking abilities in the skill tree favors a non-lethal character build and allows the player to navigate spaces that disrupt systematic and infrastructural areas of the game world. Personal computers are the most common hackable objects that leave important information for quests, passwords and dialogues that develop a rich and expansive game world. In *Human Revolution*, the email text serves an objective purpose and a narrative purpose, making it an integral part of the ludic/narrative hybridity through hacking and reading emails. Navigating through emails resembles the way text adventures construct a narrative while accommodating reader interaction. However, the emails are always couched within broader contexts of action, narrative, and the player's criteria for worthwhile information—they are never just an immanent mini-game, the way hacking is presented in the *Bioshock* series. Other textual elements of the narrative are delivered in a way that is believable in the game world such as the digital newspapers, posters and television news. The text disrupts the player's subject position in a way similar to cinematics, but functions as a user interface, which requires interactivity and a reading of design affordances that approximate a sort of rule-based play. James Paul Gee's *What Video Games Have to Teach Us About Learning and Literacy* is notable as a user experience manual that applies language-acquisition principles to the design of environments in which players must learn and negotiate unique sets of rules. *Human Revolution* bankrupts traditional notions of ludology and generated narratives—for instance, Gee's methods for managing feedback and gradual changes in difficulty require certain variables that do not apply to email-reading, which is qualitative rather than quantitative. Though part of a broader structure of function and reward (knowledge derived from reading in-world alter the player's assumptions and opportunities as they continue through the narrative), email-reading is not itself a structure of function and reward as fighting or collection might be. Instead, email is a system of signs referring to the readerly narrative world around the player—and yet email-reading is a necessary process in playing the game.

Action-oriented games have a tradition of utilizing narrative as the backdrop for the action or as a way to inform the aesthetic, leaving cut scenes, reading lore or lengthy dialogue sections of the game to be treated as optional. Ultimately, most games can be completed by killing everything that needs to be killed and/or completing the required amount of quests. The onus is also on the player to decide how they want to engage with the text and how they approach games regardless of genre. Björk and Juul discuss how players negotiate and manipulate rules within the game world:

> a player-centric approach faces the serious problem that players, ironically, do not behave the way they should: players do not believe that they are creating games by themselves. Rather, players demonstrably discuss the merit of different games and rule variations [e.g., Bergström 2010], and will even claim to prefer a specific game for the experiences that they think the game gives them.

There is a fine line to be drawn between what players will make out of a game and what the developers intend them to be doing. Genre will dictate how a game should be played and what to expect from it narratively (if there is narrative at all) but players will still strive for an experience they prefer no matter what game they are playing. We see the PC gaming market flourish with the capabilities players have to mod and customize their games, sometimes with the developer's support. Even without tampering with the game's code, players can find alternate ways to progress through a game, either by avoiding main story quests, wandering around the game world, or turning it off. However, there is always a limit to how long or enjoyable partaking in these alternate features are and ultimately, will function within the parameters set by the developer. The maps of the *Half-Life* series are a perfect example of the implementation of this concept in that seemingly large, open maps are divided by tunnels or doors for loading screens and careful use of lighting and items (which believably exist in the world) coax the player into the direction of the main action. Thus, the intentioned path is always more appealing, but the world appears expansive and realistic at the same time.

In the case of *Human Revolution*, the emails are an integral part of the exploration of the world. Players can ignore hacking computers, but in the perspective of ludic strategy, they would be hard-pressed to miss the experience points and narrative rewards from engaging with them. Additionally, opting to scroll through emails till a quest alert appears will give the player the essential information they need to progress through the game, but not engage with the environment. *Human Revolution* rewards its players for engaging with the text and punishes those who do not. For example, during a quest in which Adam investigates Megan Reed's death, he must approach and interrogate police officer Chet Wagner in the station. The player can hack into his personal computer and find out details of Wagner's own misconduct on the job to use as blackmail. If they player does not read all the details of the email, they will not know which dialogue options to pick to win the argument. Another instance involves hacking a computer that is not related to a quest in which the player can discover that the new upgrade at the L.I.M.B. clinic will actually be detrimental to the health of the augmented human. The player can refuse to go through with the upgrade but those who did not read the email and get the upgrade will result in their vision and abilities being disabled in a later boss fight. These two examples prove that accomplishing success in *Human Revolution* comes from the player's willingness to engage with the narrative, just as much as the combat.

Augmented Argumentation: Cinematic Engagement and the Social Boss Fight

One of the most prominent examples of ludic/narrative fusion in *Human Revolution* is the implementation of "social boss fights." During the events of the game, Adam will encounter non-combatant opponents who must be persuaded in some form to let him through an area, or give him information he needs for a mission. Unlike a cinematic cutscene that is normally a passive experience, the social boss fight requires the player to take an active part in conversation by making the proper dialogue choice within a tree of options. However, the choice is not limited to opposing morality diametrics as found, for example, in the *Mass Effect* series with the paragon/renegade dynamic. Instead, there is always an optimal choice, resulting in the completed objective while also appeasing the opponent into submission. To be able to make the most effective decision, the player must pay attention to the tone of the opponent's voice and body language to determine how they will react to certain types of statements. A social augment can be purchased to further help in this analysis to determine personality type, read eye movements and breathing patterns and give the player a psychological profile of the opponent. The level of involvement in the conversation is crucial to the immersive experience for the player. It is important to consider Michael Nitsche's concept of "presence," described as, "the mental state where a user subjectively feels present within a video game space as the result of an immersion into the content of the fictional world" (203). Immersion in any game has to do with the impact the player-character and by proxy, the player, has in the game world. In the case of player presence in dialogue systems, conversations with NPCs (Non-Player Characters) cause appropriate reactions regarding the current scene and possibly further actions within the game. If the player cannot interact on a social level with the characters in a game, then their presence is perceived as useless and unimportant to the game and thus, narrative elements of games are often overshadowed by actions that have a more obvious impact in the world. *Human Revolution* emphasizes the importance of gameplay features during all types of conflict by being able to access social abilities in a game where the genre traditionally puts dialogue as a secondary, and sometimes optional feature.

One of the most intuitive and complex social boss fights occurs when Adam has to convince Wayne Haas, his former S.W.A.T. team member, now precinct desk sergeant to let him into the morgue to examine a body. As the conversation progresses, the player learns that Haas suffers from an addiction to painkillers from being commanded to kill a dangerous fifteen-year-old after Adam refuses to do so. Haas is initially hostile towards Adam and blames from for putting him through the traumatic experience. The player can choose calm Haas down, resolving the conflict between the two, be aggressive and fail the fight or, through careful observation of the scene can point out the painkiller bottle in the trash and blackmail him for entrance into the morgue.

If Adam threatens Haas with blackmail, he will be angered and turn up later in the game to try and kill Adam, leading to further choices impacting the fate of Haas. Ultimately, the social boss fight leads to objective completion and characterizing Adam as someone in a position of power that can be wielded against the more vulnerable members of society. The conversations also show the consequences of the player's narrative choices beyond the typical ludic signs of a favored response from an NPC or amount of experience earned. The social boss fight turns narrative into a game and the cinematics into a more prominent, involved element of the video game.

Too often, the traditional video game cutscene becomes the indicator for the break in the play; the controller can be put down because player input is not required. This is not to say that cinematics are unwelcome in video games; there are not many players out there that can deny the spectacle and wonder created from fully rendered scenes like the ones in many of the *Final Fantasy* games or the dramatic events of the lengthy *Metal Gear Solid* scenes. However, both of these game series follow a tradition of setting as visual spectacle, an avenue for showcasing the actions of the highly-stylized, archetypical characters. These game worlds are highly static, acting as a backdrop for paths to get to the next scene of action. Furthermore, navigating these settings do not offer much if any world building and instead, it will often be the NPCs that will tell the player where they are and what happens there. Michael Nitzche comments on the use of game spaces without extensive functionality: "Except for their footsteps, players barely touch the surrounding space. They are allowed to look but not to play with the game space" (206). Interactive sims bring about questions of how games are played and how games are developed. The advent of network-connected games developed an avenue for game creators to connect with players and update their games as often as they would like. Fully interactive game spaces involve intensive development that is unnecessary to the game's main action, especially when high-budgets and low turnarounds are not just the norm, but often expected by consumers and development teams. In an interview with the *Human Revolution* art director Jonathan Jacques-Belletête, he states that, "The whole multi-path thing is really expensive to develop, because you're creating data that the player might not see.... I've worked for companies that won't allow for a single piece of content to be developed that the player might not see" (Smith, 2010). The attitude that is exuded from the kind of development teams that Jacques-Belletête describes not only a symptom of the industry, but how design shapes player behaviors that are discouraged from game world exploration. Developers will use NPCs to replace elements of an interactive game world such as artwork, architectural design, moveable object, etc., which evoke cultural and environmental characteristics of the setting which is why these background characters often appear boring, mundane and sometimes useless to the player.

On the other hand, *Human Revolution* keeps the player involved throughout the narrative process; it gives meaning to the player's presence within the world along with the rewards and consequences afterwards. The social boss fights also put emphasis on elements of conflict outside of combat seeing as how traditional boss fights almost always require the player to kill a more challenging, higher-ranked enemy character, while cutscenes do not detract from the way the player wishes to approach combat in the game. Games have the potential to be a lot more than just about taking a passive role in the narrative, killing to unlock a new scene; the social boss fights are just one example of how different types of conflict can be featured in a game.

Human Revolution takes liberties to put narrative control in the player's hands by re-appropriating narrative directly into visual and audible experiences during gameplay. The game employs the filmic technique of "show, don't tell" to lessen the amount of exposition and to allow the player to absorb the narrative and the game world through exploration and observation. Most of these elements of the game re-experiences are produced through walking around the game environment, talking to NPCs, looking at architecture, posters and even ceilings which are specifically designed to fit the futuristic renaissance aesthetic. *Human Revolution* is not a sandbox game in the sense that the player is given the tools to do whatever they chose; there are certain areas of the game in which guns cannot be drawn, for example. Sandbox games with narratives can fail if the developers have a specific direction in mind while giving the player the illusion that their choices matter. To filmic metaphors, the player is the cinematographer, and the developers are the set designers who work together to create the narrative of the game. The decision to make the player the active agent in narrative delivery is in a way, very consumer-friendly. *Human Revolution* is mindful of the how the player's time is spent within the game and how much of the game's world they wish to take in instead of being locked into a block of time in which gameplay stops. Even cutscenes can be skipped. However, putting the player in control means that things can easily be unintentionally missed. These types of conflicts often arise from learned behaviors in certain genres. Looking up and down in *Human Revolution* is a gameplay habit often required to be able to find secret passageways, ladders and events involving NPCs and if the player is not vigilant with this type of behavior, they will not experience them. Therefore, for video game narratives experienced as-designed require, not necessarily the limiting of player agency, but a requirement of looking actions within the game world.

When player agency is taken away through non-interactive cutscenes, the game will still accommodate for player choices in the game. For example, one of the ways in which *Human Revolution* accounts for lethal and non-lethal playthroughs is by using cutscenes that reflect non-violent or defensive conflict situations. These cutscenes are positioned separate from the gameplay in that they are fully-rendered and therefore have a different, more polished look than the rest of the game's visuals, but also in that they are separate from the violence that the player can enact during regular gameplay. *Human Revolution* breaks genre barriers through use of cutscenes by leaving potential violence up to the player to enact. Steve Wilcox describes the way the original *Deus Ex* negotiates multiple gameplay styles within a genre that traditionally favors killing to complete quests. He states, "*Deus Ex* explodes the enthymeme of 'kill, reward' into the now obviously faulty syllogism of 'killing is necessary to complete the objective, objectives should be rewarded, therefore, killing is worthy of reward'" (Wilcox). By representing Adam in cutscenes without a gun, the game is challenging the generic notion of the FPS hero as a gun-toting murderer. The purpose of these fully rendered cutscenes is to establish the setting or to introduce a new conflict, usually a boss fight. Not only are these cinematics wondrous displays of spectacle but they also mark the beginning and end to chapters in the game and prime the player for their next task. To accomplish the task of accommodating both kinds of play styles in the game, any fully rendered cutscenes will not depict Adam holding a gun. Although this artistic detail could easily be missed, players choosing not to fire a single bullet will not experience narrative-breaking dissonance that often comes from the result of gun-toting heroes common in the genre. Adam is portrayed cinematically as deadly, his arms, which are prominently shown throughout most scenes, are fully augmented and sport a retractable arm blade which is deployed in threatening situations. He also has implanted eye covers that hide his expressions and emotions. Part of the function for displaying these and many other argumentations on Adam's body is to present him as a proponent for customization. Adam reflects, in general, the involvement the player has with how he approaches combat, no matter the build. Yes, Adam is deadly, but in cutscenes he never threatens characters with a gun. *Human Revolution* is not perfect in this regard; the highly-criticized mandatory boss fights, even after being re-mastered in the *Director's Cut* version, favor the lethal approach, forcing stealth build players to kill, potentially for the first time in the playthrough. The player cannot sneak around these bosses or engage with them in a social boss fight that creates a rift in the narrative experience. Quite simply, it makes no sense for pacifist Adam to even directly approach threatening enemies in the manner portrayed in the cutscenes.

While it is hardly necessary to make cinematics completely interactive, the developers constructing those scenes need to be aware that when core gameplay begins, narrative does not stop.

"It's not the end of the world, but you can see it from here...": Ludic Signals and Gameplay

The objective of *Human Revolution*'s final mission is to shut down a radio signal causing augmented humans to act in a manic rage. What makes this mission unique is how the game communicates with the player in regards with how they handle the swarms of non-militant enemies, who act and communicate very differently from the soldiers Adam has been confronting thus far. Firstly, "the crazies" (as described by the developers in the *Director's Cut* commentary) act panicked and lost, and display schizophrenic characteristics that are highly contrasted with the soldiers who only talk about their jobs, and are usually masked. "The crazies," similar to soldiers, will attack Adam if they spot him; however, most do not carry guns and do little damage when attacking. While the player can continue to use lethal and non-lethal approaches as per usual, killing the crazies will not garner any experience points. This is unlike any other kill made earlier in the game which is matched with an on-screen text notification. The lack of the ludic signal is unusual for this game experience because it is inconsistent with the combat reward system established up to this point. The ethical implications of killing those who are of not sound of mind and body are also connected to this system of signals. While killing thugs and enemy guards is deemed okay through normal allocation of experience points, "the crazies" are presented as innocent victims of the overarching narrative. They are connected to Adam, who could have suffered the same fate if not for the intervention of Meghan in the previous mission. The game effectively sends a message of consequence to players who have been killing their way through objectives through the removal of ludic rewards. It is a shocking scene because gameplay-wise, it is unusual to have narrative direction in the middle of combat and also bring out ethical questions of killing in a genre where the action is the primary draw for the average gamer. Non-diegetic signs transcend gaming genre conventions and also signify a need to empathize with "the crazies," thus creating a type of ludic dialogue between the developers and the player.

As game studies move from the fragmented debates between combative disciplines and approaches into a more solidified area of study with its own lexicon of terms and theories, more scholars will be able to focus on how games are both ludic and narrative entities. We should be framing our analysis beyond the ludology/narratology and treating each game as a product of diverse teams who collaborate to create an experience for many to enjoy. Those most successful of these games take into consideration genre conventions that will draw those audiences in and subvert those expectations through the inclusion of interactive narrative. We can think of Björk and Juul's "intentional stances" as a way to mediate between the intent of the developer and the player approaching a game informed by genre conventions and mechanical trends in the industry. It is one thing for a developer to make a narrative-based game, but another to try and shape players' decisions against what is familiar within other genres. That is not to say that all cinematics should be gamified, or that baseless killing has no place within gaming, but instead, should not be the default in all game development.

Works Cited

Aarseth, Espen J. *Cybertext: Perspectives on Ergodic Literature*. Baltimore: Johns Hopkins University Press, 1997. Print.

Björk, Staffan, and Jesper Juul. "Zero-Player Games." *JesperJuul.net*. Web. 12 Feb. 2015.

Bogost, Ian. *How to Do Things with Videogames*. Minneapolis: University of Minnesota Press, 2011. Print.

Bogost, Ian. *Persuasive Games: The Expressive Power of Videogames*. Cambridge, MA: MIT Press, 2007. Print.

Bogost, Ian. *Unit Operations: An Approach to Videogame Criticism*. Cambridge, MA: MIT Press, 2006. Print.

Bogost, Ian. "Videogames Are a Mess." Digital Games Research Association Conference. Uxbridge. 1 Sept. 2009. *Ian Bogost*. Web.

Carr, Diane. "Ability, Disability and Dead Space." *Game Studies*. Gamestudies.org, Dec. 2014. Web.

Deus Ex: Human Revolution. Feral Interactive, Eidos Montreal. Feral Interactive, Eidos Interactive, Square Enix, 2011. PC.

Frasca, Gonzalo. "Ludologists Love Stories, Too: Notes from a Debate That Never Took Place." *DiGRA '03—Proceedings of the 2003 DiGRA International Conference: Level Up* (2014): n. pag. Digra.org, 2014. Web.

Frasca, Gonzalo. *Videogames of the Oppressed: Videogames as a Means for Critical Thinking and Debate*. N.p.: n.p., 2001. Print.

"Gamasutra's Top 12 Games of the Decade." *Gamasutra*. UBM Tech, 30 Dec. 2009. Web.

Gee, James Paul. *What Video Games Have to Teach Us About Learning and Literacy*. New York: Palgrave Macmillan, 2003. Print.

"IGN's Top 100 Games of All Time." *IGN*. IGN Entertainment, 2007. Web.

Iverson, Sara. "In the Double Grip of the Game: Challenge and *Fallout 3*." Game Studies. Gamestudies.org, Dec. 2012. Web.

King, Geoff, and Tanya Krzywinska. *Screenplay: Cinema/Videogames/Interfaces.* London: Wallflower, 2002. Print.

Murray, Janet Horowitz. *Hamlet on the Holodeck: The Future of Narrative in Cyberspace.* New York: Free Press, 1997. Print.

Nitsche, Michael. *Video Game Spaces: Image, Play, and Structure in 3D Game Worlds.* Cambridge, MA: MIT Press, 2008. Print.

Papazian, Gretchen, and Joseph Michael Sommers, eds. *Game On, Hollywood! Essays on the Intersection of Video Games and Cinema.* Jefferson, NC: McFarland, 2013. Print.

"PC Gamer's Top 100 PC Games of All Time." *GamesRadar.* PC Gamer, 22 Mar. 2013. Web.

Ruggill, Judd Ethan, and Ken S. McAllister. *Gaming Matters: Art, Science, Magic, and the Computer Game Medium.* Tuscaloosa: University of Alabama Press, 2011. Print.

Sisler, Vit. "Digital Arabs: Representation in Video Games." *European Journal of Cultural Studies* 11:2 (2008). Web.

Smith, Quintin. "*Deus Ex: Human Revolution* Interview." *IGN.* 6 Oct. 2010. Web.

Targett, Sean, Victoria Verlysdonk, Howard J. Hamilton, and Daryl Hepting. "A Study of User Interface Modifications in World of Warcraft." Game Studies. Gamestudies. org, Dec. 2012. Web.

Walther, Bo. "Cinematography and Ludology: In Search of a Lucidography." Dichtung Digital. Brown University. Web.

Wesp, Edward. "A Too-Coherent World: Game Studies and the Myth of "Narrative" Media." Game Studies. Gamestudies.org, Dec. 2014. Web.

Wilcox, Steve. "Persuasive Processes: Procedural Rhetoric and Deus Ex." *First Person Scholar.* The Games Institute, 5 Dec. 2012. Web.

The Biopolitics of Gaming
Avatar-Player Self-Reflexivity in Assassin's Creed II

TOM APPERLEY *and* JUSTIN CLEMENS

In this essay we discuss key gameplay elements of one of the most important and influential videogame series of recent years, Ubisoft's *Assassin's Creed* series. We propose that an essential part of the success of this game is due to its making a significant and innovative intervention in the meta-reflexive thematization of the avatar-form: the imaginative staging of the experience of the user and consequently the user's necessary relationship to the game software and hardware is the underlying theme of the narrative itself. Within this staging, the concerns of narrative and the ludic parameters of the game world are extraordinarily strongly aligned. This alignment further offers a strong interpretation of the "real world" in which the game is played: that is, what Michel Foucault called "biopolitics."

This alignment brings together what Jesper Juul describes as the fictional and rule-based elements of digital games. All games and experiences of gameplay in his discussion combine a process of an unfolding interplay of narrative and rules. While narratives and rules work together to shape the experience of gaming, it is unusual for digital games to have such a strong thematic alignment between these key elements. More often the narrative and rules are quite formally separated into sequences of play and narrative "cut scenes," although there are several exceptions to this deliberate separation, notably *Half-Life* (Valve Corporation). Even so, the relationship between fiction and rules has been a key theme of game studies scholarship since the emergence of the field. Against this backdrop, we argue that the *Assassin's Creed* series can tell us a great deal about the form of digital games: not simply as the interplay of rules and fiction, but as a complex techno-cultural form that meta-reflexively communicates truth about itself, game players and technologically-mediated play.

In this essay, we focus on a particular formal element of digital games: the avatar. The figure of the avatar has become central in the ongoing discussions in game studies regarding the relationship between narrative, game design, play, and even marketing, but in this essay we hope to take the discussion of the avatar into less well-charted terrain. Through examining the avatars used by players in *Assassin's Creed II* (Ubisoft Montreal) we will focus on several important factors that demonstrate that games can be more than the interplay of fiction and rules. First, we discuss key information about the game *Assassin's Creed II* before turning to the concept and technology of the avatar. The second part of the essay outlines a critical framework developed on the basis of this attention to the avatar, using the concepts of "focalization," "localization," "integration," and "programming."

Assassin's Creed II

The *Assassin's Creed* series has generated a large number of games, twelve at time of writing, with the thirteenth scheduled for release at the end of 2015. It has been a great success for Ubisoft, commercially, although the critical success of the series has been less consistent. This informs our choice of *Assassin's Creed II* as exemplary of the series, as it is the most critically-acclaimed (and also the best-selling, reaching 9.5 million units sold in 2010). But unlike most blockbuster games, *Assassin's Creed II* has a critical meta-reflexivity which suggests that on some levels it is profoundly experimental, while still having many features that also indicate it was designed to appeal to a general audience.

The fictional premise of the game is now well-known. Desmond Miles, a young man of indeterminate ethnicity is subjected to a series of hi-tech experiments by a corporation called Abstergo in order to gain access to the genetic memories of his ancestors. His ancestors were not only members of an infamous secret order Assassins, but were also involved in a number of important clandestine events which had profound shaping effects on the present. The order of Assassins, loosely based on the historical order, have fictional elements, particularly the longevity and reach of the order—which as the series of games has unfolded has moved from the Middle East to Italy and onto the New World—but also the strong Gnosticism of their beliefs. Abstergo is gradually exposed as a part of a shadow empire of an opposing secret society, a fictionalized version of the historical Knights Templar, with whom the Assassins have an ongoing, deep-historical struggle. By accessing Desmond's memories, the Templars hope to be able to uncover information kept secret from them and gain control of an important artifact, the Apple of Eden—the source of human knowledge.

At the start of *Assassin's Creed II*, Desmond escapes from the Templars with the help of modern-day Assassins and begins to explore his ancestor's memories on a voluntary basis. He and his companions hope that by reliving their memories he will develop the skills of a highly trained Assassin himself, through a phenomenon they describe as the "bleeding effect." Desmond interacts with his ancestors' memories through a technology known as Animus 2.0, whereby inside the machine he relives the memories of his fifteenth century ancestor, Ezio Auditore da Firenze, a disgraced Florentine nobleman. When Desmond is reliving these memories, the player no longer uses him as an avatar, and instead operates Ezio directly, moving between the two avatars at major fictional plot-points.

This key plot point aligns the fictional and rule based elements of the game, placing the ambiguous positionality of the avatar—and its integration with other avatars generated by the "animus" as it is called in the series—as the central experience of playing the game. The player plays as Desmond, or as Desmond "playing" Ezio. A key role of the player in advancing through the structure of the game and the narrative requires the maintenance of an equilibrium between the two positions of Desmond and Ezio. This is demonstrated most prominently by the mechanic of "synchronization." This device is unique to the series, and is used to describe the closeness of the relationship between Ezio's actions and Desmond's memories of his ancestor that are being extracted from the Animus 2.0. For example, should Ezio suffer a serious injury he is desynchronized, which, rather than acting as a "death" metaphor, is represented as a deviation from the "actual events" of the ancestral memory. Injury is not the only potential cause of desynchronization. Other possible causes include leaping from or falling from heights, entering unmapped areas, or even being discovered in the process of an assassination. Moreover, since Ezio follows the creed of the Assassins—which includes a doctrine of the minimization of harm to non-combatants—he becomes desynchronized if he kills too many "innocents." In this respect, synchronization requires that players refrain from certain actions, even if they appear possible or even advantageous—because they are not part of Ezio's memories.

This simple device has complicated ramifications for the interpretation of *Assassin's Creed II*. Synchronization provides the narrative logic for the programmed rules that restrict the players' freedom of action within the game world. There is a complicated layering of the primary avatar of the player, with the secondary avatar—who functions in the game as the player's avatar, but is in fact the avatar of an avatar. This layering creates a strong contrast between the different avatars, their capacities and actions. Desmond has little freedom of action. Although he is no longer the prisoner of a faceless corporation, he has little option but to try to recreate the memories of his ancestor for the Assassins, so that they can reach the fabled prize of the "Apple of Eden" before the Templars. Ezio, however, quickly develops into a skilled assassin with many resources. While Ezio's actions are limited by the need to be synchronized with Desmond's memories, the experience of using Ezio as an avatar in the game is markedly different. Ezio often has many choices about what his next action is and a repertoire of skills, technologies and allies to aid him; Desmond spends most of his time constrained within a hidden cavern, and has no real choice but to continue to use the Animus 2.0.

The Avatar

In his recent study of the transformations of *Character and Person* across media ranging from classical poetry to contemporary online environments, John Frow notes that: "In the worlds of digital gaming and screen-based virtual reality (and increasingly in military robotics), the inscription of participants into discursive places happens through the manipulation of a representation called an avatar" (41). Frow's book is substantially interested in the particularities of the techniques by which different kinds of genre and media at once represent, construct and integrate their users into their own forms of presentation. In this regard, he is concerned to detail how the avatars of contemporary gaming differ structurally and pragmatically from their precursors. To this end, Frow specifies the following features that, in general and taken together, characterize avatars. An avatar:

- is the primary interface between the user and the world, in the sense that the player of the game acts on the world of the game through the avatar;
- can range in abstraction from a cursor (see also: Jenkins and Fuller) to a user-simulation, from a simple ASCII character as used in early rogue-likes to the highly detailed and customizable avatars found in recent BioWare games like *Dragon Age: Inquisition.* In some cases games—like *Tony Hawk's Underground* (Neversoft)— have allowed players to create avatars from digital photographs (whether of themselves or someone else);

- has abilities that are correlated with the affordances of its world (see also: Myers); the avatar is designed for the game world and the game world for the avatar. The capacity of the avatar defines the player experience of the game world. Players of *Grand Theft Auto: Vice City* (Rockstar North) soon realize Tommy Vercetti can't swim, which means driving a car into even the smallest canal will be fatal, and adjust their approach accordingly;
- an avatar is explicitly integrated into the malleability, reversibility and replayability of its world. In this sense through transformation in the avatar the game world is also transformed (Myers 19); for example in *Dragon Age: Inquisition*, many areas of the gameworld are unavailable until the player acquires the perk "deft hands, fine tools," which can only be achieved by accumulating influence, which the player gradually achieves through completing quests. Once the perk is acquired, rogues within the player's party will be able to pick previously impossible locks and open access to new areas. An extreme example of integration is the game series *Skylanders* (Toys for Bob), where the avatar's items, abilities and experience are stored on a plastic figure of the avatar containing a digital storage device; this information can be communicated to another device using near field communications (see: Jayemanne et al.);
- makes a user vicariously visible for other users: it is not just a site for identification for the player, but also for spectators and spectator/players (see Newman). Simon has noted that motion-based games, in particular, make the body of the user spectacular in a way which opens players to new forms of surveillance, while also offering them new margins of play (Apperley "The Body of the Gamer"). The visibility created by the avatar is different, in the respect that it is limited to the screen, also that it is much simpler to record and distribute the performance of an avatar. Indeed this form of video recording of avatars during game play has become widely popular on many online platforms;
- is neither strictly first- nor third-person (see also: Apperley "Genre and Game Studies," 15–16). Scholars note that players identify in a first-person manner even with third-person avatars like Lara Croft or Mario during play, and even afterwards these avatars are identified by players as an "I" (see: Atkins 44–45; Consalvo 331; Schliener 222–224).

Avatars also serve a range of extra-diegetic functions. They are important for embedding gameworlds "in a broader globalized commercial culture" (Frow 44). The figure of the avatar becomes an iconic intellectual property that is used to promote gaming brands. The association of Mario with Nintendo in the eighties was followed by SEGA's iconic Sonic the hedgehog in the 90s; other significantly iconic avatars are Lara Craft from the game series *Tomb Raider* (Core Design) and Master Chief from the *Halo* series (Bungie). These avatars have extended the presence of games into other media and media events, becoming what Marsha Kinder calls "transmedia commodities" by means of licensed products, such as: the *Super Mario World* cartoon series that ran on NBC in 1991, films like *Lara Croft: Tomb Raider* (West) and *Prince of Persia: The Sands of Time* (Newell), and numerous other product placements, advertisements and toys.

In order to discuss the avatar in *Assassin's Creed II*, we use Frow's observations to extend the understanding of the formal significance of the avatar beyond a discussion of character. We want to understand the technology of the avatar and the role it plays in framing the experience of gameplay, through a discussion of its role in *focalizing* the experience of the player, *embedding* that experience in a local context, *integration* of the player in the game world, and in *programming* the players' behavior.

Focalization

Focalization is a familiar term from literary studies (Genette), but to which we give a particular inflection in the context of digital games (see also: Thon). The term in general denominates the various strategies through which narratives are at once focused through the experiences of a character, as that character's experiences simultaneously facilitate the reader or viewer's (or even player's) engagement with the narrative. This is exemplified in *Assassin's Creed II* through the device of synchronization. As the player using Ezio as an avatar progresses through the game they are constantly reminded of the off-screen presence of Desmond, as every time they are injured or otherwise make a mistake in the game they are warned of their immanent desynchronization with Desmond's genetic memories of these events. After all, the player is playing Desmond playing Ezio. But this relationship is a reflection—albeit a complex one—on all avatar-based digital games, which are experienced through the quality of the performance of an avatar over which the player has control. Focalization is a double articulation through which the avatar character becomes the prime vector of the narration as it also becomes the key operator of identification and use by its player. *Assassin's Creed II* plays with this doubling by multiplying the narrative and rule-based coded layers that establish focalization.

As digital games often establish a regulated movement between so-called "first-person" and "third-person" operations, in addition to permitting a vast range of operations unavailable to prior media, focalization becomes increasingly complex as it becomes ever more essential to ensure the player's integration. The underlying complexity in *Assassin's Creed II* rests entirely on the double avatar of Desmond/Ezio, even if the facts of their relationship are difficult to process (or believe), the process of playing the game is absolutely familiar. Yet this interplay of avatars establishes a player's relationships with the space and time of the game. Synchronization defines Ezio's movements in the game. For example, some areas appear to Ezio but, as he approaches them, the player (as Desmond) is warned that the area is not available in current memory. This may mean Ezio has never traveled there, or that he will be only able to travel there later in the game. Continuing to proceed into the area will cause Ezio and Desmond to become desynchronized. Desmond and Ezio also operate in different timelines, a more-or-less contemporary 21st century and the late 15th century, respectively. Moving between these times is facilitated by the doubling of the avatar, and Ezio's status as a memory of Desmond allows *Assassin's Creed II* to delve in and out of his life to access only key memories. Focalization illustrates how the avatar has become the primary and privileged mode of access to many mainstream digital games, and that it operates according to a set of complex strategies that suggest a need for theorization that goes beyond the application of narrative.

Localization

Avatars are also crucial for how digital games establish new forms of *localization*. They are able to sustain users across an unprecedentedly wide range of circumstances. As gaming anthropologists have shown, there are extraordinary variabilities and particularities in time, place, and person during the "play" of digital games (Apperley "Gaming Rhythms"), that have sustained a diverse field of ethnographic investigations (see: Boellstorff; Boellstorff et al.; Nardi; Pearce and Artemesia; Taylor "Play Between Worlds"; "Raising the Stakes"). This mutability of the avatar, the ability for it to provide a locus of action and identification for people in such a wide spectrum of highly individualized contexts is a crucial factor in the popularity of individual games. However, mass appeal has been identified as a factor that limits diversity in avatars (Williams et al.), with a large majority of avatars in "blockbuster" big-budget games being young, white, male, and heterosexual. Players, however, often subvert these apparent norms (Schleiner), and there is also a growing movement for diversity in representations in independent game design (Anthropy), and among the playing public more generally.

If focalization enables the double-articulation of the character with the narrative and the user with the game, localization designates a simultaneous, asymmetrical, transient double-positioning, whereby the "real" user is established in a locale in the "real" world (particularly significant for so-called locative gaming), and as a "real time" in-world actor who can appear as such to other in-world actors. If many of the possible decisions regarding one's localization are of course external to the games, the games themselves now work to integrate these elements into their play. Despite manifold claims to be "immersive," games rely on players being able to shift between being "inside" and "outside" of the game, or even vastly different qualities of activity within the game. In part—of course—this is out of necessity, games have to fit into people's lives, so they must have some minimal respect for time in forms of features like "pause" and "save" that allow people to respond to the needs of their bodies. But importantly, this also responds to how people play games in a milieu of other media and activities and may share their play activities across social media. This extends to live-streaming video, gathering information about the game through such sources, and the use of FAQs, wikis, and "let's play" videos. Different parts of the game will require different levels of intensity of play, which may change how they are localized, for example, once the Auditore family villa in Monteriggioni has been unlocked, it can be used as Ezio's headquarters. This shifts the scope of the game from the individual actions of Ezio to focusing on a small economic system. The player can invest in improvements in Monteriggioni, and collect income from the town. The villa itself becomes an archive of Ezio's activities, displaying portraits of people he has assassinated and the various artwork, armor and weapons he has collected during the course of the game. This makes the experience of playing in Monteriggioni markedly different from the other parts of the game. Rather than focusing on careful perception, combat, and climbing, the game changes emphasis during this stage. The experience becomes somewhat more contemplative; looking over the villa is a more reflective and aesthetic experience than the careful scanning for enemies. Furthermore, the economic element is conducted through a map, moving decisions outside of the real-time intensity that otherwise characterizes *Assassin's Creed II.*

Integration

Thirdly, the avatar is reflexively targeted by game designers as the crucial instrument for the *integration* of *affect* with cognitive intentionalization and identification, without itself being the only or even primary object of that intention-identification. In other words, as a player is consciously focusing on a particular in-game task or sequence of tasks, this form of focus comes to be linked to a particular affect or set of affects. The affect is not the *object* of the intention, but is generated and integrated through the repetition of the tasks as its accompaniment. One of the things that all new media in general and contemporary gaming in particular work at doing is a kind of reterritorialization of cerebrality itself through binding affect to action according to each game's specific constraints. This work is done by refocusing the videogame "experience" on emotions and action, or rather a calibration of them. Thus game design places an extraordinary emphasis on producing emotion from the player in response to the narrative tasks and events of the videogame. Games are not simply the performance of individualized and combined actions in the form of pushing buttons and twisting joysticks to control an on-screen object/avatar. Rather, games seek to combine and align the active controlled elements of the interactive media with emotional responses that are both built by an investment in play through action and give meaning and depth to it. The so-called "immersiveness" of new media such as video games is certainly a form of immersion, but not in the sense that it is usually understood.

Again, the double avatar of Desmond/Ezio demonstrates how emotional responses to avatars are built by and through investments in play. There is a strong antipathy to Desmond and passion for Ezio among players and commentators.[1] The problem is that Desmond is boring. The fiction that he is a character may be compelling, but he doesn't really do anything but exist as a vehicle for the story. Strangely enough, one of the key aspects that makes Desmond so boring is his very proximity and similarity to the player herself. Just as the player must be in "real life," Desmond is without the skills of his ancestors, is at the mercy of in-game events, and is compelled to spend most of his time immobilized in the animus. He is thereby in a strict structural homology with the player, who must also be immobilized in front of the game console in order to access the game at all. Desmond's replaying of his ancestors' experiences also offers a homology with the player's own situation, with one absolute difference: Desmond allegedly becomes more and more powerful within the diegesis himself as he undertakes more and more synchronizations, because he can gain real physical skills through the "bleeding effect," whereas the player only becomes better at playing the game itself. Presumably nobody has ever gained "Assassin" skills in real life through playing *Assassin's Creed II.*

Ezio, in comparison, is a highly skilled figure, and these skills transfer into a wide repertoire of potential actions for the player of the game. As a result, moving between the two avatars is a notoriously jarring experience. Ezio shifts easily between stealth modes and highly athletic and acrobatic activity, whereas Desmond plods, operating on a very narrow selection of actions. This serves to signify the importance of Ezio for the game; Desmond is practically nothing more than a vacuous plot device for accessing Ezio. Desmond is significant only because of his connection to Ezio, just as any player is made an actor in a game world through their avatar.

But what is crucial to note is the drive towards the *integration of affect with cognition* that digital games enable, to a degree historically unparalleled. Whereas certain forms of media in fact work to dis-integrate affect and cognition, digital games tend to work to integrate both intensely and intensively. For instance, one of the primary ethical aims of ancient Stoic philosophy was to produce a radical detachment from affect by means of thought-exercises that worked to encourage affect's subordination to a cognitive logic of necessity. Or, to give an example closer in many ways to the present inquiry: Immanuel Kant's aesthetics turns around the power of form to simultaneously unleash an affect of pleasure in the subject which is not tied to any particular kind of cognition; instead, the form inspires a reflexive and non-teleological process of cognition (which Kant calls "free play") which then gives the subject a certain "indifference" to the claims of affect itself. Digital games take an antithetical route from these philosophical operations in freighting the contingent playful tasks of the avatar with certain affects, which are sutured together and to the player through the necessary repetition of such tasks in the game. In part, this integration can be attributed to a push towards the maturation of the medium, which many critics and designers feel relies overmuch on identification with an object/avatar through a sense of control and not necessarily an emotional identification. Games augment and extend embodied control into virtual spaces, but as yet do little to expand the range and depth of potential emotional experiences in the same way as literary and cinematic fictions.

Programming

Finally, an irreducible requirement for each digital game is that it must be programmatic insofar as it must train—or, more precisely, *retrain*—its user, whether in major or in minor ways, to be able to use it successfully. Many elements of the form of digital games are directed to this end. Games, as Anthropy and Clark (4) note, have made increasing use of tutorials at the expense of providing an engaging experience. Tutorial sequences often are focused at the beginning of the game and familiarize players with how to control the avatar and recognize opportunities and hazards. Anthropy and Clark's bone of contention is how even the most simple and apparent actions are insinuated into a pedagogical framework, rather than being left for the player to intuit. But aside from this game-designed concern, we argue that the pedagogical frame of the tutorial is absolutely crucial for the player's identification with their on-screen avatar. These tutorials place a fettered vehicle at the player's disposal: the potential for action is limited, but the limit is deferred. A player with a background in playing digital games recognizes the tutorial for what it is: a moment when they may be told something that either they already know or are able to discover for themselves. But this moment disciplines players into an avatar whose functions are shaped by particular limits, which are gradually expanded and even transformed over the course of the game. By limiting and channeling the control players have over avatars during the beginning of the game and other key programmed interludes, the player is conditioned into understanding their absolute identification with the avatar. The notion that this identification centers around a particular performance of the avatar which, if not achieved, control over the avatar will be withdrawn through desynchronisation in the case of *Assassin's Creed II*, or death in many other games. Identifying with the avatar in this particular frame is a *prima facie* requirement for being able to play the game, but only as it is intended to be played.

This programming that takes place is necessarily up against the inertia of the user's existing sensorium, and extends this sensorium through the avatar. Thus the pedagogical links the existing techniques at a meta-level by providing access to the basic operations of focalization, localization and integration through a combination of narrative and rule-based techniques through the centrality of the avatar. As a technical device the avatar enables continual modulations, modifications, and monitoring of user retraining through the indefinite repetition of basic movements melded with the serial dosing of affect in a graded hierarchy of internally-ratified accomplishments. This, we suggest, is the true significance of the avatar as a device, far beyond any consideration of narrative or character. This is not to say that the character of the avatar and the narrative of the game more broadly are in any way insignificant, merely that this area is not where the cultural innovation of gaming lies. Rather, considering this aspect of the avatar is important for understanding the form of contemporary digital games as entertainment technologies and as experiences of the users. *Assassin's Creed II* is noteworthy in the sense that its dual-layered play reflects the challenging relationship between player and avatar, and the narrative of the game emphasizes that the association between the mastery of the avatar and biopolitical destiny are preordained.

Biopolitics

Assassin's Creed II is exemplarily biopolitical in a number of interesting ways. It should be considered simultaneously as a self-reflexive critique *and* an extension of the biopolitical regime described in detail by many contemporary theorists. According to Foucault's canonical description, "biopolitics" designates a form of governmentality in which life itself becomes the central object and target of techniques and technologies of power (see Foucault). As such, this "life" is both pre- and supra-individual: pre-individual, in that the life of each body must be shaped, organized and directed according to quite diverse forms of interiorization (one of Foucault's famous examples is the use of confession regarding sexuality, which at once makes the subject feel free in their expression, as it seduces that subject into particularly intense forms of self-monitoring behaviors); supra-individual, in that the life of the social body emerges as the object of all sorts of expertise that constantly intervene upon segments of that body in the name of the whole (for instance, population studies, statistics, policing procedures, etc.).

Assassin's Creed II is set in a recognizably contemporary biopolitical world, and it explicitly presents a scenario in which the control of life is the primary object of technology. First of all, its diegesis is governed by the transhistorical struggle of giant multinational corporations such as Abstergo (the "front" for the Templars in Desmond's present), for the control of crucial technologies (such as the "Apple of Eden") that have a special power over life and death. This is a world of esoteric genomics, technics and sinister commercial interests. Second, the progressive synchronization of the split avatars of Desmond and Ezio in the course of the game is itself an explicit narrative and allegory of the operations of biopolitical control. Third, the playing of the game itself integrates the player into the Abstergo-type system of contemporary gaming, which it stages by way of Desmond's incarceration in the animus. Fourth, the game itself proclaims that it was constructed by a multinational team of persons of different genders, ethnicities, and religious backgrounds; that is, the very paradigm of neoliberal deracinated labor.

In doing so, the game offers a unique and striking deconstruction of the differences between genes, genealogy, experiences and memories. In the end,

Desmond is to become the sum and expression of his entire genetic ancestry, as well as their experiences, skills, personalities and interests. Here, one would also have to note the almost-absolute focus on the male lineage: whatever else it may be, and no matter how radical and inventive its techniques, *Assassin's Creed II* also recreates a kind of supercharged patriarchal heroics. Diegesis, narrative, action and construction are thus all integrated by the game in such a way as to function as a veritable paradigm of contemporary biopolitics.

Conclusion

The tentative model that we have presented can function as a heuristic and probative tool in the study of an assortment of avatars in a wide range of historical and contemporary avatar-based digital games. This is certainly true of *Assassin's Creed II*, albeit with a crucial difference. This game, and the rest of the *Assassin's Creed* series, renders the issues in a way that self-reflexively stages the processes of focalization, localization, integration and programming for its players. This is a peculiarity of the series, but this offers crucial transparency on this important aspect and elements of the player/avatar relationship.

Digital games regularly present several self-reflexive moments as part of the construction of the player's relation to their avatar. While the original *Assassin's Creed* (Ubisoft) established the basic parameters for the series, it is *Assassin's Creed II* that offers a qualitatively different modality of self-reflexivity, which is tantamount to a paradoxical self-analysis of its own operations. In doing so, it establishes a new limit in game design, in which a mystical allegory of the impact of alien technology upon anthropogenesis becomes indiscernible from the player literally incarnating that allegory in and by playing the game. This allegory, moreover, integrates the globalized post-industrial conditions of its own production, distribution and reception in such a way as to expose these conditions as contingent, yet simultaneously render them absolute. At this point, the very "freedom" that the diegesis shows the avatar struggling for becomes indistinguishable from the total systemic control of contemporary biopolitics, in which patriarchal genetic inheritance comes to coincide with personal memory through the agency of inhuman technology.

Acknowledgments

This essay forms a part of the research project DP140101503 Avatar and identity (Justin Clemens, Tom Apperley and John Frow 2014–2016) that is funded by the Australian Research Council. Research assistant: Robbie Fordyce.

Note

1. For example, see this poll in *The Escapist*: http://www.escapistmagazine.com/forums/read/9.305125-Poll-Assassins-Creed-Anyone-else-hate-Desmond

Works Cited

Anthropy, Anna. *Rise of the Videogame Zinesters: How Freak, Normal, Amateurs, Artists, Dreamers, Dropouts, Queers, Housewives, and People Like You Are Taking Back an Art Form*. New York: Seven Stories Press, 2012. Print.

Anthropy, Anna. and Naomi Clark. *A Game Design Vocabulary: Exploring the Foundational Principles Behind Good Game Design*. Boston: Addison-Wesley, 2014. Print.

Apperley, Thomas. *Gaming Rhythms: Play and Counterplay from the Situated to the Global*. Amsterdam: Institute of Network Cultures, 2010. Print.

Apperley, Thomas. "Genre and Game Studies: Towards a Critical Approach to Video Game Genres." *Simulation & Gaming* 37.1 (2006): 6–23. Print.

Apperley, Thomas. "The Body of the Gamer: Game Art and Gestural Excess." *Digital Creativity* 24.2 (2013): 145–156. Print.

Atkins, Barry. *More Than a Game: The Computer Game as a Fictional Form*. Manchester: Manchester University Press, 2003. Print.

BioWare. *Dragon Age: Inquisition*. Electronic Arts, 2014. Digital Game.

Boellstorff, Tom. *Coming of Age in Second Life: An Anthropologist Explores the Virtually Human*. Princeton: Princeton University Press, 2008. Print.

Boellstorff, Tom, Bonnie Nardi, Celia Peace, and T. L. Taylor. *Ethnography and Virtual Worlds: A Handbook of Method*. Princeton: Princeton University Press, 2012. Print.

Bungie. *Halo: Combat Evolved*. Microsoft, 2001. Digital Game.

Consalvo, Mia. "Zelda 64 and Video Game Fans: A Walkthrough of Games, Intertextuality and Narrative." *Television and New Media* 4.3 (2003): 321–334. Print.

Core Design. *Tomb Raider*. Eidos Interactive, 1996. Digital Game.

Foucault, Michel. *The History of Sexuality, Volume One*. Trans. R. Hurley. Harmondsworth: Penguin, 1978. Print.

Frow, John. *Character and Person*. Oxford: Oxford University Press, 2014. Print.

Genette, Gerard. *Narrative Discourse: An Essay in Method*. Ithaca, NY: Cornell University Press, 1980. Print.

Jayemanne, Darshana, Bjorn Nansen, and Thomas Apperley. "Postdigital Play, Hybridity and the Aesthetics of Recruitment." Referred conference proceedings of the Digital Games Research Association, 2015. Web. 13 April 2015.

Jenkins, Henry, and Mary Fuller. "Nintendo® and New World Travel Writing: A Dialogue." *Cybersociety: Computer-Mediated Communication and Community*. Ed. Steve Jones. Thousand Oaks, CA: Sage, 1996. 57–72. Print.

Juul, Jesper. *Half-Real: Video Games Between Real Rules and Fictional Worlds*. Cambridge, MA: MIT Press, 2005. Print.

Kinder, M. *Playing with Power in Television and Videogames: From Teenage Mutant Ninja Turtles to Muppet Babies*. Berkeley: University of California Press, 1991. Print.

Myers, David. *The Nature of Computer Games: Play as Semiosis*. New York: Peter Lang, 2003. Print.

Nardi, Bonnie. *My Life as a Night Elf Priest: An Anthropological Account of World of Warcraft*. Ann Arbor: University of Michigan Press, 2010. Print.

Neversoft. *Tony Hawk's Underground*. Activision, 2003. Digital Game.

Newell, Mike. *Prince of Persia: The Sands of Time*. Walt Disney, 2010. Film.

Newman, James. *Videogames*. London: Routledge, 2004. Print.

Pearce, Celia, and Artemesia. *Communities of Play: Emergent Cultures in Multiplayer Games and Virtual Worlds*. Cambridge, MA: MIT Press, 2009. Print.

Rockstar North. *Grand Theft Auto: Vice City*. Rockstar Games, 2002. Digital Game.

Simon, Bart. "Wii Are Out of Control: Bodies, Game Screens and the Production of Gestural Excess." *Loading.... A Canadian Journal of Game Studies* 3.4 (2009): 1–17. Web. 2 February 2015.

Taylor, T.L. *Play Between Worlds: Exploring Online Game Culture*. Cambridge, MA: MIT Press, 2006. Print.

Talyor, T. L. *Raising the Stakes: E-Sports and the Professionalization of Computer Gaming*. Cambridge, MA: MIT Press, 2012. Print.

Thon, Jan-Noël. "Perspective in Contemporary Computer Games." *Point of View, Perspective and Focalization: Modeling Mediation in Narrative*. Eds. Peter Hühn, Wolf Schmid, and Jörg Schönert. Berlin: de Gruyter, 2009. 279–299. Print.

Toys for Bob. *Skylanders: Sypro's Adventure*. Activision, 2011. Digital Game.

Ubisoft Montreal. *Assassin's Creed II*. Ubisoft, 2009. Digital Game.

Valve Corporation. *Half-Life*. Sierra Entertainment, 1998. Digital Game.

West, Simon. *Lara Croft: Tomb Raider*. Paramount Pictures, 2001. Film.

Williams, Dmitri, Nicole Martins, Mia Consalvo, and James D. Ivory. "The Virtual Census: Representations of Gender, Race and Age in Video Games." *New Media and Society* 11.5 (2009): 815–834. Print.

BioShock Infinite

The Search for Redemption and the Repetition of Atrocity

Amy M. Green

BioShock Infinite, released in 2013, underscores the limitations of a purely ludological approach to video game studies. The game, rich with symbolism, serves as a singular example of how a video game can combine traditional elements of storytelling with the visual tools of the video game medium to create a haunting and profound narrative suited to narratological analysis. Unfortunately, video game scholars divide along ludological and narratological lines and this proves limiting in that it prevents those approaching video games from different theoretical frameworks from coming together to examine gaming holistically. That being said, ludology casts too narrow a net, on its own, to fully articulate the scope of what video games are capable of providing, as narrative experience, to gamers. *BioShock Infinite* covers a broad swath of thematic ground, from religious extremism, to racism, to explorations into the nature of reality, to the application of quantum physics. Yet most importantly, the game explores brutally and tragically the darker aspects of human nature. Specifically, the game explores the failure of its central characters, however well-intentioned, to leave behind cycles of violence and atrocity. For all of the game's grandeur of setting—the floating city of Columbia, Vigors granting magic-like powers, and the like, *BioShock Infinite* is, at its core, an intimate portrait of human tragedy and failure. The issue proves central to all of the game's main characters, with special emphasis on protagonist Booker DeWitt, whom the player controls via a first-person view of the world through his eyes. The repeated references to the Battle of Wounded Knee, culminating in a long set piece in which the gamer fights through a propagandistic and racist rewriting of the battle, haunt the game while tied to a real-world event, one rendered both mimetically and ahistorically.

BioShock Infinite offers such a complex and interwoven narrative that a brief synopsis of the plot here proves necessary. Booker DeWitt, the game's protagonist and a private detective, travels to the floating city of Columbia to retrieve a young woman named Elizabeth. Presumably, he does this because of his dire financial straits and gambling debts. Unfortunately, Elizabeth has been held captive for all of her nineteen years in a prison dubbed "The Tower of the Lamb" by Columbia's totalitarian ruler and self-styled messiah, Prophet Comstock. To complicate matters, the Vox Populi foment rebellion and the overthrow of Comstock's racist and repressive regime. Comstock's Columbia resembles pre–Civil War America, complete with slavery, overt and institutionalized racism onto which is grafted Comstock's own revisionist rewriting of American and Columbian history. As a specific result of Comstock's rewriting of the Battle of Wounded Knee and the Boxer Rebellion, Captain Cornelius Slate, once his loyal adherent, rebels and seeks out DeWitt to engage in a suicide battle.

The game's narrative builds over some 35–40 hours of gameplay time and it is not until the very last 20 minutes or so of the game that all of the narrative threads come together to form a cohesive whole. The revelations at the end also recast many previous events in a new light. A repeating piece of dialogue haunting Booker demands of him, "Bring us the girl and wipe away the debt." Yet the very question of whose guilt and whose debt is not so easily answered. To further complicate matters, the narrative of *BioShock Infinite* utilizes some of the more mind-bending and complex aspects of quantum physics, specifically those related to multiple universes or timelines existing simultaneously with one another. In the world of the game, the narrative proposes that every action one takes, or does not take, splits a different timeline off of the main one. This all coalesces in the revelation that Booker is Prophet Comstock, albeit from one of these alternate timelines. He seeks out Elizabeth, his biological daughter and thus Comstock's, because this version of him sold her to Comstock to pay off gambling debts. What drives this Booker, and seemingly countless other versions, to self-destructive behavior all centers back on his experiences at Wounded Knee.

A final important plot point centers on Elizabeth herself. Because Comstock brought Elizabeth to his timeline from Booker's thorough a device capable of bending space-time, she retains an ability to open up what she calls "Tears," rifts into any one of these innumerable timelines. Some Tears, as Elizabeth says, open into worlds that are almost entirely identical to hers. Others, importantly, are drastically different. This places in Elizabeth's hands the power to see into other timelines and to have a chance at redeeming Booker's past. The Luteces, twins Rosalind and Robert who function as recurring NPCs, are also late in the game revealed to be trying to exorcise their own demons. It is their scientific genius that harnesses the power of Tears and allows for Prophet Comstock to kidnap Elizabeth. Yet their solution to assuage their guilt proves both imperfect and highly morally dubious. They are the ones who send Booker into an alternate timeline to rescue Elizabeth, in order to try to undo their actions.

BioShock Infinite, despite being a first-person shooter ludologically, is most importantly a story about the frailties of human nature and the ambiguity of morality. Ian Bogost raises the provocative idea that gamers and academics alike might "seek to understand how videogames reveal what it means to be human" (53). As much as that can mean an exploration into the more positive aspects of human nature, it can also mean incursions into darker territory. *BioShock Infinite*'s lengthy playtime allows for a fully immersive investigation into the failure of people who otherwise seem to want to transforms their lives, but instead end up recreating their previous failures. Repetition of atrocity and the failed quest for atonement form the thematic backbone of the game. The game begins with a blackscreen and dialogue that comes from near the end of the game, but has no initial context. Elizabeth asks, "Booker, are you afraid of God?" to which he responds, "No. But I'm afraid of you." Immediately after this, the game presents, again without full context, a quote reading, "The mind of the subject will desperately struggle to create memories where none exist," attributed to Robert Lutece. Here begins an absorbing commentary about the desire and agency for change versus the actual will to follow through. However much Comstock co-opts Christian imagery for his own gain, Columbia is otherwise a world without Christianity or any state-sanctioned religion, built instead around the cult of personality he has created. The quote also proves telling in that the game does not rely on the idea of divine punishment for sins. Instead, these characters commit atrocities and inflict emotional and physical wounds on one another as if it were habit.

In the literal sense, Robert Lutece's quote speaks to the phenomenon that once Booker gets pulled through the Tear by the Luteces, his memories scramble and he starts to form a new narrative from the pieces. Symbolically, however, this represents Booker's own past, rife with violence and the commission of atrocity, and his ultimate refusal to deal with it by trying to expunge that person, that Booker, in favor of creating Comstock. The effort proves futile and Comstock is no less dangerous, troubled, or ruthless than the man he tried to leave behind. It is also here at the start, with the opening images of Booker tossed on the churning waters while being rowed by the Luteces, otherwise disguised by their rain gear, that the symbolic importance of water first presents itself, as it does throughout the game, as failed baptism. Booker's transformation into Comstock begins, in some of the timelines, in the immediate aftermath of Wounded Knee, with him being born-again and baptized in a river. Not all Bookers accept the baptism, but even those who do find little peace. Booker himself goes on from Wounded Knee to work as a union breaker for the notorious Pinkerton's National Detective Agency—based on the real-world Pinkerton's—only to find himself fired due to his penchant for violence. Whether Booker chooses baptism or not, he cannot summon the will to become a better person. Indeed, he seems to reflect little on what this might mean and in the case of Comstock, favors instead a world where no one will question what he does. This theme not only carries through *BioShock Infinite*, but is also the major theme of both of the game's DLC (Downloadable Content) episodes, *Burial at Sea* parts 1 and 2. Although the purpose here lies in examining atrocity and redemption in the main game, the DLC storyline content directly correlates in a few major places, specifically those which transform the manner in which the gamer views events from the main game. Chief among these is Daisy Fitzroy's threatened murder of Jeremiah Fink's young son and its consequences for Elizabeth, which will be discussed in detail further on.

Booker DeWitt, Elizabeth, and the Lutece twins are all, to some extent, seeking some sort of salvation. Perhaps, albeit to twisted ends, Comstock seeks some sort of salvation of his own. Unfortunately for him, that means turning his own self-disgust outward and downward to the world below Columbia. In the process of seeking salvation, they make everything worse. When taken in their totality, the intricately crafted plot points of the narrative require a narratological approach to the game over a ludological one. The gameplay itself is not otherwise remarkable in terms of how the gamer maneuvers through the environment. *BioShock Infinite* is a corridor First-Person Shooter (FPS), meaning that in many battle sequences, enemies will tend to cluster and Booker moves forward, as if down a hallway, through these areas. Booker wields Vigors from his left hand and guns from his right, again not a novel form of gameplay, as the two previous *BioShock* games followed a similar structure. That being the case, the game instead leaves behind novel or overly complex gameplay mechanisms in favor of building an immersive world and plot.

Video games contain what literary theorist Roland Barthes describes as "cardinal functions"—interlocking plot events—and "catalysers," complementary events (51). In the specific case of *BioShock Infinite,* these take the form of essential background material, propaganda, architecture and art work, found objects like audio recordings called voxophones, and encounters with Non-Player Characters (NPCs). All provide the catalysts critical to the full development of the cardinal functions. Claude Bremond constructs an over-arching geography for understanding the main elements of plot narrative more generally. He breaks down plot into simple narratological structures: the goal, actualization or impediment to objective, and then the goal attained or not attained (63). Applied to *BioShock Infinite*, such a set of working parameters proves that the game is necessarily intended as narratological in nature. The player is encouraged to learn and to see and to explore the narrative, which in this case is, in many ways, self-directed. While the game has certain goals and destinations moving the player in a particular direction, he or she is otherwise free to explore each area of the game fully. Further still, there is no external narrator per se, although a number of characters like Comstock and Fink, and even everyday citizens of Columbia, do present points of view via player interaction or voxophones. The player *becomes* the narrator in part by constructing the order in which the narrative events are taken. Granted, the player cannot re-order the events of the main plot. However, all of the exploration-based events, including finding artifacts and the exploration of landscape, create the fictive world in its totality. To that end, the game is designed in such a way that exploration is a clear end goal of each area. After a level is cleared of enemies, for example, no further threat exists to the player—he or she can explore as desired. Celestino Deleyto's statement "A film narrative does not need the existence of an explicit narrator" (219) can easily be applied to video games, which vary in terms of point of view. Film is static, however, in that its choices are already made. What is foregrounded in a shot by the director is that way forever in the final artifact. The gamer, however, can actively manipulate the game world and is encouraged to do so when playing *BioShock Infinite*.

The growing concept in academic studies of video games that "a refor-mulated version of the question of ludology and narratology might ask if games need to produce stories, while acknowledging that they might be able to do so" (Bogost 70) is at least grudgingly moving toward what many gamers already know to be true. *BioShock Infinite*, unlike titles which begin *in medias res* with almost immediate combat, begins entirely free of conflict. Once the player reaches Columbia, he or she arrives during its 1912 Raffle and Fair, a spectacle reinforcing Comstock's racist and autocratic rule of Columbia and his manipulation of historical events to that end. So the player who refuses to participate in the narratological process of exploration is the player who is out of sync with expectation. Graeme Kirkpatrick asserts, "Play is what enables us to conjure something out of nothing" (14). Yet the same might be said of the act of reading wherein the reader creates entire landscapes, worlds, people, actions, and the like based on the power of the narrative. Video games use the act of gaming—the act of play—as the conduit into powerful forms of creation. A gamer who refuses exploration when exploration is the clear intention might be likened to someone who skips through entire chapters of a book or fast forwards through large sections of a film.

While Grant Travinor's article precedes the release of *BioShock Infinite*, many of his observations reflect on this game as much as they do the first and second games of the series, the subject of his writing. He says of *BioShock*, "The completeness of the picture that the player gets depends on their own curiosity in searching out evidence. It is also a key part of the fictional narrative of BioShock that the player must discover their own nature in the game-world" (94) and these same gameplay mechanisms and choices form the backbone to unfolding the tangled history of *BioShock Infinite*'s Booker, Elizabeth, and Comstock. This also forms another foundational argument for "reading" the game narratologically, not ludologically.

The opening sequence of game play also introduces the player to daily life in Columbia and the larger thematic concerns of the narrative. Elizabeth Duquette discusses Frederick Jackson Turner's placement of the image of the American frontier as critical to exceptionalism: "Turner's argument establishes a link between geography and character; fundamentally masculinist, the American self is rejuvenated by contact with, and domination over, primitive peoples and the land itself" (474). Turner, writing in 1893, says of the frontier, "This perennial rebirth, this fluidity of American life, this expansion westward with its new opportunities, its continuous touch with the simplicity of primitive society furnish the forces dominating the American character" (2). For Turner, American expansion wins the day because the constant contact with those that are lesser, in this case native peoples living on the ever-expanding Western boundary of the country, builds character as American will dominates all others. While any number of propagandistic art pieces from the days of frontier expansion might show the Lady Columbia guiding America ever westward, it would be men leading the charge. Comstock's Columbia functions precisely along these lines, with Columbia literally existing as a separate entity from America, all but unreachable to those in the world below, except with specific permission. Those in Columbia are taught to view Americans as "primitives" with views of racial equality and inclusiveness. Further still, Columbia privileges whiteness above all other factors, with African Americans included in Comstock's world along the lines of what Turner describes as primitive peoples.

The interconnected issues of race and politics buttress much of the game and are both used by Comstock as a means of enacting social control over the people of Columbia, while revealing his own boundless capacity to hate and to turn discontent away from his regime and to the marginalized and demonized Other. He creates a white, privileged, upper-class set of elites, a lower-class set of the working poor, who are depicted primarily as Irish or Jewish and lesser than other whites, and then an underclass of the purely Other, primarily African Americans. Pointedly absent from Columbia in person are any American Indians, so much the focus of Comstock-née-Booker's turmoil. Benjamin Hourigan asks of *BioShock*, "Could *BioShock* act as a proving ground for the political beliefs of those young media consumers who are now having some of their most important cultural experiences in front of a high-def television with a videogame controller in their hands? It wouldn't be the first time that games have reached out to enmesh their players in politically potent issues" (23). Certainly, *BioShock Infinite* engages the player with uncomfortable explorations of race, the use of propaganda and myth-making in the running of government, and the tendency of human nature to be self-serving and self-justifying. All of this culminates in the game's exploration of Wounded Knee.

When early on in the game, the player reaches the Fraternal Order of the Raven, the headquarters of a Freemason-esque secret society which espouses Comstock's twisted view of the world, he or she begins to see how Comstock's choices not only continue to keep him from redemption, but also twist others to his point of view. A voxophone recorded by Comstock reveals his view that "No animal is born free except for the white man." He takes a "white man's burden" view of minorities at best, and it is a tenuous best, and at worst, he cares little if they live or die. The Order building also houses Comstock's phrenological study, a slideshow focusing on American Indians and their inferiority. For all of his outward drive to escape his past, his hatred still simmers. Interestingly, no American Indians appear in the story at all. While there are African American characters, mostly slaves or relegated to menial work, and Asian characters like the gunsmith Chen Lin, there are no American Indians. While he has at one level tried to expunge them from Columbia, presumably by forbidding their immigration, they haunt it and Comstock.

Wounded Knee looms large over both main protagonist Booker DeWitt and the entire narrative of *BioShock Infinite*. The first hint at the pall cast by this event occurs in the very opening moments of the game, as Booker is ferried across a stormy sea to a lonely lighthouse. His main possession at the game's start, a wooden memento book in which he keeps his initial case documents and revolver, bears the engraved metal plate, "Property of Booker DeWitt, 7th Cavalry, Wounded Knee." The Wounded Knee episode sits uniquely within the game as a mimesis of the fallout of the actual historical event, yet the historical event itself does not occur within the game. The game begins in 1912, some 22 years after Wounded Knee. By avoiding the direct representation of the Battle of Wounded Knee in the game, *BioShock Infinite* avoids the potential pitfall of lessening, or making too cinematic or non-impactful, the slaughter that occurred in 1890.

Critical reaction to the game's take on historicity proves important in underscoring the need for critics, both academic and not, to engage seriously with video games when their narratological purpose is explored. The case of Daniel Golding's relatively lengthy review/analysis of *BioShock Infinite* underscores the very serious lapses in scholarship and research that are all too common in publications about videogames. In this particular case, Mr. Golding is a reviewer, for *The Arts*, a subsection of the Australian Broadcasting Company's massive news website. *The Arts* is a well-respected publication with reviews of everything from film to video games and publishes wide-ranging content concerning major issues in the arts. It is distressing that such a selection as this was not at all vetted given the broad reach of the site. I was given the link to this article by a colleague, whose own research abilities I otherwise highly respect, as a credible work that I might use for a larger article on *BioShock Infinite* I am working on. The problem is that without my colleague having played the game, this individual relied on the credibility of the publisher to speak to the veracity of Mr. Golding's work and this person believed the article's contents wholesale. The main problem here, and it is not one asserted lightly at all, is that Mr. Golding clearly did not play *BioShock Infinite*. He may have played some of the game, but my greater suspicion, as someone who has played this 40-plus hour game through carefully three different times, is that he saw some of the promotional footage developer Irrational Games released about the game in advance of its release. Specifically, Golding makes the case that *BioShock Infinite* fails in any way to address the issues it raises with any depth. He identifies the main thematic elements of the game as, "Manifest Destiny, American Exceptionalism, racism, and religious conflict," and in that he is certainly correct, if not a bit limited. However, he then asserts as the thesis of his article, "You do not engage with this kind of material if you want to make something disposable." He never defines what it really means that the game is "disposable" or that these themes are "disposable," given that the narrative itself in terms of gameplay runs some 35–40 hours. A book, by this same argument, could be "disposable."

He goes on to further use the example of the game's references to the

Battle of Wounded Knee to prove this point and says that this historical event is presented "without statement." It is here that the entire argument falls apart and does that because of a lack of serious—or any—engagement with the source material and it is from here that the assertion can safely be made that he did not play the entire game. Simply put, without a much longer analysis of *BioShock Infinite*, the game does, instead, present Wounded Knee as a powerful underpinning to the entire narrative. It is the foundational event in the life of protagonist Booker DeWitt and it is his actions after the atrocities he commits at Wounded Knee that set all the other storylines in motion. Specifically, using Wounded Knee as a backdrop, the game goes on to explore the repetition of atrocity and what drives people back to cruelty, even after they claim to want to be better. The first reference to Wounded Knee appears in the opening moments of the game and are there, again, in the last moments, when Booker DeWitt faces what he has done. Instead, Golding's argument seems to be based on seeing some brief promotional footage that featured the Hall of Heroes and some of its gameplay.

Mr. Golding's work, as a whole, underscores the inherent problem that exists right now in video game studies, whether through a narratological or ludological lens, and in discussions about video games: some of those who comment and write about video games, in both academic studies and in popular publications, have not played them, or have not played them extensively enough to extrapolate one idea onto myriad game titles. One could not write a critical analysis or book review of a novel he or she never read any more than he or she could propose one overarching, universal thesis that would apply wholesale to any story ever written. It is time for the critical writing about video games to rise to the quality of the material that is out there. This applies to both formal, peer-reviewed academic pieces and those published in less formal media outlets.

The Battle of Wounded Knee is presented very seriously within the game, even though this is done by means of reflection instead of historical recreation, and by seeing Comstock's self-righteous rewriting of its history for his benefit, his deep-seated pathos stands at the forefront. The history leading up to the Battle at Wounded Knee on December 29, 1890, is long, tortured, and complex. The game also does not specifically deal with the historical lead-up to the battle, as this aspect is not a concern of its protagonist Booker DeWitt. What is important here is Booker's role at Wounded Knee specifically that night in 1890.

It is worth examining the historical events of Wounded Knee. Dee Brown quotes Oglala Lakota Chief Red Cloud as saying of the coming slaughter, "The white men were frightened and called for soldiers. We had begged for life, and the white men thought we wanted theirs" (413). The Seventh Cavalry plays a major role historically in the conflict and this is the unit to which Booker DeWitt belongs. It was the Seventh Cavalry's Major Samuel Whitside who marched the Miniconjou Lakota Sioux to Wounded Knee Creek (414).

The issue of atrocity and the repetition of cycles of atrocity underpin the game's entire narrative. The game problematizes this concept through the evolving characterization of Booker DeWitt and the narrative revealing only in bits and pieces, and only toward the end of the game, after the player has invested emotionally in both Booker and Elizabeth, a full sense of scope of what has happened. At first, Booker appears troubled, saddled by gambling debts and some vague trauma over his actions at the battle of Wounded Knee, but he otherwise is taciturn when pressed for details. Later, the gamer learns that Booker not only participated at Wounded Knee, but brutally murdered women and children. Further still, many iterations of Booker, in order to assuage their guilt, become "born again" as Prophet Comstock, the epitome of a brutal and cruel dictator. Yet the Booker the gamer knows up until these revelations has been sympathetic and he clearly feels some level of horror at what he has done. Yet the problem lies in whether or not the gamer should feel moved to sympathy, a complicated and complex manipulation of the gamer's emotions brought out by the narrative.

The reasons for Booker's reluctance to talk about Wounded Knee start to coalesce as he and Elizabeth make their way to and through the Hall of Heroes chapter of the game. The main outline of the historical Battle of Wounded Knee begins with the forced march of the Lakota Sioux back to Wounded Knee. The Cavalry's eventual plan was to deport them to prison camps. Most important, perhaps, to the slaughter which occurs has to do with the demographic of the prisoners. The American Indians marched to Wounded Knee comprised "120 men and 230 women and children" (Brown 415).

Over the course of that night, the Seventh Cavalry set up armed sentries around the encampment at Wounded Knee, with the ultimate plan being to deport the Lakota Sioux to a prison camp in Omaha. The problems began the next day, when the new man in charge, Colonel James W. Forsyth, ordered the men to be disarmed. One man, Black Coyote, refused to surrender a rifle, "shouting that he had paid much money for the rifle and that it belonged to him" (Brown 416). Black Coyote's gun went off, presumably due to the struggle for it. After that, chaos reigned. The troops began to fire at everyone. Many of the Lakota men then armed themselves, and skirmishes broke out with the soldiers. While there is some dispute, as some of the wounded died after the battle, the best estimate is that some 300 of the 350 total men, women, and children were slaughtered (Brown 417). John E. Carter of the Nebraska Historical Society places the casualties at 250 Lakota Sioux ("Wounded Knee Massacre" n.p.). Whatever the final number historians agree upon, a vast number of those killed that night were unarmed and were women and children.

When Booker and Elizabeth reach The Hall of Heroes, a nationalistic, propaganda-laden exhibit featuring both Columbia's military prowess and Comstock's own, the Battle of Wounded Knee comes to the forefront. The exhibit, featuring shining uniforms, banners encouraging both white dominance of the world and patriotism, exemplifies all that Comstock wishes were true about himself. This sequence of the game also introduces Captain Cornelius Slate, who served with Booker DeWitt at Wounded Knee. The narrative reveals Slate through a series of voxophones, some found well after The Hall of Heroes, and also as an antagonist who directly interacts with Booker and Elizabeth in combat. Since he does not know that Comstock and Booker are essentially the same person, Slate believes that Comstock has made a "vaudeville travesty of my battles." He asserts that Comstock, who has now taken credit for nearly single-handedly winning at Wounded Knee, has made "a painted whore of our past." There is a sense of the idea of fictive constructs of another level at play here, evident in Slate's fury. This is the idea of the "tin soldier" and the idea of the representation of the heroic soldier ideal versus the atrocity at Wounded Knee. Throughout the Hall of Heroes segment, Slate becomes increasingly unhinged about Comstock being a "tin soldier" and not a true representation of a soldier.

At first, the narrative seems to hint that Slate might be a true exemplar of the redeemed villain and that his rage originates from his horror over what happened at Wounded Knee and the fact that Comstock takes credit for a bloodbath. Slate's initial thoughts and words seem to skew toward him hating the fact that Comstock does not honor the men who really fought and died, however unjust the cause. Yet this becomes quickly problematized. Instead, Slate shows no remorse for the slaughter of Wounded Knee and deems his and Booker's own actions "sacred."

Marie Laurie Ryan asserts, "In its fullest realization, the emancipation of embedded stories from the main narrative line leads to a subversion of the distinction between story and discourse" (123). In the case of the role of the Wounded Knee slaughter, and all the irreconcilable histories surrounding it as a fictive aspect of the game, the focus makes Wounded Knee both story and discourse. It is a commentary on the horrors of the real-life Battle of Wounded Knee, an internal discourse used to drive DeWitt, and an external discourse with the gamer about the manipulation of history. Booker and Slate are both completely fictive constructions with connections to a real-world event, but they function emotionally within the game as if they *could have* existed in real life. Even recent events like the trials of those involved in genocide during the reign of the Pol Pot find perpetrators of atrocity either relishing their roles or trying to deny their proved participation. The roles of both men in *BioShock Infinite*'s exploration of Wounded Knee prove equally cloudy and impossible to fully reconstruct. Slate claims that he led the Seventh Cavalry, but Booker claims that he does not remember who did, which might be an example of Slate's self-aggrandizing and/or Booker's deflection of culpability.

Slate, although a relatively minor NPC character appearing in just this one segment of the game, haunts much of the game via voxophones he leaves behind. Outwardly, Slate shows his hatred for Comstock by joining the resistance group the Vox Populi. Yet their cause, to overthrow Comstock and create a more egalitarian Columbia, means nothing to him. It is not a path to redemption. Instead, he is guilty of, as he says, "trading Comstock's lie for a new one." Yet he cannot reconcile his hate for Comstock with his own image of himself. What he decides upon is a course of action that might be deemed suicide-by-Booker. He and his remaining men have lain in wait for Booker because "they want to die at the hands of a real soldier." Slate's fear lies in being made a "tin man," or a tin soldier, as he alternately says.

The Hall of Heroes contains two major exhibits, one featuring, of course, Wounded Knee and the other the Boxer Rebellion. Comstock, who is hailed as the "hero of Wounded Knee" in murals adorning the exhibit and who claims to have "razed Peking to the ground" and then seceded Columbia from the Union, and Slate now battles over both imagined histories. Slate claims he burned down Peking, not Comstock. Comstock claims credit for the event even though he was not there, as he was at Wounded Knee. It is never really clear what either man did, yet each seems singularly driven to boast. Slate wants Booker to brag to Elizabeth about what he did, but Booker refuses. The gamer learns, via one of Slate's voxophones, that the men of the 7th Cavalry went so far as to nickname Booker "The White Indian of Wounded Knee" because of the "grisly" atrocities he committed that day. Booker never speaks of this directly to Elizabeth or to the gamer in any asides. It is only very late in the game, via a found voxophone, that Comstock reveals a bit more of his actions. What Booker does say, tellingly, calls into question whether he feels remorse over his own actions, or simply wants to escape them. Elizabeth asks him, "Do you ever get used to it, the killing?" to which he answers "Faster than you can imagine." This sentiment plays out in the style of gameplay itself. *BioShock Infinite* offers no stealth mechanism for sneaking by enemies or avoiding combat. At best, a player could try to run past enemies in certain areas, but in many cases, all enemies must be defeated before Booker and Elizabeth can move on. Booker remains a killer.

The Hall of Heroes sequence ends with Slate cornered and defeated, his men all dead, as wished for, at Booker's hands. He does not, for all the narrative build up, put up a fight himself. He asks, instead, that Booker "finish it," leaving the player the moral choice to either shoot Slate or leave him. The choice itself does not otherwise impact the storyline, but it presents a compelling moral quandary for the player. Killing Slate essentially gives Slate exactly what he wants—a heroic death, at least in his mind. Leaving him alive might seem the more fitting punishment. The act of "suicide by Booker" is, in and of itself, a profound copout.

The Battle of Wounded knee is the catalyst for the transformation of Booker deWitt—this is why he goes that fateful day to be baptized, yet it feels no less of a copout and a means to deny reflection on his past. He walks away from the trauma and guilt over Wounded Knee as Comstock, soon to be Prophet Comstock. Yet Comstock does not fulfill what seems to be his initial drive: to atone for what he has done through the creation of a new life. Instead, he creates a twisted, racist, and dangerous totalitarian regime powered by propaganda and cult of personality. When Booker first enters Columbia, the docking port is a chapel indoctrinating newcomers into the worship of Prophet Comstock as both leader and deity. Within the chapel are such affirmations as, "He has led us to this new Eden." Comstock borrows heavily from Christian iconography, likening Elizabeth to the Christ-like lamb. At this point, he might be accused of cruelty and megalomania, but his plans go to further, darker places. He has composed a "prophecy," the fulfillment of which is Elizabeth's purported destiny, which vows, "The seed of the prophet shall sit the throne and drown in flame the mountains of man." The "mountains of man" referred to here is the world below Columbia, specifically America. His reasons stem from a hatred at once as all-consuming as it is irrational.

As far as the events of Wounded Knee go, Comstock has folded those into his new biography and his image as Prophet. The gamer learns, during the events of the game's early parade sequence, that after Wounded Knee, Comstock received "a vision of the future" to start over. Of the concept of American Exceptionalism, Elizabeth Duquette argues, "It has justified territorial expansion, authorized intervention in foreign wars and the domestic affairs of sovereign nations, and vigorously, sometimes aggressively, promoted free market capitalism" (473). For Prophet Comstock, he transforms this ideal into something that might best be called Columbian Exceptionalism. He couches his history and rule on the premise that America failed and turned weak. Specifically, Lincoln and the Emancipation Proclamation stand as distinct points at which Comstock deviates from traditional conceptions of American exceptionalism to form his own divergent and largely self-created history. He presents the freeing of the slaves as an abomination and instead has monuments to John Wilkes Booth.

What terrifies Prophet Comstock is Booker DeWitt, who Comstock knows is coming to rescue Elizabeth and who he paints into his own mythology as "the false shepherd." Again, his rationale runs in direct opposition to what was once his great guilt and horror over Wounded Knee. If Booker takes Elizabeth from him, then Comstock's vision of starting a fiery war with America will never come to pass. Presumably, this would leave Comstock to live out his remaining days, few in number since he reveals he has terminal cancer, without anything but his own memories of what he has done. Further still, Elizabeth will be freed from her life-long enslavement. The reason behind Comstock's irrational hatred of American Indians also comes to light late in the narrative, through a voxophone—Comstock himself is part American Indian. When his fellow soldiers bring up this point, he responds with unspeakable cruelty at Wounded Knee, even burning women and children alive inside their teepees that night. He claims that the taint of being seen as less than white ruined him. He would rather craft a careful outward image of himself than live a life of true moral agency. Fear drives him to hatred, both internal and external, which then both drive him to lash out at others, even the most innocent.

It is with Elizabeth and her own tragic story that Comstock's actions demonstrate not just a lack of remorse, but an intolerable repetition of atrocity. Threatened by her power to open Tears and desperate to indoctrinate her into her role as the "seed of the Prophet," Comstock keeps her isolated in the Tower of the Lamb, which also contains a machine called the Siphon, which prevents Elizabeth from fully asserting her powers, although she is not initially aware of this. Without the siphon, Elizabeth cannot open Tears, nor create them. He keeps her isolated from nearly all human contact, her primary companion a human/robot monstrosity called the Songbird. When Comstock's wife, who is not Elizabeth's biological mother but is forced to pretend as much, revolts against him, Comstock has her murdered. When the Lutece twins try to assuage their guilt over being complicit in Comstock's plan to kidnap Elizabeth, he has them killed. Comstock's rule also foments increasingly violent rebellion in the form of the Vox Populi.

Booker himself, who in this iteration moves away from recovering Elizabeth just for the money and instead takes on the heroic quest to free Elizabeth and to topple Comstock, has lived a troubled life. He initially takes the job for money, but later begins to see a nobler cause. However, Booker's true nature is never fully clear. He cares for Elizabeth and, even before he realizes she is his daughter, takes on a paternal and protective role. Nonetheless, he seems more enamored with the idea of the nobler cause than perhaps the cause itself. As Comstock reminds Booker via a video feed, "I see every sin that blackens your soul. Wounded Knee. The Pinkertons." The narrative calls into question the very notion that anyone can truly change his or her essential nature. Booker, in all of these instances, resorts to violence and murder. Perhaps his best hope is to frame his own violent tendencies against the idea of the just cause. There is a Booker DeWitt, perhaps, down one of those infinite timelines who does not become what Comstock becomes, but they all tie back to Comstock, so this act of the dysfunctional assuaging of guilt—which is unsuccessful—takes a place of centrality in the overall narrative. Comstock, then, down many paths of possibility, becomes even worse than the "tin soldier" who likely committed atrocities at Wounded Knee—he creates a totalitarian society built on intolerance, ruled by religious extremism via lies, and he himself becomes ruthless.

The kidnapping of Elizabeth, originally named Anna, represents the robbing of innocence, and the fact that the innocence itself cannot last. As much as Comstock acts selfishly to take her in the first place, this is only possible because Booker was willing to sell his own daughter. At the very last moment, he changes his mind and tries to get Elizabeth back, but there is nothing to be done. Terrible choices are not so easily taken back. The issue of Elizabeth, richly drawn in her own right, underscores the narrative's complexity.

Daisy Fitzroy, leader of the Vox Populi, emerges as the next major antagonist in the narrative after Cornelius Slate and while she has important plot interactions with Booker, her profound importance lies in the manner of her death and Elizabeth's role in it. Her cause is a noble one and through a number of voxophones, the player learns how Comstock framed Daisy for the murder of his wife. She was a servant in their household, a black woman, and an easy scapegoat. Her life after that was as a fugitive, and instead of being broken by Comstock, she decided to fight against him. Yet even the Vox, as they call themselves, manage to lose the moral high ground. Once the rebellion becomes an all-out war—one which the Vox begin to win handily—they slaughter everyone in their path. They hang eerily beautiful red streaming banners from the buildings in Columbia, evocative not of new hope, but of bloody chaos and death. The Fitzroy narrative thread reaches its height when Booker and Elizabeth find her holding Fink and his young son hostage. She immediately kills Fink, symbolically smearing his blood across her face, and threatens to shoot the boy. It becomes the point of no return for her and for Elizabeth. Fitzroy, once vowing only to overthrow Comstock's regime, now says that nothing will change unless she "pull(s) it up from the root," meaning the slaughter of children is fair game. As much as this represents Fitzroy's moment of greatest atrocity—she clearly will kill the boy—it represents Elizabeth's first killing. She sneaks into the room and stabs Fitzroy. In the aftermath, a somber Elizabeth cuts her hair short and asks, "How do you wash away the things you've done?" Booker has no answer. The Fitzroy/Elizabeth confrontation gains added depth in Part 2 of *Burial at Sea*. The gamer, finally allowed to play as Elizabeth, watches this scene play out as a spectator when she crosses through a Tear. This time, however, she sees what lead up to Fitzroy threatening to kill the boy. The Luteces goad Fitzroy into the act because they need Elizabeth to be toughened up a bit, to be free of her wide-eyed innocence and sense of hope. Focused as they are on physics and probability, they deduce that the only way Elizabeth will survive is through violence.

The Elizabeth the gamer meets upon her rescue by Booker, however, is already diminished and painfully naïve as to her true circumstances. Comstock's Siphon keeps her abilities in check. A fully powered Elizabeth proves fearsome and unstoppable. The first time the gamer sees Elizabeth without restraint is in a vision of a bloody future and a burning New York, the work of Elizabeth and her followers down a timeline in which Comstock fully indoctrinates her. The gamer again sees Elizabeth at her full power near the end of the game, when Booker destroys the Siphon. She becomes something, then, more than human, able not only to manifest and open Tears at will, but also able to see into every single possible timeline, what she calls the "sea of doors." She is, in profound ways, the game's great tragic figure. She, of all the characters, is a true innocent. Yet even her initial wide-eyed naïveté and exuberance over being freed both give way to violence. One of the game's great contrasting images is of Elizabeth right after her rescue, dancing for the first time in the sunlight and then the dirtied, bloodied, and somber Elizabeth late in the game asking Booker if he is afraid of God.

Comstock tries, and partially succeeds, in passing along his legacy of hatred to her. Unfortunately, his assertion that "cruelty can be instructive" comes to pass. She hates different things for different reasons, but the seed of hate is planted. When she is first introduced in the story, Elizabeth, due to her near isolation in the Tower of the Lamb, knows little of the outside world. After Booker kills a number of Comstock's men, she is horrified by the slaughter and says, shocked, "You killed all those people." Yet, piece by piece, the outside world, even Booker, corrupt her. This dark rite of passage begins when Elizabeth kills the leader of the Vox Populi and continues after Elizabeth voluntarily returns to Comstock in order to save Booker from the Songbird.

Booker, consistently the failed hero, does not successfully rescue her. Indeed, he apparently dies over and over each time at the hands of the Songbird as Elizabeth opens Tears for him to try again and again, and he only reaches her when Elizabeth musters the last of her powers to open one final Tear that moves him forward in time by a number of months. During that time, she has been ruthlessly tortured, subjected to medical experimentation, and brainwashed into compliance with Comstock's plan. This is where the idea of the multiple timelines proves useful. The Elizabeth who is not saved becomes the older Elizabeth who orders the attack upon New York, then presumably all of America. Booker encounters this older, hardened, and weary Elizabeth, one who is successfully corrupted by Comstock. As she shows Booker a vision of a burning New York, Elizabeth states: "Time rots everything, Booker. Even hope." Although Booker saves Elizabeth, he has not saved her from Comstock, not really. He has simply managed to shorten the time she was with him in this particular timeline. In other timelines, Elizabeth fulfills Comstock's prophecy. The older Elizabeth hopes to eradicate this timeline completely by bringing Booker through this last Tear she has the power to manifest. Even this desire to avoid bloodshed presents problematical implications. Elizabeth will not so much learn a moral lesson or have to make a better moral choice to resist or reject Comstock as much as she will have to avoid the choice in the first place. Yet even this Elizabeth, spared the grimmer fate, has changed. When Booker frees her from Comstock's laboratory, she immediately retaliates against the staff there by opening a Tear and killing them.

Elizabeth's own consistent compliance up until the point at which Booker rescues her early in the game proves troubling. Ivana Markova notes, "Since propaganda is commonly understood as dissemination to the general public of a doctrine or an ideology, whether religious or political, it implies that it has a sociological or political rather than a psychological meaning, because its impact is on crowds rather than on single individuals" (38). She further asserts that propaganda itself functions based on its relationship to related institutions, such as a government looking to further or maintain its power and interests and that propaganda can be separated from an interrelated concept of persuasion. While propaganda is "monologue," persuasion is "dialogue" (49). These concepts provide a useful lens for understanding how Comstock controls Columbia in the broadest sense, and Elizabeth at the individual level. Elizabeth, without being able to fully articulate why, tells

Booker that when she was young, she used to create Tears. She does not realize the reason why she can now only open existing ones and not create new ones is due to the Siphon. Yet even though she could leave the Tower of the Lamb through these Tears and escape into a new life, she always returns.

The final confrontation of the game—the one that most gamers likely await anxiously—is the one between Booker and Comstock. The game, brilliantly, avoids a gun battle or any type of real hand-to-hand combat here between the two. Comstock goads Booker by telling Elizabeth that Booker has not been truthful. After all, he has "rewritten" his memories to avoid remembering his selling of Anna. Any other combat would be futile. These two men are one in the same, separated by timeline, but not by much else. They are mirrors of each other, the self-righteous would-be liberator of Elizabeth, the self-righteous ruler of Columbia. The scene plays out quickly, as Booker repeatedly smashes the physically vulnerable Comstock's head in on a baptismal font. One more act of violence. In Suzannah Biernoff's examination of the first two *BioShock* games, she explores the origin of the Splicers and how inspiration for them, in part, comes from photographs of horrifically wounded soldiers from World War I. While that discussion does not prove relevant here, her exploration of the issue of violence adds dimension. She writes, "Although the distinction is ultimately unsustainable, it is still widely believed that 'art' is morally beneficial (except perhaps when it is too entertaining) and that computer games are not. In art (it is said) cruelty and violence are sublimated rather than simply enjoyed" (329). Biernoff sees the problem inherent in such a black and white delineation of the purpose of violence and cruelty. *BioShock Infinite* contains a number of sequences of violence, some quite brutal, some quite intimate, as is the case with Booker's killing of Comstock. The violence here merits just such careful consideration. While it is a shocking scene, it could hardly be said to be enjoyable. Indeed, for many gamers, DeWitt's killing of Comstock feels necessary, yet a weariness hangs over the scene and over Elizabeth and DeWitt. Comstock is not really dead, as he has not been expunged from all permutations of possibility. He has only been eliminated in this one particular iteration of Columbia.

It is here, in this point, that the narrative unfolds its final layer of complexity as it explores the failure of its characters to truly find agency and change. This Comstock, of the game proper, is dead, yet "he is alive in a million million worlds," as Elizabeth cautions. In some worlds, Booker does not opt to get baptized as a means to assuage his conflicted feelings toward Wounded Knee. That Booker may or may not, then, sell Elizabeth to Comstock via the Luteces. However, any number of Bookers do take the baptism and become Comstock. Elizabeth's solution, as she takes Booker through a

Tear to the creek where he does or does not take the baptism, is to drown him. At first glance, such a narrative plot point—that there exist multiple possibilities—might appear to be interesting, but relatively straightforward and simple. Closer inspection proves it is anything but. Zach Waggoner references Jean Beaudrillard's conception of the simulacra, notating that they are "copies without originals" (38). The unanswered question, then, lies in determining what constitutes an "original" Booker DeWitt. Certainly aspects of his personality appear to be locked down, especially his actions at Wounded Knee. Elizabeth never speaks of any Tears in which there exists a Booker who avoided Wounded Knee, or did not kill there. Instead, the copies all share in common a series of traits, especially a predilection toward violence.

Perhaps, then, no one in *BioShock Infinite* can rightly claim the mantle of hero. Instead of heroes, broken people trying to find a way to be just slightly less so populate the narrative. Roland Barthes states, "A narrative is never made up of anything other than functions: in differing degrees, everything in it signifies" (49). In the case of this narrative, the plot threads are so tightly constructed so as to fit all of the seemingly disparate narrative threads together in one devastating series of endings. If the game offers any true sense of hope, it proves fleeting and indistinct. After the end credits, the gamer is playing as Booker again, back in his office where the game started. This time, Booker hears a baby cry and runs to her room. As he opens the door, the screen goes white. There may be a possibility that one Booker does not sell Anna to the Luteces, but this also implies at the same time that Elizabeth's plan to eradicate all permutations of Comstock from the timeline did not work. At its core, *BioShock Inifnite* is an example of epic, thematically deep storytelling. The game simply would not allow for an analysis focusing solely on its ludological elements. The narratological perspective in approaching the game is the only one allowing for its richness of storytelling to be considered to its fullest advantage.

Works Cited

Barthes, Roland. "Introduction to the Structural Analysis of Narratives." *Narratology: An Introduction*. Eds. Susana Onega and José Angel García Landa. London: Longman, 1996. 45–60. Print.

Biernoff, Suzannah. "Medical Archives and Digital Culture: From World War I to *BioShock*." *Medical History* 55 (2011): 325–330. Print.

Bogost, Ian. *Unit Operations: An Approach to Videogame Criticism*. Cambridge, MA: MIT Press, 2006. Print.

Bremond, Claude. "The Logic of Narrative Possibilities." *Narratology: An Introduction*.

Eds. Susana Onega and José Angel García Landa. London: Longman, 1996. 61–75. Print.

Brown, Dee. *Bury My Heart at Wounded Knee.* New York: Bantam Books, 1972. Print.

Card, Claudia. "Surviving Long-Term Mass Atrocities." *Midwest Studies in Philosophy* 36 (2012): 35–52. Print.

Carter, John E. "Wounded Knee Massacre." *Encyclopedia of the Great Plains. http:// plainshumanities.unl.edu/encyclopedia/doc/egp.war.056.* 2011. Accessed August 8, 2014. Web.

Deleyto, Celestino. "Focalisation in Film Narrative." *Narratology: An Introduction.* Eds. Susana Onega and José Angel García Landa. London: Longman, 1996. 217–233. Print.

Duquette, Elizabeth. "Rethinking American Exceptionalism." *Literature Compass* 10:6 (2013): 473–482. Print.

Hourigan, Benjamin. "A Slave Obeys, a Player Chooses." *IPA Review* (March 2009): 20–23. Print.

Irrational Games. *BioShock Infinite.* 2K Games, 2013. PlayStation 3.

Kirkpatrick, Graeme. *Aesthetic Theory and the Video Game.* Manchester: Manchester University Press, 2011. Print.

Markova, Ivana. "Persuasion and Propaganda." *Diogenes* 55:37 (2008): 37–51. Print.

Ryan, Marie Laurie. "Cyberage Narratology: Computers, Metaphor, and Narrative." *Narratologies.* Ed. David Herman. Columbus: Ohio State University Press, 1999. 113–141. Print.

Travinor, Grant. "*BioShock* and the Art of Rapture." *Philosophy and Literature* 33:1 (April 2009): 91–106. Print.

Turner, Frederick Jackson. "The Significance of the Frontier in American History." Presented to *The American Historical Association* on July 12, 1893. Accessed on-line at http://nationalhumanitiescenter.org/pds/gilded/empire/text1/turner.pdf. 1–9. Web.

Waggoner, Zach. *My Avatar, Myself: Identity in Video Role-Playing Games.* Jefferson, NC: McFarland, 2009. Print.

"All that's left is the choosing"
BioShock Infinite *and the Constants and Variables of Control*

Matthew Wysocki *and* Betsy Brey

ELIZABETH: "Look at that. Thousands of doors, opening all at once. My god, they're beautiful."
BOOKER: "What, the stars?"
E: "See? Not stars, they're doors."
B: "Doors to?"
E: "To everywhere, all that's left is the choosing."
B: "What are all these lighthouses? Why are we ... who are...?"
E: "There are a million, million worlds. All different and all similar. Constants and variables."
B: "What?"
E: "There's always a lighthouse. There's always a man. There's always a city."
B: "How do you know this?"
E: "I can see them through the doors. You. Me. Columbia. Songbird. But sometimes, something's different ... yet the same."
B: "Constants and variables."

BioShock Infinite is the third installment in the *BioShock* series, all created by Ken Levine and published by 2K Games. Though it is not a sequel to the previous games, it does share many of their themes and gameplay mechanics and does allow for a brief visit to Rapture, the site of the first two *BioShock* games. The preceding conversation between protagonists Elizabeth and Booker that occurs near the game's conclusion confirms the existence of "multiverses" but also outlines a central theme of this game, that the player has "a million" options available in how they proceed through the game while also confirming that in any playthrough, they will always experience a man, a lighthouse, Elizabeth, Columbia, and Songbird. Every time they play something is different, yet always the same. This is the meaning of constants and variables. But through this scene and this game, the developers of *BioShock* continue to explore and expand how we can conceptualize and theorize about the issues of player control and agency with regard to video games.

Since the newer *BioShock* features all of its major narrative development during cutscenes, it could be read as a game that reinforces how little has changed with regard to control. *BioShock Infinite* implies that a multiverse of possibilities exist and "All that's left is the choosing" of which path to take. But since this revelation happens during a point when the player is more spectator than agent, it appears that all a player can do is watch as the game makes choices for them. It may have infinite in the title, but it appears finite in its options. However, as this discussion explores, the choosing of paths, those sections of gameplay that must be done in order to activate the cutscenes, are crucial for our understanding of when we say a player does and does not have agency. By focusing on gameplay as the object of study within discussions of control, we see that agency is a unique and personal experience for each player, allowing a multiverse of agencies and paths through story. The game, as a static text, is a constant. But each gamer's own choices, as variables, allow each player control over their own path. There may be a framework in place that must be followed, but there is a multiverse of options with regard to how to traverse it.

Theories/Discussions of Control and Gameplay

Questions of control are on the forefront of game studies, both within the games as texts/experiences, as well as within the discipline as a whole. Voorhees argues that polarizing debates, such as the ludology/narratology debates, only act to hinder the continued growth of game studies. He puts forth that the purpose of study and the domain of study are being confused by this question, enacting a false dilemma that limits the discipline to an either/or answer (9–11). The purpose of studying games varies within the interdisciplinary field of game studies, asking different questions requiring different approaches. To limit the questions to either a focus on ludic concerns or narrative ones serves to limit the findings of research. The sheer number of different genres, purposes, and audiences for games cannot be understood through a single binary of ludic or narrative (Nitsche 1–2).[1]

In the end, the debate of narratology versus ludology has acted to open the emerging discipline with the outcome of leading to a new false dichotomy of game versus player.

As a field, game studies employs theories and practices from a multitude of disciplines, but at what should we direct these theories—the player or the game? Studying the player can be associated with communication and media studies. Some player-as-object-of-study research can seek to understand non–virtual world behavior through mediated and gaming practices. Limperos, et al., note that the majority of this type of research focuses on the effects of the game on a player (Vorderer and Bryant), such as emotional impact on players (Schneider et al.) and potential negative/anti-social, or positive/pro-social behaviors associated with game play (Smith; Lee and Peng; Fischer, Kubitzki, Guter, and Frey) including issues of violence in games (Anderson et al.; Weber, Ritterfield, and Kostygina; Ferguson). Motivation also proves to be a topic covered by player-as-object-of-study scholars, questioning the selection process in choosing a game (Hartman and Klimmt; Raney, Smith, and Baker), entertainment seeking and use (Ohler and Nieding; Klug and Schell; Sherry et al.), and in-game decision-making (Bowman, Joeckel, and Dogruel; Penny; Hartman and Vorderer). Ethnographic studies also focus on player-as-object-of-study. William Bainbridge's 2010 The Warcraft Civilization focuses on the impacts and implications of roleplaying in Blizzard's *World of Warcraft* series.

However, as Voorhees notes, such approaches delegate the power of meaningfulness entirely to the player, nearly eliminating the possibility of control by the game itself (13). It can be argued that these methodologies overlook the place of the creator(s) and of the rule structures of the game played. Furthermore, if the control of a game experience falls solely in the hands of the player, why do gamers frequently express dissatisfaction with game narratives, most clearly illustrated by the *Mass Effect* ending controversy?

In contrast, studying the game has often been the focus of many different interdisciplinary fields, ranging from sociology, literary studies, computer science, digital design, psychology, and many more. Proponents of the game-as-object-of-study argue players are "subject to power, maneuvered, positioned or manipulated by games" (Voorhees 13). Because games are predesigned and prescribed code sets, Bogost refers to games as "models of experience" as opposed to depictions of experiences. To play a game, according to Bogost, is to control prescribed actions within the rules (4)—after all, "a videogame constantly asks its players to act ... only a small number of acts are really supported in the game world" (Bogost 48–49). Research concerning questions of space, narrative, and design (Jenkins; Nitsche; Lee, Park, and Jin; Sellers; Schell; Zimmerman and Tekinbas) also tend to focus on the game-as-object-of-study. Critical examination of games themselves as cultural and technological artifacts, such as studying the ideologies of and approaches to topics ranging from gender, race, philosophies, sexuality, or politics (Cuddy and Nordlinger; Murray; Brathwaite; Cassell and Jenkins; Bogost, "Persuasive Games"), explore these themes and issues within digital spaces, but this kind of study is reflective, mirroring the undercurrents of critical questions and concerns. Additionally, while not true of all games-as-objects-of-study research, some tend to privilege the game-text as absolute; all there is of a game is contained within its code, and the player loses any and all potential influence. But games without players are simply code.

Losing the player means losing play, perhaps the defining factor of a game.

Both the game and the player have been, and will continue to be, studied separately. But this is merely another binary, another either/or simplification. Nitsche encapsulates the idea well, arguing that the ludology/narratology debate is one of many possible approaches (41), and no single theory or approach could fully explain, explore, or define the study of games (1). In the case of player versus game, Voorhees offers a hybrid approach, arguing the overlapping area of gameplay, between the player and the game, can help reveal new implications and ideas for games studies.

Gameplay for Ang, building off of much early work in game studies, is a consequence of the interaction between paidea ("education": with no clear objective) and ludic ("play": with clear victory or defeat) rules. "First, gameplay emerges from and must conform to the paidea rules that describe the semantic of the game. Second, gameplay is oriented toward the ludus rules that describe the structure of the game" (315). This reveals the nature of interaction that exists as paidea rules are set forth by the game designer. They function to restrict what the player is or is not allowed to do, while ludic rules allow the player to bring forth complexity in their gameplay. Caldwell also provides a definition that positions this idea of player and developer both being involved in negotiating and creating the gameplay. He states that gameplay:

> [I]s a way of quantifying the operations of a kind of economy of desire that operates between the player and the game itself. This economy has, as its constitutive elements, such factors as attention span, pleasure, ratio of novelty to repetition. These elements are in constant circulation in a game and the resulting economy is responsible for a good deal of the dynamism of the experience: in other words, the gameplay [para 10].

The player brings in motivations and needs to the experience, and likewise, the game provides its own lures. The interactions between these is where gameplay may be located.

Working from this, Voorhees states that gameplay consists of "the negotiation of the determinant structure of the game and the agentic capacity of the player" (15). Based on this position, we see that rather than controlling the limits of the field, gameplay looks for meaning and significance in the interface of the parts rather than the parts themselves—not just the game, not just the player, not just the narrative, not just the ludic or paideic elements, but the possibility space where the parts meet. Bissell makes the comparison that "the best part of looking at a night sky, after all, is not any one star but the infinite possibility of what is between stars" (12–13); rather than seeking any individual story, game mechanic, design element, character, or player, the study of gameplay focuses on the interface between those elements (Voorhes 16). Voorhees defines gameplay as a process in which the player "manages the distribution and application of the abilities, motivations and understandings they bring to the game" (16). But Voorhees clearly argues that gameplay is not a rout process—it cannot be "objectively identified" and it is not a "thing" or "phenomena" (16). This process shows the concessions of power between the game and the player, passing back and forth to elicit discourse and interaction.

Voorhees puts forth that gameplay remains a crucial element for the proper understanding of control in game studies. "An often used but poorly defined term, gameplay displaces both player and game with an emphasis of the interfacing of the two. However, gameplay is more than simply an intersection between an agentic player and the structure of the game; gameplay is the agonistic struggle—playful but consequential—out of which meaningful human action emerges" (16). By rethinking game studies in this manner, this places more control in the hands of the player, but also in the structures that oversee the games we play, balancing both player and game by focusing on gameplay.

The question of control in gaming is one that Levine's *BioShock* series has provided much insight into. Wysocki and Schandler contend that the "Would you kindly?" cutscene in the first *BioShock* asked questions about what levels of control gamers have when playing video games. Inherent in that game is the idea of a man choosing but a slave obeying (2013). Wysocki and Schandler write, "Perhaps the only real choice, the only real level of control that a player truly has is the choice to play or not to play. But in choosing not to play, the gamer is denying their identity as a gamer.... [T]he gamer must do as the game tells them. What else are you going to do, turn it off and not play?" (206). But gamers do turn it on, and gamers do choose to press play.

As one of us (Wysocki and Schandler) has developed previously, control is much more than opting whether or not to turn the game on or off, arguing that:

The word control has many implications when it is used in connection with video games. Obviously on a basic level, unlike other media, if a player does not control the game, there is no experience. You must participate to keep the story moving forward. While other media might require their audience to be mentally active, they remain physically passive. Their agency consists of little more than pushing play on a remote control or turning a page. A video game demands response. Buttons and joysticks must be manipulated, paths must be mapped out, and flaming barrels must be jumped. Failure to do so means failure to continue the gaming experience [196].

There are many times when gamers choose not to continue a game—the story does not catch their interest, the game mechanics are difficult, the gameplay does not fulfill their expectations; there are many reasons why some players never complete a game. By making these choices, they are making the decision to end the game and therefore, end the game experience. However, for players who wish to continue their game experience, they have no option but to literally play along with whatever the game asks them to do, obeying whatever the demands the game code doles out. Wysocki explains how this relationship of control extends far beyond the player, stating:

much of the video game industry focuses on questions of control. How can they improve the methods of "playing" to make the gamer feel more connected? How can the player "control" the game in a way that makes them feel more like they are "there"? Each generation of game console that gets released redesigns the game controller in small or large ways. And Nintendo, Sony, and Microsoft have released motion controllers designed for new ways of involved game experiences. In fact the unique nature of the Wii propelled a mediocre game, Wii Sports, into a best selling title based upon being packaged with a Wii motion controller [2].

Immersion and narrative connectedness depend on the player being able to ignore the physical means of their control and become absorbed into the experience. The gameplay must absorb the means of play; a player must forget the screen, the controller, and themselves. Developers know this and seek to increase the transportative quality of games through these physical means of control, the idea seemingly being that the more nature and fluid the control, the better the game experience.

Bogost also considers how to conceptualize gameplay as a way to help define the concept of control, though instead of calling it gameplay, he uses the phrase "possibility space":

In a video game, the possibility space refers to the myriad configurations the player might construct to see the ways the processes inscribed within the system work. This is really what we do when we play a video game: we explore the possibility space its rules afford by manipulating the symbolic system it provides. The rules do not merely create the experience of play—they also construct the meaning of the game [Procedural, 43].

Similar to Wysocki and Schandler's work on the first *BioShock*, Bogost is speaking to how the rules and structures of the game function as systematic elements of control. But both Bogost and Voorhees are also putting forth the idea that within play is a large part of when players are deciding what the experience means to them and where their agency lies. As we shall discuss, we feel that the lighthouse scene in *BioShock Infinite* can be read as a statement about the importance of the crucial element of gameplay as location for player control.

The Synopsis

BioShock Infinite is a first-person shooter video game developed by Irrational Games and published by 2K Games. It was released worldwide for the Microsoft Windows, PlayStation 3, and Xbox 360 platforms on March 26, 2013. Irrational Games and creative director Ken Levine based the game's setting on historical events at the turn of the 20th century, such as the 1893 World's Columbian Exposition, and based its story on the concept of American exceptionalism. Featuring the floating city of Colombia, *BioShock Infinite* serves up a new, dynamic and memorable setting, arguably equally iconic to the previous game's setting, Rapture.

Players enter Colombia as former Pinkerton agent Booker DeWitt, sent to the floating air city to find a young woman, Elizabeth, who has been held captive there for most of her life by a man named Zachary Comstock, the founder and spiritual leader of Columbia. Though Booker rescues Elizabeth, the two become involved with the city's warring factions: the elite Founders that rule Columbia as a utopia for white Americans, and the Vox Populi, underground rebels. During this conflict, Booker learns that Elizabeth possesses strange powers to manipulate "Tears" in the space-time.

Over the course of the game, players learn, among many other things, that Booker DeWitt in some universes becomes Zachary Comstock after being born again through baptism. Comstock becomes sterile due to experiments in exploring multiple dimensions and, desiring an heir, locates Anna, the daughter of Booker DeWitt and therefore, technically his own biological daughter. DeWitt sells Anna, through agents, to Comstock to wipe away a debt. In Colombia, the infant Anna becomes Elizabeth and is raised as Comstock and his wife's daughter, groomed to take Comstock's place and wage war against millions of innocents on the earth's surface. Only in retrospect do two of Comstock's agents understand what they have put in motion, and decide to put a stop to it, plucking DeWitt out of his universe hoping that he may be able to recover Elizabeth and restore peace. It is determined that the only way to prevent the creation of Columbia is to kill Booker before his transformation into Comstock. In essence, to remove two variables at once from the multiverse—preventing an apocalyptic and destructive war but ensuring there will never be a lighthouse, there will never be a man, there will never be a city.

The Implications of Constants and Variables

At different times the player is given very specific binary options. Some examples: Booker can choose for Elizabeth to wear a cage or a bird choker, when asked by the Lutece twins. Booker either kills or spares Slate. At the ticket booth, Booker either pulls a gun on the ticket booth taker or has his hand stabbed by him. Booker can call the coin flip right after entering Columbia either heads or tails. Booker can choose to throw the baseball at the black and white couple during the Raffle Square Stoning scene, or at Fink (or potentially the player can choose neither—not react fast enough for the game to register a decision). While these have the appearance of important choices, eventually the player should realize they are false alternatives, having no concrete impact on the game. For example, regardless of the player's attempted choice for Booker in the Raffle Square Stoning scene, the police notice the brand on Booker's hand and grab him before he throws the ball. If Booker is stabbed in the hand, it does not influence the player's combat abilities—there is only the aesthetical alteration to his hand of a bandage. Elizabeth happily wears either the bird or the cage choker without comment or consequences beyond her appearance. Slate is either killed by Booker or killed by other means, but either way, Slate dies with no further impact on the story. Each of these binaries, the selection of heads or tails (literally at one point), does not impact the story. Beyond narrative impacts, decisions do not have gameplay impact, either. The game is not easier or harder to play depending on the player's choices. Many times in games, some choices lead to positive results—perhaps an upgraded weapon or a refreshed ammo stock—and some lead to negative results. However, decisions in BioShock Infinite are more or less equally rewarded, leading to no gameplay impacts. On a narrative level, the fact that all decisions are equally rewarded, other than minor changes in dialogue, denies the possibility of leading to the trope of the "good" or "evil" ending.[2] Returning to the Raffle Square scene again, no matter what the player opts to do, he or she is rewarded with the same item later in the game. These kinds of scenes act to fool with player's expectations of how choice in a game should work. Games are constructed space. Each detail is within that space because someone put it there. Players are accustomed to game material having a purpose. Those details traditionally have impact. These dead-end decisions toy with the player's expectations of game narrative because players are not used to having irrelevant material placed in a game. However, these kinds of choices do act to emphasize the decision-making process. Simply by the act of continually forcing players to make decisions, the story and gameplay makes *BioShock Infinite* players very aware of choices, calling attention to the main narrative itself.

Identically to *BioShock*, *BioShock Infinite*'s key revelation happens during a cutscene. However, there is a difference when these scenes occur. The "Would You Kindly" cut scene occurs at roughly the mid-point of *BioShock* and Wysocki and Schandler argued that continuing the game highlighted the lack of control that gamers have. The player is made aware of their manipulation and then must continue to satisfy the script of the game in order to complete it. They are not free to make choices outside of what has been programmed. There is no option to abandon Rapture or avoid seeking revenge against Atlas, despite the player knowing the game is continuing to manipulate their actions. In the same vein, Bissell argues *BioShock*, "offers the freedom to luxuriate in Objectivism's enlightened selfishness, the game's fiction denies the gamer that same freedom.... Rather than mock the gamer, *BioShock* could just as easily be commenting on itself, its game-ness, thereby allowing the gamer to feel what he or she wants to feel" (1153–54). Through the set rules, the player is allowed the chance to consider the ramifications of their manipulation. As Bissell reminds readers, "you get controlled and are controlled" (39). The act of playing *BioShock*, or any game, requires a player to give up control, to obey the algorithms of the game, even as these algorithms cast the illusion of control. What players have is not total freedom, but rather, a set of rules to explore. Only through meeting the requirements of the game can the game be experienced.

In *BioShock Infinite*, the "Constants and Variables" reveal occurs during the conclusion of the game. Booker has dealt with Comstock in the current reality the gamer finds herself or himself in, but Elizabeth reveals that he remains a threat in other realities. The player is required to progress through a series of scenes, occasionally moving Booker along his path, where the full depth of the truth is revealed and the dialogue from the beginning of this chapter occurs. Ryan argues that this discussion reveals the essence of video games:

Infinite discusses the ideas of "constants and variables"—the fact that, in each reality, some things will remain the same and some things will be different. If we step outside of the game world, we find that every single playthrough begins and ends at the same point: from baptismal waters upon entering Columbia to the baptismal waters you finally drown in. In much the same way *Bioshock* [sic] commented on the single-player experience in video games, *Infinite* takes an even more meta approach.... *Infinite* comments on the nature of video games. It always presents the same game world and the same set of events. There is no escaping that loop. You can consider the video game world the constant and the player the variable, as each time they play, they progress slightly differently [para. 2].

It is in this variable progression that the true control available to players is revealed. The framework of beginning and ending remain, but the player chooses their path within those constants. While the game cannot be experienced if one does not meet its requirements, the player chooses how to meet them. This is part of the essence that separates games from other media.

It could be argued that while a decision in this scene is made, it is not the player's. Booker, the character, makes the decision to die, sacrificing his life to prevent the repercussions of the Constants his very life creates. Because this moment is narrated in a cutscene, the player has no control to implement. The choice is not the player's, the choice is Booker's, as a character in a story, not an avatar in a game. Booker's ability to make independent choices of the player's desires highlights the player's apparent lack of control. But it must be pointed out that it was the choices the player made and the struggles the player overcame through their actions that allowed Booker the character to fulfill his role in this narrative. By playing the game their way, the player exercises their control in the game world. Furthermore, at numerous times, the game acts to remind its players that this periodic lack of agency does not mean a lack of power. As mentioned, during the course of the game players are given the choice to execute or spare the character Slate (a variable). Later they face the repercussions of this choice (a constant). Regardless of the decision made, Slate's fate is a grisly one. Still, Elizabeth reminds Booker, "a choice is better than none, Mr. DeWitt. No matter what the outcome."

During the ending cutscene of the game, Booker, faced with infinite lighthouses with infinite doors observes, "There are so many choices." Elizabeth responds, "They all lead us to the same place, where it started." Booker attempts to reinforce some sense of autonomy and states, "No one tells me where to go." Booker, representing the player, attempts to assert free will. But throughout this game, and arguably every game, some aspect of the game is based on telling us where to go. Elizabeth has already told Booker, "They all lead to the same place." Players will always end up in the river at the end of the game. What is left to players is determining how to get there. Players play for the variables. By creating a game that can be read as a reminder of that fact, Levine continues to both tear down and redefine what is possible with gaming. The constants of cutscenes or conversation trees not only can have impact on gameplay, but in a game like *BioShock Infinite*, we feel the Constants do have emotional impact upon players (though you may not have been as impressed), while also providing the framework that allows the game experience to happen. The Variables of play are where the player positions themselves as agents affecting the medium of video games. This is ultimately what *BioShock Infinite* reinforces through this moment. Ryan, in conclusion to his essay, states, "You may put the pieces of the puzzle together differently than I, but in the end, we will always drown." But we counter that in the end, we will always drown, but in games we are free to choose how we put the pieces of the puzzle together. Video games contain both elements of Constance and Variance together, and creating a game studies language that seeks to meld the elements, rather than focus on them separately, is crucial to move our field forward.

Notes

1. For an illustration of game purposes, see Ian Bogost's *How to Do Things with Videogames* (Minneapolis: University of Minnesota Press, 2011).
2. The original *BioShock* does feature a "good" and "evil" ending, but as discussed in Wysocki and Schandler as well as within this argument, the ending is complicated by the game's dialogue on choice.

Works Cited

Anderson, C.A., A. Shibuya, N. Ihori, E.L. Swing, B.J. Bushman, A. Sakamoto, H.R. Rothstein, and M. Saleem. "Violent Video Games Effects on Aggression, Empathy, and Prosocial Behavior in Eastern and Western Cultures: A Meta-Analytic Review." *Psychological Bulletin* 136 (2010): 151–173. Print.
Ang, C. S. "Rules, Gameplay, and Narratives in Video Games." *Simulation and Gaming* 37 (2006): 306–325. Print.
Bissell, Tom. *Extra Lives: Why Video Games Matter.* New York, NY: Pantheon, 2010. Print.
Bogost, Ian. *How to Do Things with Videogames.* Minneapolis: University of Minnesota Press, 2011. Print.
Bogost, Ian. *Procedural Rhetoric: The Expressive Power of Videogames.* Cambridge, MA: MIT Press, 2007. Print.
Bowman, N.D., S. Joeckel, and L. Dorgruel. "Uphold Morality, or Finish the Game? The Influence of Moral Institutions on Decisions in Virtual Environments." Paper

presented at the Media and Morality Symposium of Broadcast Education Association, Las Vegas, NV (May 2011).

Brathwaite, B. *Sex in Video Games*. Rockland, MA: Charles River Media, Inc., 2006. Print.

Caldwell, N. "Settler Stories: Representational Ideologies in Computer Strategy Gaming" *M/C: A Journal of Media and Culture* 3.5 (2000): Online.

Cuddy, Luke, and John Nordlinger. *World of Warcraft and Philosophy: Wrath of the Philosopher King*. Chicago: Carus Publishing, 2009. Print.

Ferguson, C.J. "Evidence for Publication Bias in Video Game Violence Effects Literature: A Meta-Analytic Review." *Aggression and Violent Behavior* 12 (2007): 470–482. Print.

Fischer, P., J. Kubitzki, S. Guter, and D. Frey. "Virtual Driving and Risk-Taking: Do Racing Games Increase Risk-Taking Cognitions, Affect, and Behaviors?" *Journal of Experimental Psychology*: Applied 13 (2007): 22–31. Print.

Hartmann, T., and P. Vorderer. "It's Okay to Shoot a Character: Moral Disengagement in Violent Videogames" *Journal of Communication* 60 (2010): 94–119. Print.

Jenkins, Henry. "Game Design as Narrative Architecture." *First Person: New Media as Story, Performance, and Game*. Eds. Noah Wardrip-Fruin and Pat Harrigan. Cambridge, MA: MIT, 2004. 118–130. Print.

Klimmt, Christoph, and Tilo Hartman. "Effectance, Self-Efficacy, and the Motivation to Play Video Games." *Playing Video Games: Motives, Responses, and Consequences*. Eds. Peter Vorderer and Jennings Bryant. Mahwah, NJ: Lawrence Erlbaum Associates, 2006. 153–69. Print.

Klug, G. Christopher, and Jesse Schell. "Why People Play Games: An Industry Perspective." *Playing Video Games: Motives, Responses, and Consequences*. Eds. Peter Vorderer and Jennings Bryant. Mahwah, NJ: Lawrence Erlbaum Associates, 2006. 104–114. Print.

Lee, Kawn Min, Namkee Partk, and Seung-A Jin." Narrative and Interacitvity in Computer Games." *Playing Video Games: Motives, Responses, and Consequences*. Eds. Peter Vorderer and Jennings Bryant. Mahwah, NJ: Lawrence Erlbaum Associates, 2006. 304–322. Print.

Lee, Kwan Min, and Wei Peng. "What Do We Know About Social and Psychological Effects of Computer Games? A Comprehensive Review of the Current Literature." *Playing Video Games: Motives, Responses, and Consequences*. Eds. Peter Vorderer and Jennings Bryant. Mahwah, NJ: Lawrence Erlbaum Associates, 2006. 408–426. Print.

Limperos, Anthony M., Edward Downs, James D. Ivory, and Nicholas D. Bowman. "Leveling Up: A Review of Emerging Trends and Suggestions for the Next Generation of Communication Research Investigating Video Games' Effects." *Communication Yearbook* 37 (2013): 348–77. Print.

Murray, Janet. "From Game-Story to Cyberdrama." *First Person: New Media as Story, Performance, and Game*. Eds. Noah Wardrip-Fruin and Pat Harrigan. Cambridge, MA: MIT Press, 2004. 2–11. Print.

Nitsche, Michael. *Video Game Spaces: Image, Play, and Structure in 3D Game Worlds*. Cambridge, MA: MIT Press, 2008. Print.

Ohler, Peter, and Gerhild Nieding. "Why Play? An Evolutionary Perspective." *Playing Video Games: Motives, Responses, and Consequences*. Eds. Peter Vorderer and Jennings Bryant. Mahwah, NJ: Lawrence Erlbaum Associates, 2006. 115–131. Print.

Penny, Simon. "Representtion, Enaction, and the Ethics of Simulation." *First Person: New Media as Story, Performance, and Game.* Eds. Noah Wardrip-Fruin and Pat Harrigan. Cambridge, MA: MIT Press, 2004. 71–84. Print.

Raney, Arthur A., Jason K. Smith, and Kaysee Baker. "Adolescents and the Appeal of Video Games." *Playing Video Games: Motives, Responses, and Consequences.* Eds. Peter Vorderer and Jennings Bryant. Mahwah, NJ: Lawrence Erlbaum Associates, 2006. 191–209. Print.

Ryan, Jackson W. "*BioShock Infinite*: Constants and Variables." *Dusty Cartridge* (2013). Online.

Scheider, E.F., A. Lang, M. Shin, and S.D. Bradley. "Death with a Story: How Story Impacts Emotional, Motivational, and Physiological Responses to First Person Shooter Video Games." *Human Communication Research* 30 (2004): 361–375. Print.

Sellers, Michael. "Designing the Experience of Interactive Play." *Playing Video Games: Motives, Responses, and Consequences.* Eds. Peter Vorderer and Jennings Bryant. Mahwah, NJ: Lawrence Erlbaum Associates, 2006. 10–26. Print.

Sherry, John L., Kristen Lucas, Bradley S. Greenberg, and Ken Lachlan. "Video Game Uses and Gratifications as Predictors of Use and Game Preference." *Playing Video Games: Motives, Responses, and Consequences.* Eds. Peter Vorderer and Jennings Bryant. Mahwah, NJ: Lawrence Erlbaum Associates, 2006. 263–281. Print.

Smith, Stacy. "Perps, Pimps, and Provocative Clothing: Examining Negative Content Patterns in Video Games." *Playing Video Games: Motives, Responses, and Consequences.* Eds. Peter Vorderer and Jennings Bryant. Mahwah, NJ: Lawrence Erlbaum Associates, 2006. 64–87. Print.

2K Games. *BioShock Infinite.* 2K Games, 2013. Multiple platforms.

Voorhees, Gerald. "Criticism and Control: Gameplay in the Space of Possibilities." *Ctrl-Alt-Play: Essays on Control in Video Gaming.* Ed. Matthew Wysocki. Jefferson, NC: McFarland, 2013. 9–20. Print.

Vorderer, Peter, and Jennings Bryant. *Playing Video Games: Motives, Responses, and Consequences.* Mahwah, NJ: Lawrence Erlbaum Associates, 2006. Print.

Weber, René, Ute Ritterfield, and Anna Kostygina. "Aggression and Violence as Effects of Playing Violent Video Games?" *Playing Video Games: Motives, Responses, and Consequences.* Ed. Peter Vorderer and Jennings Bryant. Mahwah, NJ: Lawrence Erlbaum Associates, 2006. 408–426. Print.

Wysocki, Matthew. "Introduction." *Ctrl-Alt-Play: Essays on Control in Video Gaming.* Ed. Matthew Wysocki. Jefferson, NC: McFarland, 2013. 1–7. Print.

Wysocki, Matthew, and Matthew Schandler. "'Would You Kindly?' *BioShock* and the Question of Control." *Ctrl-Alt-Play: Essays on Control in Video Gaming.* Ed. Matthew Wysocki. Jefferson, NC: McFarland, 2013. 196–207. Print.

Zimmerman, Eric. "Narrative, Interactivity, Play, and Games: Four Naughty Concepts in Need of Discipline." *First Person: New Media as Story, Performance, and Game.* Eds. Noah Wardrip-Fruin and Pat Harrigan. Cambridge, MA: MIT Press, 2004. 154–164. Print.

A Whirl of Warriors
Character and Competition in Street Fighter
NICHOLAS WARE

The fighting game genre, oddly, began not with an original game but with a sequel. Capcom's *Street Fighter II*, released into Japanese arcades in 1991 and quickly spreading out to the rest of the world, was one of the biggest arcade hits ever (Rignall) and spawned sequels, side games, and home adaptations for nearly every video game machine ever created. The original *Street Fighter* game, released in 1989, barely made a dent in the marketplace and can be found largely only in historical completist compilation home releases. *Street Fighter* was technically a two-player game, but only technically. There were not multiple characters to select. If a one-player game occurred, the player inhabited Ryu. If he or she was challenged, the challenger was always Ken, identical to Ryu in all ways except visual design. A victory by either player led that player to once again controlling Ryu in his quest to become the number one fighter in the world. It was largely designed as a straight-forward affair.

Street Fighter II was neither the first *Street Fighter* nor the first fighting game, but it set the standard for the genre that has followed in its considerable footsteps. Fighting games existed as early as 1976 with a Sega game called *Heavyweight Champ* (Ashcraft 94), but *Street Fighter II* was, and remains, the genre's breakthrough moment and "the game to beat" (Ashcraft 97). The shift from *Street Fighter*'s single-player focus was the main catalyst for the sequel's success and the genre's growth. While *Street Fighter* was Ryu's story, *Street Figher II* featured eight (and, as more iterations were released, eventually sixteen) playable characters. Each of these characters had a back story, a unique fighting style, and a narrative that could be followed in single-player mode. The decision to allow multiple playable characters was made to encourage competitive play; this decision paid off enormously when it came to *Street Fighter II*'s economic returns, popularity, and design influence. However, it also created a complication in storytelling that the entire genre has reflected: fighting games have multiple, competing narratives occurring simultaneously. In *Street Fighter II*, there is no way to know which of the eight possible "endings" of the game—each of the eight playable characters defeating the ultimate villain and winning the World Warrior tournament—is "real" until a sequel answers those questions. In a way, fighting games have become a perfect genre to explore our highly questionable question of narrative vs. gameplay. If one is so much more important than the other, why has the fighting genre, which defies traditional storytelling yet embraces mythos, characterization, and aesthetic as a way of enriching gameplay (and vice-versa) been so successful at both telling tales and creating compelling gameplay? How does *Street Fighter* serve its two masters?

Two Masters: Narrative

Any reader enjoying this volume can see that narrative and gameplay are not diametrically opposed, but rather two elements of many in the colloid solution that makes up a gaming experience. *Street Fighter II*, emblematic of the fighting game genre as a whole, embodies the push, pull, and eventual coexistence of narrative and gameplay by serving two masters, and serving them well. The first is the narrative master. When viewing *Street Fighter II* as a narrative object, it's important to understand the function of narrative in *Street Fighter II*. Let me borrow J. Hillis Miller's definition from his essay "Narrative":

> There must be, first of all, an initial situation, a sequence leading to a change or reversal of that situation, and a revelation made possible by the reversal of the situation. Second, there must be some use of personification whereby character is created out of signs—for example, the words on the page in a written narrative, the modulated sounds in the air in an oral narrative. However important plot may be, without personification there can be no storytelling.... Third, there must be some patterning or repetition of key elements [qtd. in Salen and Zimmerman 380].

Under this definition, the competing narratives of *Street Fighter II* do not compromise the primary elements of narrative. Rather, they actually exemplify the third part of Miller's definition. The repetition of the fight-through-the-tournament structure of storytelling is a patterning that frames not only the individual narratives of the playable characters but also the experience of the player. Just as the player is in competition with the game's programming or another player's skill, the characters the players use are in narrative competition with the other characters. Narrative reinforces gameplay and vice-versa.

This is not only true of *Street Fighter II* as a game unto itself, but as a series of games that utilize many of the same characters over multiple narratives and gameplay systems. The primary *Street Fighter* series contains seventeen distinct games across five subseries: *Street Fighter* (just one game), *Street Fighter II* (six games), *Street Fighter Alpha* (three games), *Street Fighter III* (three games), and *Street Fighter IV* (four games). Two characters appear in every one of these games: Ryu and Ken. Many others make multiple appearances. Within the subseries narrative frameworks, many of the sequels are what could be called "tweakquels" (my own term): gameplay is altered to balance the experience across characters, new moves are added to individual characters, small new systems of gameplay are added, and brand new characters appear or familiar characters make a return. However, from series-to-series the narrative provides an experience similar to that of comic book's "retroactive continuity" or "retcon" (David). A retcon is when a new work changes or clarifies the narrative of an earlier work. In the comics world this narrative move has been occurring with major characters like Superman, Spider-Man, and Batman for over half a century. It has become a standard way to tell a story. Each *Street Fighter* series retcons the previous series by deciding a single winner of the previous game's tournament. The competing narratives are no longer competing. The one true narrative steps forward and the others drop away. Other video games that use the tournament narrative structure, such as the *Tekken* and *Mortal Kombat* series, organize themselves this way as well. Thus the pattern can repeat. There is a new tournament with new and returning entrants. Each can have his or her new storyline and new pending victory. However, once a new subseries begins, only one of those pending victories will be proven correct.

This tournament structure allows the fractured narratives of a fighting game a great deal of freedom to explore many different types of stories using different tones and strategies. While Ryu's original story in *Street Fighter* was all about testing the limits of his abilities, *Street Fighter II* includes alternate reasons to fight for alternate characters. Chun Li and Guile fight for revenge, knowing that the tournament's organizer is responsible for the deaths of her father and his comrade, respectively. Dhalsim fights for a way to bring prosperity to his Indian village, which is extremely poor. E. Honda and Zangief fight for the honor of their countries and their fighting styles. Blanka fights in the hopes that he will learn more about his past. Lastly, Ken fights to prove his worth to his rival, Ryu. While most of these stories are serious, some are treated as comedy. When Zangief defeats M. Bison, the organizer of the tournament and *Street Fighter II*'s final boss, he celebrates by doing a Russian dance with an animated Mikhail Gorbachev, who hops down from a helicopter and congratulates Zangief on honoring his nation. Three secret service types flank them in suits doing the same dance. There is no doubt the moment is played for laughs. Later iterations of the game introduced a character who is solely used as comedy—Dan, whose narratives nearly always end with him embarrassing himself. The freedom to have these stories alongside serious stories of revenge and triumph is an advantage of the fractured narrative.

Additionally, narrative elements of the *Street Fighter* series can complement existing narratives of reality. Henry Jenkins and Mary Fuller suggest that video games might act as a travelogue of sorts, allowing players to virtually visit far-off fictionalized versions of real places, forming a real (if problematic) cultural connection (62). *Street Fighter II* certainly fits this description, offering a roster of diverse World Warriors that are often stereotyped to the point of bordering on offensive, though from a uniquely Japanese position. The American and western European characters have wild shocks of blond hair (save for the black boxer clearly modeled on Mike Tyson). The female Chinese character is highly sexualized, and in one of the most problematic depictions, the Brazilian character, Blanka, is a literal beast-man. The Japanese had a prominent cultural issue with ethnically Japanese Brazilian immigrants coming to Japan during the economic boom years to work factory jobs (which were lucrative compared to even middle-class work in Brazil). Their Japanese ethnicity gave them easy access to work visas, but they retained much of their Brazilian culture and Portuguese language use, which threatened the perceived homogeneity of Japanese cultural identity which led to widespread vilification of them in the media as a negative influence on Japanese culture (Maeda 196–197). These anxieties can be seen in the characterization of the sole Brazilian character as literally inhuman. *Street Fighter*, narratively, can be seen not just as virtual tourism into the various cultures on display within the game, but virtual tourism into the Japanese psyche, for good or ill.

Two Masters: Gameplay

> Reading a book—and other forms of related aesthetic experiences, such as viewing a film—demand some measure of solitude and passivity; play, on the other hand, demands some measure of precisely the opposite.—Meyers 45

One of the arguments against the importance of narrative to the gaming experience has been the mode of consumption of games compared to those of the narrative with which we are more comfortable: books and film. However, Meyers' quote above, from "The Video Game Aesthetic: Play as Form," does not serve to show us why a book is a narrative and a video game is not, but rather requires us to understand game narrative as a component of the gaming experience. I say "the gaming experience" in order to not privilege gameplay over narrative, as the gaming experience is a combination of both these elements (and others). Video games require a different mode of consumption, there is no question. A reader or a viewer consumes a story as a single, usually linear entity. Even with the ability to pick and choose sections of these stories, the story itself remains singular and contained. A game world, however, cannot be consumed as a single entity, but rather must be explored from a vantage point. And, it must be played. Therefore, the understanding of the fighting game serves the second master of gameplay. Gameplay occurs through a deliberative mode of consumption; the player makes choices and communicates those choices to the game through an interface that produces a new situation and new choices. The loop continues until the game is completed or play ends. Books and films do not require deliberation. While continuing to read or watch is a choice, it is the only choice the reader or viewer typically has, excepting experimental "interactive" fiction and films.

By situating gameplay as a mode of deliberation instead of attention, it becomes very important for a player to be able to communicate with the video game system. After all, if decisions are needed in order to consume the media, then the media must have some method of receiving the player's decisions in order to continue the process. The myriad of devices used to communicate with video games are typically controllers: a joystick, which uses a gripped bar for movement input, or a gamepad, which uses a flattened directional pad. These controllers allow the player to extend his or herself into the game world, to become one with the technology. This mirrors Donna Haraway's idea of the cyborg, "a hybrid of machine and organism, a creature of social reality as well as a creature of fiction. [...] The cyborg is a condensed image of both imagination and material reality, the two joined centres structuring any possibility of historical transformation" (Haraway 272). This connection is important because for Haraway a cyborg identity is not a clash between the mechanical and the biological but a new hybridity. Similarly, gaming experience is not a clash between the narrative and gameplay, but a hybrid experience, one which requires not only deliberative modes of consumption but nearly always bodily interaction.

If the body is key to the experiencing of video games, then the pleasures of video gaming must lie in part within the body, and thus an understanding of *Street Fighter II*'s gameplay can arise from looking at those pleasures. *Street Fighter II*, in its onscreen representation, is about the collision of bodies with other bodies and body-produced projectiles. Ryu has the ability to use his *hadouken* attack to throw *ki* (spirit) energy from his hands towards the enemy.

The Indian yoga master Dhalsim can expel small flames that shoot across the screen. Occasionally, characters use kinetic energy to throw objects such as knives or Japanese throwing daggers at their opponents. In both these cases the thrown objects only appear when the player wishes to perform the move using a set joystick/button combination. These moves are referred to as "special moves" because they require more than a simple button press to perform. David Surman describes the moment in which a special move is performed as "characterized by two pleasure registers; first in viewing the spectacular representation of the special move and secondly in a sense of reward or gratification—a confirmation of the player's successful mastery of the videogame control inputs" (210). This second reward comes from a connection of body and mind, the deliberative choice traveling through the body, inputting the commands in the controller, and being manifested by the chosen character, filtering back through the player's eyes in the form of spectacle.

> Capcom's executive director Noritaka Funamizu notes that the control commands for the special moves were designed to correspond to the image of the referent body in motion. [...] As such, there is a performative correspondence between player actions and the representation of action in the on-screen character [211].

It is in this performance that *Street Fighter II* is consumed and enjoyed. It also allows the player to understand the game. The gameplay is the aesthetic, and vice-versa, so while the gameplay goal is to perform a super move, the information manifests both in the narrative aspects of visual feedback and an intentional affordance of interaction with the controller.

> All [controllers] are designed to provide a more or less straightforward coupling with the constraints inherent in the biological human body, and as such they provide affordances, such as lifting, grasping, and pushing. When coupled to a properly programmed game system, however, they also provide a mapping functionality that allows us to perform a wide range of actions in relation to that game system and its virtual environment. Importantly, this means that the combination of controller and game system provides both *physical affordances* and *intentional affordances*, the latter often designed to yield a sense of augmented embodiment [Gregersen and Grodal 69].

In 2010 I performed a very small-scale online ethnography of competitive *Street Fighter IV* players through the website shoryuken.com, named after a popular super move in the game. As *Street Fighter IV* was both fairly new and very popular at the time, I got a good combination of newer players and players familiar with the previous games in the series. However, the nature of the shoryuken.com site meant that all of those responding would either be competitive players or wish to be competitive players. While competitive gaming now largely happens over the Internet, many of these players were enthusiasts who went to large, live tournaments in order to compete. They relished in social competitions in which "it is likely that the individual's *self-esteem*, as well as the *individual's mood* have changed in accordance to the ongoing evaluations and social comparisons" (Vorderer et al. 4). These players' "feeling to play against an opponent likely evokes a social-competitive situation that should be especially capable to engage and to involve the user" (6). Essentially, the competition matters most to these players, not the narrative. While the game as a whole builds a hybrid experience for a larger swath of players, competitive *Street Fighter* players in this small survey purported that they often disregard the aesthetic and narrative information as a way of filtering their choices of what characters to play, instead choosing them based solely on gameplay advantages against other players' characters. Questions in the survey like "What characters do you hate to fight against? Why?" were answered based on the characters that were most difficult to defeat or the least fun to play against, not ones the player found to be lacking narrative direction or were designed in an unappealing visual manner. "If you play other genres of video games, what does *Street Fighter* (and fighting games) give you that those other genres don't, and vice versa?" was almost universally answered with a chorus about competitive arena and tuned, balanced gameplay. As one 23-year-old Caucasian male stated, "Fighting games are a high-stress genre of games. It's one on one, and the only thing that's going to keep you from winning is your own skill. It's very rewarding to get better and to win against people who you perceive as skilled, but on the other hand, it can fry your nerves sometimes if you take it too seriously. Also it can take up way too much of your time if you're really trying to get good." Character play choices included discussion of "tier," a concept about the relative power of each character compared to the rest of the playable characters (Tier 1 being the highest). At the same time, some respondents talked about a "personal play style" that was important in choosing a character. "Balrog and Gen. When I first picked up SF4 I played all the characters until I settled with Balrog. I stuck with him because he just seemed to click with my personal playstyle. I also play Gen who has great cross ups and mix ups, something I feel Balrog is lacking in his game," said a 26-year-old Caucasian male.

Hybrid: Character and Competition

In the first issue of the online journal *Games Studies*, in 2001, Jesper Juul made a case for the study of games to concentrate more on rules and less on fiction.

My point is that: (1) Games and stories actually do not translate to each other in the way that novels and movies do. (2) There is an inherent conflict between the *now* of the interaction and the *past* or "*prior*" of the narrative. You can't have narration and interactivity at the same time; there is no such thing as a continuously interactive story. (3) The relations between reader/story and player/game are completely different—the player inhabits a twilight zone where he/she is both an empirical subject outside the game *and* undertakes a role inside the game [Games Telling Stories?].

He follows that with:

Using other media as starting points, we may learn many things about the construction of fictive worlds, characters ... but relying too heavily on existing theories will make us forget what makes games games: Such as rules, goals, player activity, the projection of the player's actions into the game world, the way the game defines the possible actions of the player. It is the unique parts that we need to study now [Games Telling Stories?].

Juul's intention was to come down firmly on the side of what was then called ludology in the "narratology vs. ludology"—narrative vs. gameplay—debate. Juul's point, and it is a seductive one, was that there are elements of games that are completely absent in traditional narrative media. Why not concentrate on these elements as the purpose of games studies? Juul was more measured than most, as some tried to completely shunt games studies away from the pre-existing theories of the humanities in an effort to investigate the "new parts."

However, by 2005, Juul published *Half-Real: Video Games Between Real Rules and Fictional Worlds*, an attempt to bridge the gap in which he admitted to having swayed too far towards ludology.

Video games are *real* in that they consist of real rules with which players actually interact, and in that winning or losing a game is a real event. However, when winning a game by slaying a dragon, the dragon is not a real dragon but a fictional one. To play a video game is therefore to interact with real rules while imagining a fictional world, and a video game is a set of rules as well as a fictional world [*Half-Real* 1].

There are still plenty of issues with Juul's idea of "half-real." Juul has moved on to other discourses, as has the rest of the field. The half-real concept is his final word on the matter. Sadly, he still privileges the rules as "real" opposed to the fiction, which he never calls fake but can be inferred as the binary to "real." But he does fuse narrative and gameplay, and that is the era we find ourselves in now.

So, ten years after *Half-Real*, we can look at games as fully realized: media objects that have unique gameplay elements that certainly should be considered but which are fused with narratives and narratological concepts both within the game—the characters of *Street Fighter II*, for example—and outside the game's supposed rule-based framework, such as the narratives that communities of players build interlaced, around, and on top of existing game worlds. These are not separated in what I would call the gaming experience. While it would be lovely and convenient in order to do so, the new hybrid is complicated and messy. *Street Fighter II*—and all video games—serve two masters. The important thing to remember is not that there are two, but that they are both served, often within the same moment that is easily mistaken as leaning toward one experience or the other.

In order to discuss this phenomenon in *Street Fighter II* it is easiest to compress narrative to *character* and gameplay to *competition*. These simplifications are meant only to bracket the infinite avenues that the discussion of the meaning of the play experience with *Street Fighter II* might have. Narrative is more than character and gameplay is more than competition, but *Street Fighter*'s narrative tends to manifest best in its characters and its gameplay in competition.

The aesthetic character choices in the *Street Fighter* series directly affect the way a character will be played. Ryu, for example, visually represents a traditional Japanese shotokan karate fighter. While his signifiers are exaggerated—in the style typical of Japanese popular culture—his gi, black belt, bare feet, and headband are all indicators of his fighting style, which could well be known to a player due to his or her familiarity with the cultural and pop cultural references towards which those visual signifiers point. Similarly, the game's narrative *and* gameplay structure—the tournament—is a reference to films of the 1970s and 1980s in both the U.S. and Asia that included multiple martial artists with multiple styles from all over the world fighting each other.

> *SF2*'s International Martial Arts Tournament and its global cast of characters suggest that the cinematic model for the [fighting game] was *Enter the Dragon* (1973). [The] film revolves around a tournament organized by an Evil Mastermind. [...] The tournament structure allows narrative to progress *through* a series of fights; the climactic Hall of Mirrors would make an effective game level. The three heroes anticipate the racialcultural inclusivity of fighting games: Chinese Lee (Bruce Lee), white American smoothie Roper (John Saxon) and African-American Williams (Jim Kelly) [Hunt 198].

Street Fighter then communicates its gameplay—a series of contests within a tournament structure leading up to a climactic battle with an evil adversary—with its narrative and communicates the expectations of play with its characters' aesthetic, cultural, and pop cultural references. The aforementioned Ryu is the stoic Japanese karate fighter from so many *anime* and action films. He thus plays relatively stoically, controlling space with his projectile attacks and creating openings to counterattack. This play style, found effective, loops back and reinforces the narrative type of his character. Ryu is a Japanese karate fighter because he plays like a Japanese karate fighter. Ryu plays like a Japanese karate fighter because he is a Japanese karate fighter. These two statements mean slightly different things but taken together best express the way characterization and narrative meld with cultural expectations to inform gameplay, and the way that gameplay then reinforces the meaning of those expectations. It is in the loop that meaning is made, not more one than the other.

The aesthetics of character inform gameplay beyond their cultural ramifications. Size matters in *Street Fighter*. Larger characters, especially in earlier *Street Fighter* games, tend to be slower and more powerful. Their fighting styles tend to be reliant on strength and closing the gap between themselves and faster characters or character with projectile attacks. This connection between gameplay and visual design—which influence character and thus narrative—became so stereotypical that Rufus, a character in *Street Fighter IV*, was created perhaps simply to play against type. Rufus is corpulent to a comical degree, nearly bowling ball round, but his attacks are quick, hit multiple times, and are based on controlling distance between himself and the other player, not closing it. Size and character matter so much to gameplay that they must be made not to matter in the expected way, which makes them matter even more to inform the character; Rufus is meant to be comical, and the juxtaposition of his fighting style with his visual design supports that comedy.

Game rules that could be considered somewhat arbitrary can be justified by narrative as well, and vice-versa. In *Street Fighter* games, a single match is typically played as a first-to-win-2-rounds-wins format, with a clock in each round to encourage offensive, active play. Because the characters in *Street Fighter II* are considered to be playing in an organized tournament, they would experience similar rule constraints within the game world's fiction. The life bar, a meter which is drained when taking the opponents offense and causes a player to lose when depleted, does not necessarily match up with any fictional constraint, but can be seen as an analogy for a judge present for the fight. When time runs out, whichever player's life bar is larger wins the decision of that imaginary judge, and the round. In reality we have no life bars that indicate when we are on the edge of being knocked out, nor do we have such objective judging of damage received in an MMA fight or boxing match, but the analogy is clear. Much of the game information the player depends on for strategy is the same "game" information the character within the fiction would have to navigate in his or her fight. The rules are not so strictly real and the fiction not so strictly fictional.

The Next Great Dichotomy

Many discussions in game studies have centered on binaries. In the 1990s, much was made of the real vs. the virtual. In the oughts, narratology vs. ludology. The solution to both these so-called arguments was transforming the "vs." into an "and," as it will likely be with any binary introduced into game studies. The synthesis of all these approaches and the academic disciplines that privilege them is what game studies must turn into. If game studies mirrors games, the field will become more diverse and perhaps more contentious. The 2010s have seen games embrace new technological platforms for game distribution and game consoles advance technology and integrate into home entertainment systems. Games have embraced storytelling without sacrificing gameplay with titles like *The Last of Us* or the *Mass Effect* series. Independent titles have turned towards emotional resonance in games like *Gone Home* or social ills in *Depression Quest*. Perhaps the largest, most worrisome trend has been the battle over the "gamer" identity, as the inevitable pull of progress and artistic value pries "gamer" away from the misogynist patriarchal base that has controlled game discourse for so long. However, if we look at some of the literature from key thinkers in the last five years, we see that the trend is toward considering games not as discreet systems nor as storytelling devices, but as objects within culture that carry meaning for humans.

Jesper Juul has written about the pain and the art of failure in video games because "video games are for me a space of reflection, a constant measuring of my abilities, a mirror in which I can see my everyday behavior reflected, amplified, distorted, and revealed" (*The Art of Failure* 24). Greg Costikyan has written of uncertainty and chance in video games because "'game' is merely the term we apply to a particular kind of play: play that has gone beyond the simply, and has been complexified and refined by human culture" (Costikyan 7). Ian Bogost has written about the many ways games are created towards actionable purposes because "videogames have many possible goals and purposes, each of which couples with many possible aesthetics and designs to create many possible player experiences" (Bogost 153). All three of these thinkers are looking at video games not as a puzzle to decode, but as an object in the culture of human experience. Video games can tell us about pain, about uncertainty, about political or artistic or business action. They can tell us anything, not just "a story." Moreover, we can express ourselves through games. Games can be designed not just as elaborate systems of rules, but as art objects, as theory objects, as personalized emotional maps.

This is the new frontier beyond the narrative/gameplay dichotomy. This is the reason I would rather talk about "gaming experience." "Narrative" and "gameplay" bracket so much. That bracketing was useful when scholarship about games was scare and lines had to be drawn in the sand, or games as an area of study had to be justified within the humanities or sciences. Now that game studies has matured and grown, it is going to stop its petty arguments of us vs. them. Instead, we will see game studies both as an analytical tool for extracting meaning from games and as a theory and design tool for infusing games with meaning. Game studies is growing up, and we should all be excited about its potential.

Works Cited

Ashcraft, Brian, with Jean Snow. *Arcade Mania! The Turbo-Charged World of Japan's Game Centers*. Tokyo: Kodansha International, 2008.

Bogost, Ian. *How to Do Things with Videogames*. Minneapolis: University of Minnesota Press, 2011.

Costikyan, Greg. *Uncertainty in Games*. Cambridge, MA: MIT Press, 2013.

David, Peter. "Retcons and Stetcons." PeterDavid.net. 2 February 2001. PeterDavid.net. 11 July 2014.

Fuller, Mary, and Henry Jenkins. "Nintendo and New World Travel Writing: A Dialogue." *Cybersociety: Computer-Mediated Communication and Community*. Ed. Steven G. Jones. Thousand Oaks, CA: Sage Publications, 1995. 57–72.

Gregersen, Andreas, and Torben Grodal. "Embodiment and Interface." *The Video Game Theory Reader 2*. Eds. Bernard Perron and Mark J.P. Wolf. New York: Routledge, 2009. 65–84.

Haraway, Donna. "A Cyborg Manifesto." *The Cultural Studies Reader 2nd Edition*. Ed. Simon During. New York: Routledge, 1999. 271–291.

Hunt, Leon. "'I Know Kung Fu!' The Martial Arts in the Age of Digital Reproduction." *Screen Play: Cinema/Videogames/Interfaces*. Eds. Geoff King and Tanya Krzywinska. London: Wallflower Press, 2002. 194–205.

Juul, Jesper. *The Art of Failure: An Essay on the Pain of Playing Video Games*. Cambridge, MA: MIT Press, 2013.

_____. "Games Telling Stories? A Brief Note on Games and Narratives." *Games Studies* 1:1 (July 2001).

_____. *Half-Real: Video Games Between Real Rules and Fictional Worlds*. Cambridge, MA: MIT Press, 2005.

Maeda, Hitomi. "Elements and Degrees of SI: A Case Study of Nikkei Brazilian Immigrants in Japan." *Educational Research for Policy and Practice* 5:2 (October 2006): 195–210.

Meyers, David. "The Video Game Aesthetic: Play as Form." *The Video Game Theory Reader 2*. Eds. Bernard Perron and Mark J.P. Wolf. New York: Routledge, 2009. 45–64.

Rignall, Jaz. "Top 10 Highest-Grossing Arcade Games of All Time." *USGamer*. 5 January 2015. http://www.usgamer.net/articles/top-10-biggest-grossing-arcade-games-of-all-time. 22 January 2015.

Salen, Katie, and Eric Zimmerman. *Rules of Play: Game Design Fundamentals*. Cambridge, MA: MIT Press, 2003.

Surman, David. "Pleasure, Spectacle, and Reward in Capcom's *Street Fighter* Series." *Videogame, Player, Text*. Eds. Barry Atkins and Tanya Krzywinska. Manchester: Manchester University Press, 2007. 204–221.

Vorderer, Peter, Tilo Hartmann, and Christoph Klimmt. "Explaining the Enjoyment of Playing Video Games: The Role of Competition." *ACM International Conference Proceeding Series* 38 (2003): 1–9.

Ecological Matters
Rethinking the "Magic" of the Magic Circle

ROBERT MEJIA

This essay is an attempt to answer Richard Maxwell and Toby Miller's 2008 question of "what would happen to game studies, if, rather than rehearsing debates about ludological, narratological, and effects approaches, it confronted the fact that millions of cartridges of Atari's game adaptation of *E.T. The Extraterrestrial* [...] were buried in a New Mexico landfill" (334). Maxwell and Miller's question is pertinent as game studies has yet to take seriously the ecological context of media technology, such as: (1) "the environmental burdens of energy generation and consumption throughout a medium's life cycle"; (2) "a medium's chemical and heavy metal composition"; (3) "prior inputs from the earth extracted via mining, drilling, logging, etc."; and (4) the waste byproducts of end-of-life technological disposal (Maxwell and Miller 335; for notable exceptions, see: Dyer-Witheford and de Peuter; Kline, Dyer-Witheford and de Peuter; Mejia). What the term "gaming" references is not one single thing, but rather an assemblage of contested political, economic, cultural, and ecological practices (Mejia). The narrow conception of gaming as design (ludology) or gaming as interactive narrative (narratology) obscures how choices about design and narrative are contingent upon institutions and practices that are often far removed from conventional sites of gaming. This preoccupation with whether games are better understood through the lens of ludology or narratology seems petty when contrasted with the types of questions that can be asked of a broader conception of gaming: such as what is the ecological impact of video gaming?

What research has been done documents that the ecological burden imposed by the video game industry has grown substantially since the turn of the century. Console energy consumption, for instance, remained stagnant throughout the 1990s, with only 7–8 watts used by the Super Nintendo

171

(1991), Sony PlayStation (1994), and Nintendo 64 (1996) respectively (Horowitz et al. 12). In contrast, the 2001 Microsoft Xbox consumed 64 watts, roughly eight times as much energy as prior consoles, and the current Sony PlayStation 4 (2014) consumes 137 watts, or about twice as much energy as the original Xbox and nearly three times as much as the 55-inch LED TV you might be playing it on (Delforge and Horowitz 8; Samsung "Series 7100"). Though this energy consumption only represents one to two percent of the average American household electricity usage (Hittinger), as a collective, those roughly 150 million Americans who do own a dedicated video game console (Entertainment Software Association) consume the electrical equivalent of four large power plants or "as much electricity as all the households in the city of Houston [the fourth largest city in the United States]" (Delforge and Horowitz 3). This is a substantial amount as the United States accounts for "nearly 19% of the world total primary energy consumption" (U.S. Energy Information Administration "FAQ"). To put this into perspective, the United States gaming population consumes more electricity annually than the countries of Uruguay, Guatemala, Costa Rica, or any of the other 132 countries in the bottom 60 percent of global electricity consumption; or more strikingly, the United States gaming population consumes nearly as much electricity annually as the bottom 25 percent combined (with countries including Rwanda, Liberia, Haiti, and Somalia) (U.S. Energy Information Administration "International Energy Statistics"). In order to satisfy this seemingly insatiable thirst for energy, the United States has begun to rely on environmentally questionable energy production practices "that can develop harder-to-produce resources" (U.S. Energy Information Administration "Domestic"). Though not the sole cause of this ecological situation, video games are a part of the story.

    This is a story that warrants telling for the ecological consequence and impact of video game play is intrinsic to the question of digital play itself. Far from being an external factor, a mere question of the general need to build more ecologically efficient technologies, the ecological contexts of the production, consumption, and disposal of video game technologies is intimately bound with the pleasures associated with video game play. Though Maxwell and Miller chastise game studies scholars for their fixation on the debate between ludology and narratology (334), if we are truly concerned with the ecological impact of video game play then the relationship between ludology and narratology needs to be a part of the conversation. For if ludology can be understood as an interest in the architecture of play embedded in a given game, a form of "narrative architecture" if you will (Jenkins), then it seems ecologically relevant to explore the question of which architectural systems underwrite the narratives and virtual worlds we find ourselves engaging today.

Exploring this architectural system matters for as the influential French philosopher Henri Bergson once asked, "What should we do if we heard that for the common good, for the very existence of mankind, there was somewhere a man, an innocent man, condemned to suffer eternal torment?" (60). Bergson believed that confronted with such knowledge we would respond with one of two choices: (1) we would find it acceptable on the condition that some "magic [device] is going to make us forget it"; or (2) "if we were bound to know it [and could not forget] that this man's hideous torture was the price of our existence [then] no! a thousand times no!" (60). Though we might like to believe, as ethical readers, that were we to be confronted with such a situation, so too would we respond as Bergson (no, a thousand times no!), in actuality we live in a world full of "magical" devices that help us to forget that such a situation exists in the first place. As Sara Ahmed has noted, "the freedom to be happy can be translated into a freedom to avoid proximity to whatever compromises one's happiness. The very idea that our first responsibility is to our own happiness is what allows us to look away" (590). Digital play encourages this looking away, for at their core video games are happiness machines: though we know that somewhere someone is suffering so that we might play, video games are so fun that it becomes so easy to forget about this information.

This essay is an attempt to reorient our ecological ethics surrounding video game play by repositioning the ecological consequences and impacts of video game technologies and processes as internal to the ludic design of contemporary digital play. The aim is to illustrate why it is impossible to continue looking away regarding the ecological consequences and impacts of digital play; to illustrate the entanglement of the ecological contexts of the production, consumption, and disposal of video game technologies to such an extent that one must confront the conditions of their ludic pleasure or become conscious of the fact that they have chosen to look away—to endorse the suffering of another upon his behalf. To better illuminate the entanglement of the ecological contexts of video game technologies and processes, it is necessary to: first, explain, and reconfigure the foundational game studies concept of the magic circle as a material construct as opposed to merely an ephemeral thing, as conventionally understood; and second, discuss the ecological effects of manufacturing the data processing units required of contemporary video gaming consoles so as to illustrate how this materialist conception of the magic circle undergirds the narrative pleasures derived from the experience of video game play.

My argument is that the pleasure of contemporary video game play is embedded in the ecological configuration of our current moment. Conventional accounts of ludology and narratology treat play as an ephemeral thing, and thus obscure this point. To the extent that we live in a moment of ecological strife and suffering, then a materially informed ludic analysis of the substructures of our narrative pleasure is an ethically necessary act.

The Magic Circle as a Material Construct

The construct of the magic circle was established as a part of game studies in 1938, when the Dutch Historian Johan Huizinga observed that "all play moves and has its being within a playground marked off beforehand either materially or ideally, deliberately or as a matter of course" (10). This delimited space grants the field of play a sense of liminality—a sense of being betwixt and between, a space where the rules of everyday life no longer apply. And yet, play is not without rules, for rather "play demands order absolute and supreme" as "the least deviation from [these rules] 'spoils the game,' robs it of its character and makes it worthless" (Huizinga 10). This is because as a liminal space, the site of play has a specific purpose, which is to "equalize" the social status of all participants and create the opportunity for new social statuses to emerge (Turner 58–59). By way of example, for instance, every four years the World Cup offers the opportunity for countries across the globe to compete as relative equals on the basis of their athletic skills. On this stage, in this delimited space of the soccer field, countries as disparate as Costa Rica and the Netherlands and Algeria and Germany—ranked 80th, 17th, 49th, and 4th in terms of economic size, respectively (International Monetary Fund)—can come together and compete as plausible equals in the quest for global recognition. Play is therefore never innocent, as in inconsequential, for it is always a "contest *for* something or a representation *of* something" ([emphasis original] Huizinga 13). The magic circle, then, is the name we give to the rules, parameters, and substructures by which this contest and representation is enabled.

The concept of the magic circle became a formal part of video game studies in 2004, with the publication of *Rules of Play: Game Design Fundamentals* by Katie Salen and Eric Zimmerman. In this influential text, Salen and Zimmerman offered three perspectives by which to evaluate the structure of the magic circle: rules, play, and culture (96–97). Evaluating the structure of the magic circle from the perspective of rules conceives of the site of video game play as a closed, rigid space with no or only minimal interaction with its surrounding environment. From the perspective of play, a semi-enclosed space whereby "players bring a great deal in from the outside world: their expectations, their likes and dislikes, social relationships, and so on" (Salen and Zimmerman 96). In other words, though the rules governing the game may have minimal correspondence with the outside world, the structure of the magic circle is penetrated by the cultural perspectives brought in to the game by players and audiences. From the perspective of culture, however, the structure of the magic circle is an "extremely open system," whereby the rules, parameters, and substructures of gaming are informed by and in turn inform the larger cultural context (Salen and Zimmerman 97). That is, from the perspective of culture, one can interpret a game like golf, for instance, as a statement about the relationship between technology, nature, and humanity: precise tools of play, well-manicured greens, and affluent leisure time.

Though Salen and Zimmerman's rearticulation of the magic circle operated as a spectrum, from a closed rule-based system to an open cultural system (96–97), most scholars have collapsed the definition to mean that the magic circle refers to a closed rule-based approach to game studies (Consalvo; Juul; Malaby). This misreading has led to a series of untenable theoretical statements made about the nature of play. The problem, however, may not necessarily be the concept of the magic circle, for many of the more egregious claims predate the publication of Salen and Zimmerman's *Rules of Play*. As Henry Jenkins documents:

> a blood feud [has] threatened to erupt between self-proclaimed Ludologists, who wanted to see the focus shift onto the mechanics of game play, and the Narratologists, who were interested in studying games alongside other storytelling media [1].

That said, though the problem may not lay with the magic circle, the general tendency has been either to suggest abandonment of the concept altogether (Consalvo; Malaby) or its reconfiguration as an even more enclosed construct: "we could alternatively describe a game as a puzzle piece. [...] Seen as a puzzle piece, a game may or may not fit in a given context" (Juul 63). Neither proposal is satisfactory, however, as each perspective lacks an adequate understanding of the construct of magic in and of itself.

Though it is popular to conceive of magic as an ephemeral thing (Karshner), the religious studies scholar Bernd-Christian Otto reminds us that ancient magicians did not "believe in possessing supernatural abilities as part of their personality, lineage or psycho-spiritual training (*à la* Harry Potter). They merely operated as mediators between their clients and the gods while expecting the latter to fulfill the requested need" (333). This point is reiterated by the prominent social anthropologist Marcel Mauss's observation that "magic—which we have shown to be more concerned with the concrete—is concerned with understanding nature. It quickly set up a kind of index of plants, metals, phenomena, beings and life in general" (176–77). So though the effects of magic are often grounded in faith—in a god, nature, et cetera— just like a placebo, magic requires a "mediating substance" by which to facilitate this effect (Tambiah 193). Indeed, as Mauss argues, the effectiveness of magic may have had as much to do with these mediating substances as by pure faith alone, for it was under the guise of magic that real technical experiments and discoveries were made (175–76); after all, the better magician is the one who can actually produce tangible "magic."

As S. J. Tambiah, Michelle Rosaldo, and Kimberly Stratton each document, however, not just any mediating substance will do when it comes to the practice of magic, tangible or otherwise. Rather, "the contrast in the meanings of the material symbols used is clear-cut" (Tambiah 194). For instance, in the Babylonian Talmud, an important collection of rabbinic teachings, one lesson documents the protection of two rabbis from "magical assault both by their knowledge of [a warding] spell and by their peculiar dietary observance that marks them as distinct and specially protected" (Stratton 363). These two practices, faith and diet ("mediating substance") go hand in hand, for as Kimberly Stratton notes, "to understand fully the meaning of this passage [on magic] one has to know [that] this brief narrative appears in the middle of an extended discussion about proper diet. [...] The narrative [...] is used here by the [narrator] to undergird the legitimacy of rabbinic observances" (365). Likewise, as Michelle Rosaldo notes, focusing instead on the Ilongot of the Philippines, since the mediating substances required of a particular magical practice are quite specific—and not easily interchangeable with one another— then it is not surprising that these magical devices are environmentally specific as well:

> The sick person sits with a boiling pot of herbs under a blanket, and [...] calls for the help of two spirits, the *palasikan*, "those who go upstream," and the *lampoon*, identified as spirits of high places. [...] The plants collected tend to be associated with one or the other of these spirits. One set, composed largely of grasses which grow by the water, are linked to the *palasikan*. The second set [...] are associated with the *lampoon*, whose "high places" may well be associated with the orchids, which grow high on trees [87].

Combined with the lesson from the Babylonian Talmud, this example from the Ilongot illustrates that magical devices are sensitive to and contingent upon the ecological configuration of the surrounding environment: animals, plants, and other "mediating substances" are not spread haphazardly across the globe but rather often require specific habitats; and to the extent that access to these specific mediating substances is denied, then so too is the magical act itself denied.

To the extent that magic ought to be understood as a faith-based material practice, contingent upon environmentally specific mediating substances, then we can now offer a more comprehensive, materialist conception of the magic circle that is capable of encompassing not just the liminality of the concept (in terms of rules, play, or culture) but also its ecological impact as well. This new conception of the magic circle argues that the space of play operates as a liminal space that is undergirded by very specific and unique ecological structures. Just as the magic associated with the Babylonian Talmud and the Ilongot required specific mediating substances, so too do contemporary gaming platforms require their own specific "magical devices" in order to produce their magical effect. Conventional accounts of ludology and narratology miss this point. Hence, the remainder of this essay focuses on illustrating why this materialist conception matters by illuminating the ecological specificity of one such mediating substance of the magic circle of video gaming: the data processing units.

A (Brief) Ecological Analysis of the Video Game Console

The advent of a new console marks an important moment in the structural reconfiguration of the magic circle. The reason is because the console itself, as I have been arguing, exists as the material manifestation of the magic circle enabling the creation of a liminal space whereby the social status of all participants is relatively equalized and the possibility of new social statuses can emerge. To be clear, the existing social status of all participants does not disappear upon engagement with the magic circle, but rather the way in which those existing social statuses are translated into the liminal space is contingent upon the design of the platform or interface (Stanfill). The console as magic circle translates users into players, whom are subsequently offered or denied a range of new identities and social statuses of which to adopt for the sake of play. Hence, the magic circle is not democratic: not everyone is allowed to be a gamer. This point is perhaps made clearer by way of considering the development of the original Microsoft Xbox controller which was purposely designed "for people with large hands, like North Americans, particularly North American men" (Dyer-Witheford and de Peuter 81). Combined with its complex array of buttons and dual-analog sticks, the Microsoft Xbox was designed to appeal to a particular population of gamers and likewise was inaccessible to other gaming populations, such as those who would later find comfort with the Nintendo Wii. Hence, the advent of a new console marks an important point in the structural reconfiguration of the magic circle precisely because it marks the moment when the lines are drawn regarding who can participate as a gamer and which new social statuses are privileged.

The current generation of video game consoles, which include the PlayStation 4, Xbox One, and Wii U, marks one such moment in the historical reconfiguration of the magic circle. The classification of game consoles in terms of generations is a misnomer, however, as it groups platforms by their historical period and not their structural configurations; it presumes that consoles share similar design characteristics by virtue of their time period, when in fact their differences are often as important as their similarities. For instance, the Super Nintendo and Sega Genesis are both classified as fourth-generation consoles and yet the magic circle and subsequent social identities offered by each system differed substantially: the slower processor speed but larger RAM allocation (amongst other important technical differences) meant that games played slower but possessed smoother animation on the Super Nintendo than the Sega Genesis. This seemingly small difference mattered substantially as game franchises were often vastly different even when released on both platforms. For example, *The Adventures of Batman & Robin* was released on the Super Nintendo as a methodical beat 'em up with some platforming elements whereas the Sega Genesis version played as a run and gun game (Clockwork Tortoise; Konami); this difference in the technical capacity of the magic circle matters for it means the difference between Batman being imagined as a reluctant crime fighter versus an overexcited vigilante.

That said, the idea of a console generation matters for the label carries substantial normative influence about what it is that a particular configuration of the magic circle ought to look like. When it comes to the current generation of video game consoles the Wii U is often not considered to be a legitimate "next gen" (eight generation) console (Tassi). This status (or lack thereof) designates certain types of gaming practices as legitimate and others illegitimate. Regarding the latest generation of video game consoles, the processing of photorealistic graphics and advanced artificial intelligence are considered the hallmarks of contemporary gaming. This has placed an even greater emphasis on console processing power, even more so than past generations; even the "illegitimate" Wii U has adopted high-definition graphics as its output standard. Hence, though a variety of video game components could be analyzed for their ecological impact, for the sake of this analysis, I will focus primarily on the manufacturing of data processing units.

The Central Processing Unit (CPU) and Graphics Processing Unit (GPU) are the most important components of a video game console. These two data processing units are responsible for everything from rendering graphics and processing virtual world physics to controlling non-playable character behavior (artificial intelligence) and interpreting player controller inputs, and more. So important are these data processing units to the practice of contemporary video gaming that the idea of a video game generation is closely tethered to a console's processing power (which is why the PlayStation 4 is considered a legitimate next generation console but the Wii U is not). Since console generations are valued in terms of the power of their CPUs and GPUs, legitimate gaming is defined in terms of its graphical capabilities and artificial intelligence programming capacity; powerful data processing units enable the rendering of real-time photorealistic graphics and the enactment of more convincing non-playable character behavior. This emphasis is why, outside of the Nintendo Wii and Wii U, advances in controller input has remained relatively stagnant for consoles since the PlayStation 1's dual analog controller (1997), whereas visual capabilities have increased by orders of magnitude.

These advances in graphics rendering and other data-extensive operations are the result of advances in data processing unit design. Though CPUs and GPUs represent fundamentally different computer engineering philosophies—with "CPUs designed [...] to provide fast response times to a single task" whereas GPUs are built for "applications that have a larger degree of parallelism" (Lee et al. 451)—they each are integral to contemporary gaming practices. The integration of advanced physics engines in video games, for instance, benefits from the fast computational ability and memory architecture of modern CPUs (Lee et al. 457). Complex graphics rendering, on the other hand, benefits from the ability of GPUs to process multiple calculations simultaneously (though comparatively slower, e.g., 1.3GHz versus 3.2GHz, a modern GPU possesses hundreds to thousands of cores versus between four to eight for most modern CPUs [Lee et al. 451; NVIDIA]). Considering the power of these data processing units, it might be surprising to learn that the CPU and GPU for the PlayStation 4 fit on a die measuring only 19 × 18.3 mm, a space smaller than the size of a quarter (Sayed). Perhaps even more surprising, since so much sophisticated circuitry is embedded on dies such as these, manufacturing these components requires the use of highly toxic acids in order to account for the increased "sensitivity [...] to contamination and impurities" (Honeywell 1; see also Grossman 56–60). The use of these chemicals is not only potentially dangerous to those whom work in close proximity to them (in the manufacturing facilities), but improper storage and disposal of these acids and their residue can contaminate water supplies (Grossman 7, 67). Contaminated water extends more than a mile north from a former

AMD manufacturing site in Sunnyvale, California, for example, and is now a Superfund hazardous waste site (EPA). Hence, the magical properties of scientific design, in terms of the creation of photorealistic graphics and other gaming practices, are dependent upon a manufacturing process that is "not clean. Period" (Grischuk 70).

The ecological toxicity of CPU and GPU manufacturing extends beyond the use of highly toxic acids, however. The production of data processing units rely on "finished metals potentially derived from Conflict Minerals [such as] tin, tantalum, tungsten, and gold" in order to manufacturer their products (AMD 35): tantalum and tungsten "are part of the 'wiring' connecting transistors and act as a barrier to maintain the integrity of the transistors inside the chip itself"; tin is used to connect the chip to the circuit board; and gold "is highly conductive and used [...] when a very pure connection between components is required" (Intel "Conflict"). These metals are considered potential conflict minerals as extraction of these resources have been linked to war and political instability in the Democratic Republic of the Congo (DRC), as this central African nation is "richly endowed" with these resources and hence these metals are "extracted mainly from mines on the eastern boarder of the DRC" (Coakley 1; Intel "The Conflict"). Each of the various factions in the DRC have "ruthlessly exploited the mineral wealth from territories under their respective control," resulting in the death of tens of thousands monthly at the height of the war and the estimation that "75 percent of children born during the war have died or will die before their second birthday" (Montague 102–03). Even today, it is estimated that (at best) 33 percent of the mines in the DRC are controlled by military groups (in contrast to a 2010 report by the United Nations that found that "almost every mineral deposit" was occupied by military forces [von Billerbeck]).

Because of the ongoing war, resource extraction from the DRC remains lucrative for metal suppliers and buyers as the presence of military groups and other exploitative practices keeps the labor cost of extraction artificially low: the miners who labor under harsh conditions, often without shoes or masks, make less than $1 USD (Dizolele). Alternative labor options are limited for populations in the DRC as the mines have proven to be particularly lucrative for the military forces, with the price of columbite-tantalite—an important ore used in many electronic devices—going for $400 USD per pound in the early 2000s (Dizolele). As a result, this combination of market- and military-pressure has resulted in the neglect or outright plundering and destruction of alternative small businesses and agricultural industries in the east (Hayes and Burge). This has meant that at some mining sites, the only food source available is wildlife; at one such location, an illegal mining operation at the UNESCO World Heritage Site of Kahuzi-Biega National Park, "3,700 elephants and most of the 8,000 eastern lowland gorillas [an endangered species]" have been killed (Hayes and Burge 35). Though Western governments and electronics manufacturers such as AMD and Intel have pledged to "break the link between the trade in minerals and ongoing conflict and human rights abuses in Central Africa," Sarah von Billerbeck argues that the policy of "conflict-free" mining is an ambiguous concept that privileges Western interests over those of the DRC (von Billerbeck). Armed forces or not, the fact of the matter is that Western demand for consumer electronics has contributed to the destabilization of the DRC's economy, environment, and political system.

Mining, however, is not the only means by which to procure the resources needed for advanced consumer electronics; the recycling of scrap metal is an increasingly lucrative avenue as the cost of recycling can, in some cases, be substantially lower than mining and more resource efficient as well (Grossman 27–31). Though this would seem to be, and undoubtedly is, an improvement over conventional mining practices, particularly those associated with the DRC, this alternative is not as rosy as it would seem. The reason is because the vast majority of electronics recycling is shipped to countries with lax labor and environmental protection laws thereby forfeiting most if not all of the ecological benefits associated with recycling (Discovery News; Greenpeace; Grossman 185). Indeed, AMD's hazardous waste production increased by roughly 50 percent, from just under 100 metric tons in 2011 to over 150 metric tons in 2012, after "scrap products sent off-site for precious metal reclaim [were reclassified] as hazardous waste" (AMD 50–51). So, as Greenpeace notes, "although recycling can be a good way to reuse the raw materials in a product, the hazardous chemicals in e-waste mean that electronics can harm workers in the recycling yards, as well as their neighbouring communities and environment" (Greenpeace). Indeed, in Guiyu, China, a town of 150,000, lead levels found in the Lianjiang River were "2,400 times higher than levels deemed safe by the World Health Organization" (Grossman 185). As a result of this water and air pollution, "80 percent of Guiyu's children experience respiratory ailments, and are especially at risk of lead poisoning," and another 45 million people in the surrounding region are at risk due to living downwind and downstream (McAllister). Hence, as Walt Grischuk argues, "the reality is that part of the reason countries, such as the U.S., have cleaner air is because they now get their products, steel, concrete, and printed circuit boards from China rather than having dirty factories on their own land" (Grischuk 71).

The ecological hazards mentioned above are not confined to the production processes associated with the manufacturing of CPUs and GPUs.

The use of toxic chemicals, conflict minerals, and production of hazardous waste are just some of the many ecological effects that undergird the video game and electronics industry. Though the focus here has been on a handful those ecological impacts associated with CPU and GPU manufacturing, these effects and others operate across the various components that are essential for contemporary gaming practices. For instance, in 2013, one worker was killed and several others injured and hospitalized after a series of hydrofluoric acid leaks at a Samsung facility in South Korea responsible for manufacturing computer memory (Souppouris). And in 2013, after multiple environmental and occupational safety and health violations at this Giheung/Hwasung manufacturing facility, Samsung withdrew its application to the South Korean government to designate the facility as a "green company"—representing a failure to comply with its own "Planet First strategy, which aims for business activities that respect people and nature" (Samsung *Half Year* 115). This failure to obtain certification and adhere to its own "Planet First strategy" matters for gamers as Samsung is the memory supplier for Sony's PlayStation 4 (Sayed). Hence, though this analysis has focused on the ecological consequences of manufacturing data processing units, the ecological effects of gaming practices extend across the totality of hardware production, use, and disposal.

Conclusion

Because the satisfaction offered by video games operates in a digital environment, it can be difficult to remember the ecological infrastructure that undergirds such pleasure. The pleasure of play operates as a magical space whereby players are transformed into superhuman warriors, treasure hunters, athletes, or any other number of fantastical social positions of which they would otherwise be unable to occupy. Though this transformation might seem like magic, in the ephemeral sense, magic has long been linked to concrete ecological practices, what S. J. Tambiah has called "mediating substances" (193). And just like ancient magic, so too, as I have documented, does the modern magic of contemporary video gaming require its own collection of mediating substances in order to create the magical spaces it offers. Hence, magic and technology, far from being incompatible constructs, actually share much in common. Indeed, as Marcel Mauss has argued, magic can be thought of as the middle ground connecting technology with religion (106). Technology becomes magic when it is no longer solely interested in making things happen but instead is also interested in reenchanting the everyday and mundane, creating a space for the fantastic.

The concept of the magic circle, then, offers an effective middle-ground from which to acknowledge both the pleasure and satisfaction derived from video game play *and* the ecological arrangements that make such play possible. The integration of advanced physics engines and photorealistic graphics rendering and more is contingent upon the production of advanced technologies whose sophistication belies its ecological impact. As Eric Williams, Robert Ayres, and Miriam Heller argue, though "the microchip is often assumed to be a prime example of dematerialization since value and utility is high while the weight of the product is negligible" the weight of fossil fuels and chemicals used "in production total 630 times the mass of the final product, indicating that the environmental weight of semiconductors far exceeds their small size" (6609). Equally important, the ecological impact of high-tech electronics manufacturing "tends to increase with advances in the technologies" as a result of the need for evermore refined and purified materials (Bossuet 198). Though this notion of refinement and purification may suggest cleaner manufacturing processes, as Elizabeth Grossman argues, these initiatives are "designed to protect chips, not to protect those who are making them" (90). This, then, is the reality of contemporary gaming: so that we might experience pleasure, somewhere, someone is suffering to produce the mediating substances required for the magic circle of gaming. The suffering of another is the prerequisite for contemporary video game play; we must not forget this.

Though this analysis is highly critical of the ecological impact of contemporary gaming, it is not a wholesale dismissal of the industry as frivolous entertainment, however. There are other sectors of society, including other media industries, that are just as troubling, if not more so, than the video game industry (Maxwell and Miller; Shadman and McManus). Likewise, play is an important cultural practice due to its ability to equalize the social status of (some) participants and create the opportunity for new social statuses to emerge (Huizinga 12–15; Turner 58–59). Indeed, the influential scholar of play, Johan Huizinga, has argued that play carries a "*significant* function" that is central to culture, and hence cannot be wished away (1). Play is magical, and video games are especially magical. For all their differences, the ongoing interest in conventional ludology and narratology is driven by this desire to better understand what makes video games so magical. And yet, this magic comes at a cost; a cost of which conventional ludology and narratology are unable to offer an account. Incorporating a materialist conception, as I argue, illustrates that these costs can be located in the mediating substances required to produce the magic circle we call play. Knowing this, however, requires a return to the question raised in the introduction: "What should we do if we heard that for the common good [...] there was somewhere a man, an innocent man, condemned to suffer eternal torment?" (Bergson 60). Though it is beyond the scope of this essay, fortunately, something can be done (see: Bossuet; Intel "The Conflict"). Such interventions, however, are contingent upon how you answer Bergson's question: what will you do?

Works Cited

Ahmed, Sara. "Killing Joy: Feminism and the History of Happiness." *Signs: Journal of Women in Culture and Society* 35.3 (2010): 571–94.

AMD. *Corporate Responsibility Report*, 2014.

Bergson, Henri. *The Two Sources of Morality and Religion*. Trans. Audra, Ashley R. and Cloudesley Brereton. Notre Dame, IN: University of Notre Dame Press, 1932/1997.

Bossuet, Lilian. "Sustainable Electronics: On the Trail of Reconfigurable Computing." *Sustainable Computing: Informatics and Systems* 4 (2014): 196–202.

Clockwork Tortoise.*The Adventures of Batman & Robin*. Sega, 1995. Sega Genesis.

Coakley, George J. *The Mineral Industry of Congo (Kinshasa)*. U.S. Geological Survey, 2000.

Consalvo, Mia. "There Is No Magic Circle." *Games and Culture* 4.4 (2009): 408–17.

Delforge, Pierre, and Noah Horowitz. *The Latest-Generation Video Game Consoles: How Much Energy Do They Waste When You're Not Playing?*: Natural Resources Defense Council, 2014.

Discovery News. "India's Poor Risk 'Slow Death' Recycling E-Waste." *Discovery News*. Web. June 20, 2013.

Dizolele, Mvemba Phezo. "Congo-Kinshasa: Coltan Treasure—A Blessing and Curse." *Africa News* 2007, sec. Business Daily.

Dyer-Witheford, Nick, and Greig de Peuter. *Games of Empire: Global Capitalism and Video Games*. Minneapolis: University of Minnesota Press, 2009.

Entertainment Software Association. *2014 Sales, Demographic and Usage Data: Essential Facts About the Computer and Video Game Industry*, 2014.

EPA. "Advanced Micro Devices, Inc." *Pacific Southwest, Region 9: Superfund*. Web. October 17, 2014.

Greenpeace. "Where Does E-Waste End Up?" Web. October 17, 2014.

Grischuk, Walt. *Supply Chain Brutalization: The Handbook for Contract Manufacturing*. Charleston, SC: BookSurge, 2009.

Grossman, Elizabeth. *High Tech Trash: Digital Devices, Hidden Toxics, and Human Health*. Washington, D.C.: Island Press, 2006.

Hayes, Karen, and Richard Burge. *Coltan Mining in the Democratic Republic of Congo: How Tantalum-Using Industries Can Commit to the Reconstruction of the DRC*. Cambridge, UK: Fauna & Flora, 2003.

Hittinger, Eric. *Power Consumption of Video Game Consoles Under Realistic Usage Patterns*, Carnegie Mellon, 2011. Web.

Honeywell. *Hydrofluoric Acid*. 2003. Web.

Horowitz, Noah, et al. *Lowering the Cost of Play: Improving the Energy Efficiency of Video Game Consoles*. Natural Resources Defense Council, 2008. Web.

Huizinga, Johan. *Homo Ludens: A Study of the Play Element in Culture.* London: Routledge & Kegan Paul, 1938/1949.

Intel. "The Conflict Mineral Journey." Web. October 17, 2014.

_____. "Conflict Minerals in Your Daily Digital Life." Web. October 17, 2014.

International Monetary Fund. "World Economic Outlook Database." International Monetary Fund. Web. October 11, 2014.

Jenkins, Henry. "Game Design as Narrative Architecture." Web. 16 March 2009.

Günzel, Stephan, Michael Liebe and Dieter Mersch, eds. *The Magic Circle and the Puzzle Piece.* Philosophy of Computer Games, 2008. Potsdam University Press.

Karshner, Edward. "Thought, Utterance, Power: Toward a Rhetoric of Magic." *Philosophy and Rhetoric* 44.1 (2011): 52–71.

Kline, Stephen, Nick Dyer-Witheford, and Greig de Peuter. *Digital Play: The Interaction of Technology, Culture, and Marketing.* Montreal: McGill-Queen's University Press, 2003.

Konami. *The Adventures of Batman & Robin.* Konami 1994. SNES.

Lee, Victor W., et al. "Debunking the 100x Gpu Vs. Cpu Myth: An Evaluation of Throughput Computing on CPU and GPU." *Proceedings of the 37th Annual International Symposium on Computer Architecture* (2010): 451–60.

Malaby, Thomas M. "Beyond Play: A New Approach to Games." *Games and Culture* 2.2 (2007): 97–113.

Mauss, Marcel. *A General Theory of Magic.* New York: W.W. Norton & Company, Inc., 1902/1972.

Maxwell, Richard, and Toby Miller. "Ecological Ethics and Media Technology." *International Journal of Communication* 2 (2008): 331–53.

McAllister, Lucy. "The Human and Environmental Effects of E-Waste." Population Reference Bureau. Web. October 17, 2014.

Mejia, Robert. "Playing the Crisis: Video Games and the Mobilization of Anxiety and Desire." Dissertation. University of Illinois at Urbana-Champaign, 2012.

Montague, Dena. "Stolen Goods: Coltan and Conflict in the Democratic Republic of Congo." *SAIS Review* 22.1 (2002): 103–18.

NVIDIA. "What Is GPU Computing?" Web. October 18, 2014.

Otto, Bernd-Christian. "Towards Historicizing 'Magic' in Antiquity." *Numen* 60.2–3 (2013): 308–47.

Rosaldo, Michelle Zimbalist. "Metaphors and Folk Classification." *Southwestern Journal of Anthropology* 28.1 (1972): 83–99.

Salen, Katie, and Eric Zimmerman. *Rules of Play: Game Design Fundamentals.* Cambridge, MA: MIT Press, 2004.

Samsung. *Half Year Report*: Samsung, 2014.

_____." Series 7100 Specs." Web. October 17, 2014.

Sayed, Rashid. "Inside the PlayStation 4: Motherboard Components Explained." Gaming Bolt. Web. October 11, 2014.

Shadman, Farhang, and Terrence J. McManus. "Comment on 'the 1.7 Kilogram Microchip: Energy and Material Use in the Production of Semiconductor Devices.'" *Environmental Science & Technology* 38.6 (2004): 1915–15.

Souppouris, Aaron. "Samsung's Marketing Brings Attention to Factory Deaths as Well as Devices." The Verge. Web. October 17, 2014.

Stanfill, Mel. "The Interface as Discourse: The Production of Norms through Web Design." *New Media & Society* (n.d.): 17.

Stratton, Kimberly B. "Imagining Power: Magic, Miracle, and the Social Context of Rabbinic Self-Representation." *Journal of the American Academy of Religion* 73.2 (2005): 361–93.

Tambiah, Stanley J. "The Magical Power of Words." *Man* 3.2 (1968): 175–208.

Tassi, Paul. "EA CEO Doesn't Think Wii U Is a 'Next Gen' Console." *Forbes*. Web. October 14, 2014.

Turner, Victor. "Liminal to Liminoid, in Play, Flow, and Ritual: An Essay in Comparative Symbology." *The Rice University Studies* 60.3 (1974): 53–92.

U.S. Energy Information Administration. "Domestic Production Satisfies 84% of Total U.S. Energy Demand in 2013." Web. October 2, 2014.

_____." Frequently Asked Questions." Web. September 30, 2014.

_____." International Energy Statistics." Web. September 30, 2014.

von Billerbeck, Sarah. "Is the News About Congo's Conflict Minerals Good?" *The Washington Post*. Web. October 17, 2014.

Williams, Eric D., Robert U. Ayres, and Miriam Heller. "The 1.7 Kilogram Microchip: Energy and Material Use in the Production of Semiconductor Devices." *Environmental Science & Technology* 36.24 (2002): 5504–10.

Conclusion
Of Lumpers and Splitters
Matthew Wilhelm Kapell

It is good to have hair-splitters and lumpers. (Those who make many species are the "splitters," and those who make few are the "lumpers.")— Charles Darwin, Letter to Joseph Dalton Hooker, 1857 (Darwin 518)

In a volume with the conceit that the "debate that never happened" in game studies is one that should have occurred it is important to note that the specific idea of such a debate is nothing new. The general framework of deliberation this book addresses is one first described by Charles Darwin in biology but which has occurred in a multitude of disciplines since. In paleontology it is one that fossil hunters describe as a debate between those who, when confronted with a new fossil, either claim it to be something wholly new or categorize it into an existing category. The Lumpers of game studies see digital games as part of a long history of narrative types while the Splitters see them as wholly new and in need of their own, unique category. The purpose of this book is to ponder those categories in the examination of specific games and question how those categories, if more fully debated, might enable a better understanding of digital games, specifically, and games as a general construct of human activity.

The anthropologist Freeman J. Dyson explained this phenomenon more generally, noting, "observers of the philosophical scene may be splitters or lumpers. Splitters like to name many species; lumpers like to name a few" (Dyson 238). And, since the introduction to this volume used anthropology's own fizzled debate on the emic/etic approaches, perhaps anthropology—briefly!—can be used to further explain what this volume hopes to accomplish. The philosopher of anthropology, Benoît Dubreuil, explained the distinction between Lumpers and Splitters by noting that "[t]he former tend to model reality along a few generalized classes or distinctions, whereas the latter have a propensity either to divide models into multiple classes to gain precision or to reject generalizations altogether in favor of particularistic accounts" (Dubreuil 140).

Both Dyson and Dubreuil are concerned with questions of the philosophy of anthropology and both find it worthwhile to examine why, for example, a new hominine fossil might be classified by one paleoanthropologist as part of a long-standing species and why another might offer up a new species name or, even, an entirely new genus. However, what both are not interested in would be the politics of the modern academy and what young scholars must do to assure their career paths. But let us imagine, for just a moment, a young tenure-line anthropologist working in the field. Doing so strongly suggests much for the game studies "debate that never happened."

Finding a new fossil, our fifth-year lecturer or assistant professor of anthropology is confronted with a choice. Her department will be putting her name forward for tenure soon, and we can imagine she has published a few journal articles but is worried about the final decision for tenure. While her department may be fully in support she is aware that her dean, and likely a provost, a president, a rector, chancellor or vice-chancellor, and perhaps even a board of governors will have to vote to offer her tenure—and that none of those people are anthropologists. So, worried about her career she must look at her new discovery from the perspective of what will make it appear important to those outside of her field.

How would we expect her to think about the new fossil she's just uncovered? How would we imagine that tenure decision would take place if, in one application for tenure, it includes the statement, "Has described a member of the well-known species x?" Would a better tenure application include the statement, "Has described a wholly new genus, never before classified by anthropologists?" Which will make her work appear more significant to a rector who has a doctorate in economics or a vice-chancellor with degrees in English?

Importantly, I am not suggesting that such claims are made with conscious intent on the part of this hypothetical young scholar. But, given years of work, intense study, and often significant hardship both socially and financially, it should be unsurprising for a person to think that their discovery is, truly, unique. In anthropology—and biology, and paleontology, and a host of other fields—the Lumper and Splitter debates are well-established and understood. Thus, new proposed species are examined in the literature with great care and conferences often proceed around questions of "is this different enough to warrant a new name?"

Without such debates those claiming their work is wholly new face too little criticism and their ideas become significant only for the fact that no one works to appraise them in the larger context of previous scholarship.

Or, to put this in game studies context, for the purposes of similar decisions for young scholars, who stands the better chance of seeing their work classified as important in academies throughout the world? Will it be those who lump digital games into a category of narratives spanning several thousand years or those who claim their approach, by definition, makes irrelevant all scholarship that preceded it?

There is an ideological, political, and cultural bias—in the academy and outside it—in favor of those who can claim their work to be entirely and radically "new." And since the debate never happened, increasingly, the scholars who classify themselves as ludologists are gaining preeminence. Their claim that their approach is important because digital games are distinct from previous types of human activity nicely fits into cultural models, after all. No one would imagine a marketing slogan such as "Modest Improvements to a Previous Product" but Apple's "Think Different" was an important moment in computer history.

Ludologists are offering their own "Think Different" model of scholarship, and it makes them popular. Until now the only thing allowing narratologists to retain any prominence is the well-understood word "narrative" when compared to the poor neologism "ludic."

Ludic Autopoiesis

In a discussion of the differences between historical narratives and fictional ones Hayden White worried about the historian's desire to force narratives on to events that do not easily fit into narrative structures. Fictional narratives, though, should not experience such difficulties, White thought, writing that in "a discourse having to do with manifestly imaginary events, which are the 'contents' of fictional discourses, the question poses few problems. For why should not imaginary events be represented as 'speaking themselves'?" (White 4). For White, an intellectual historian, narrative could be disruptive to complete historical understanding but, at the same time, it was necessary for the creation of a work that could be both understood and appreciated. While historians, by and large, follow narrative rules in writing histories, a few stand out for refusing to do so—but their prominence is maintained in their position relative and in opposition to more traditionally structured histories.

The most ardent ludologists in game studies do not follow this model. It is central to their claim that a discussion of the ludic shows the study of games to be a form of human activity, as noted in the Introduction, "descended from go or chess" (Jones 4)—making narrative approaches not just misguided, but useless. Thus, their scholarly output does not merely reject traditional narratives and even metanarratives, it treats them as unimportant to the object of study, itself. In other words, ludology offers game studies the opportunity to be a new field that was born from a near vacuum of ideas. This scholarly attempt at autopoiesis is problematic for a number of reasons but the most important is the inherent lack of institutional reflexivity in the claim, itself.

If ludological analysis is indeed a *new* form of analysis jettisoning previous approaches as dysfunctional and ineffectual then, of course, there should be no reason to worry about that previous scholarship. The test of that approach, as detailed briefly in the Introduction here, can be seen in the essentially *ad hominem* statements ludic scholars use in their critiques of narratologists. But it also can be reminiscent of what Alex Callinicos said of similar claims during the cresting of the wave of postmodernity in academe. "Postmodernism," Callinicos wrote, "is precisely the condition in which such metanarratives turn out to have the popularity of popular narratives, to be the source of their own legitimacy, a cluster of language-games merging into the heterogeneity of ordinary discourse" (Callinicos 93–94). The ludic approach is, in my mind as editor (but not in the writing of the various contributors here) exactly that: an approach that offers both its own legitimacy in its claim of originality and its own metanarrative which is, simply, the rejection of narrativity.

Freeman Dyson, in his own discussion of Lumpers and Splitters, offered that Lumpers are, by and large, Platonists and Splitters are simply materialists. "Materialists imagine a world build out of atoms," Dyson notes, while, "Platonists imagine a world built out of ideas" (Dyson 238). In this formulation, and as applied to game studies, narratologists see in games a revision of the long-standing idea of the narrative—of the *story*. But ludologists are convinced they have uncovered a new atom of human analysis, different from all others. Thus, their approach to the study of such games must, itself, be new, significant, and—dare we say this?—uniquely important.

Like our imaginary young paleoanthropologist, above, they have an excellent reason to claim their importance—but recognizing the institutional needs for such claims in an emergent field such as game studies strongly implies that their claims come with a large, inherent bias.

There are a number of fields of inquiry that are littered with such autopoietic claims and there is no space to rifle through that dustbin of intellectual history here. What is worthy of space in a conclusion, however, is the underlying purpose of this volume in assessing the claim that ludology is a new approach to an essentially new human activity in the realm of digital games. Since the claim that it is "new" hinges on the position that other approaches are misguided it should be easy to show ludic scholars detailing how narratology (or any approach) fails in the truth-test of utility. But, as was noted in the Introduction to this volume, such ludic analyses tend to be far more *ad hominem* with claims of *prima facie* obviousness than they are *ideo sequitur* conclusions.

While throwing about various Latin phrases may imply a certain formality to the ludological approach (or my critique of it), however, this is not the intent, here. Too many ludologists work to discredit their non-ludologist colleagues by simple dismissal and spend their time making claims that their conclusions are so obvious as to not be open for debate. This inevitably leads to the position that ludology is both new, and important. So, another Latin phrase—apologies!—may be worthwhile: *ex nihilo nihil fit*: Nothing comes from nothing.

The recognition that, indeed, nothing comes from nothing is the driving force behind this volume. The Introduction details the various contributors' approaches to their individual topics. But each was also asked to examine how each side of the narratology/ludology debate would be of use in their analysis. A reader who has gotten this far will have noted that many of the contributors used the term "ludonarrative" to explain what they were undertaking. This was not a term that I discouraged as the idea behind it is something I've used in my own work in the past (cf. Kapell). But each contributor defined the term in the way that would best serve her or his own contribution here.

But the use of the term implies something else. It implies that the debate that never happened did, in fact, happen—and that the solution has been the term ludonarrative. This is not the intent. Nor is it the conclusion this work wants to imply. Instead, the use of ludonarrative throughout may be seen as a synthesis of the competing ideas of ludic and narrative approaches—but it is not the only synthesis (or the only next step) in such analyses.

But such a synthesis is, this book argues, necessary. In the Introduction and here in the Conclusion I've used anthropology, linguistics and, to a lesser extent, history to note the significance of academic debates for disciplines. In the case of the emic/etic debate of anthropology in the middle of the last century a casual reader may conclude that the fact that those fields still exist bodes well for the lack of coherent debate in games studies. However, the real take-away is not this at all. Each of those disciplines had long histories behind them, and significant institutional momentum (cf. Ross 143–171). Game studies *does not*. If this field is to exist longer it must engage in a process of codification of its central themes and its central theses. Otherwise it will exist for but a brief time, known for the occasional "cult of personality" of a few main thinkers more than those thinkers actual ideas, and find that those doing game studies in the future will be tokens in departments of media, or English, or some humanistic social science.

Game studies, then, has proceeded in far too disorderly a process. Marshall Sahlins, in a critique of postmodernism, noted that it tended to "stifle ... creativity for fear of making some interesting structural connection ... or a comparative generalization" (Sahlins 48). Similarly, the high priests of game studies have done the same to their now junior colleagues—stifled them. If an enterprising graduate student attempts to make a comparative generalization—especially if that comparison is to an old narrative—they will find that their presentation at a conference is scheduled for the final morning and their submitted journal article is rejected. You will find, as a result, some of those papers in this volume—because they deserve to be read and thought about.

Mature fields of inquiry, in other words, welcome competing ideas and work to further their paradigms. Mature disciplines also eventually agree on central themes based on the ideas presented, not the individuals presenting them.

It is, frankly, time for game studies to grow up.

Works Cited

Callinicos, Alex. *Against Postmodernism: A Marxist Critique*. New York: St. Martin's Press, 1991. Print.

Darwin, Charles. "Letter to Joseph Dalton Hooker." *The Life and Letters of Charles Darwin, Vol. 1*. Ed. Francis Darwin. London: Zhingoora Books, 1857. 517–518. Print.

Dubreuil, Benoît. *Human Evolution and the Origins of Hierarchies: The State of Nature*. New York: Cambridge University Press, 2010. Print.

Dyson, Freeman J. *Dreams of Earth and Sky*. New York: New York Review of Books, 2015. Print.

Jones, Steven E. *The Meaning of Video Games: Gaming and Textual Strategies*. New York: Routledge, 2008. Print.

Kapell, Matthew. "Civilization and Its Discontents: American Monomythic Structure as Historical Simulacrum." *Popular Culture Review* 13.2 (2002): 129–136. Print.

Ross, Dorothy. *The Origins of American Social Science*. Cambridge: Cambridge University Press, 1991. Print.

Sahlins, Marshall. *Waiting for Foucault, Still*. Chicago: Prickly Paradigm Press, 2002. Print.

White, Hayden. "The Value of Narrativity in the Representation of Reality." *On Narrative*. Ed. W.J.T. Mitchell. Chicago: University of Chicago Press, 1981. 1–24. Print.

About the Contributors

Tom **Apperley** is a senior lecturer at the University of New South Wales, Australia. He is the author of the open-access print-on-demand book *Gaming Rhythms: Play and Counterplay from the Situated to the Global*. He is working on the Australian Research Council grant "Avatars and Identities" with Justin Clemens and John Frow.

Emily Joy **Bembeneck** earned a Ph.D. in classics from the University of Michigan. She works in the experimental teaching programs at the University of Chicago where she works closely with faculty across disciplines to engage students through the use of technology. Her research interests involve games and narrative, with a focus on the use of characters and choices to create compelling experiences in both video games and literature.

Betsy **Brey** is a doctoral student at the University of Waterloo. She is in the Department of English Language and Literature, working with game studies and narrative. Her research focuses on gameplay mechanics and narrative immersion. She is a member of the editorial staff at FirstPersonScholar.com and researcher at University of Waterloo's Games Institute.

Justin **Clemens** is an associate professor in the School of Culture and Communication at the University of Melbourne. He is working on two Australian Research Council grants: the first, with Tom Apperley and John Frow on "Avatars and Identities"; the second, on contemporary Australian poetry.

Mark **Filipowich** is a curator and co-coordinator of the Blogs of the Round Table feature at *Critical Distance*. He is a master's degree candidate at the University of Western Ontario in information and media studies.

Amy M. **Green** received a Ph.D. in literature from UNLV in 2009. She specialized in Shakespeare and 19th century American literature. Her work has evolved and she focuses on popular culture studies, particularly the narratological study of video games. She is especially interested in the expanding presence of video games as a compelling source of narrative, one that is necessarily participatory by nature.

Matthew Wilhelm **Kapell** has edited or co-edited six books in various areas of media and cultural studies. Holding master's degrees in anthropology and history and a doctorate in American studies, he has taught extensively in the United States and Great Britain in those disciplines, as well as media studies, film studies, and war and society. He has also published on British colonial law in Africa, the 1943 Detroit race riots, human genetics, and the literary history of science fiction.

Lindsey **Joyce** is a Ph.D. student at the University of Texas at Dallas studying interactive narrative systems. She is managing editor at both *Five Out of Ten Magazine* and *Haywire Magazine*, as well as a published games critic. She also co-edited the forthcoming *Videogame Cultures* e-book collection with Inter-Disciplinary Press.

Vince **Locke** is an adjunct English instructor at Delta College, where he teaches composition and literature and often themes his classes around video games. He has presented papers on philosophy and games at the Far West Popular Culture Association conference and maintains a gaming blog called Thought Puzzles and Power Ups.

Robert **Mejia** is an assistant professor of media studies at the State University of New York, Brockport. He received a doctorate from the Institute of Communications Research at the University of Illinois at Urbana-Champaign. He has published on the politics of the digital divide, mobile technologies, gaming, artificial intelligence, and philanthropy.

Alexandra **Orlando** is a Ph.D. student at the University of Waterloo specializing in narratology and game studies. Her research interests include the intersection between film theory and game cinematics, e-sports and East Asian game studies. She is the author of "Hybrid Player-Characters: Ludonarrative Cohesion in *BioShock: Infinite*" (*First Person Scholar*, 2015).

Eric W. **Riddle** has a graduate degree in English and has begun a Ph.D. program in 18th and 19th century British literature. He has academic interests in Gothic literature as well as popular culture studies and has written on film, zombie culture, and video games.

Matthew **Schwager** graduated from Montana State University after completing studies in English literature, music technology, and graphic design. He studies experimental digital media at the University of Waterloo, Ontario. He has published on game studies and has had work featured in *Print* magazine.

Andrew **Wackerfuss** is a historian in the Washington, D.C., area, working during the day for the United States Air Force and at night as an adjunct professor at Georgetown University. His work combines themes of military history, gender history, and political violence, with video games and zombies making increasingly regular interruptions.

Nicholas **Ware** is a Ph.D. student in texts and technology at the University of Central Florida. He has present and upcoming publications on a variety of games studies issues including sex and romance in games, the presentation of sports fandom in games, and the metareality of professional wrestling games. He teaches courses ranging from game history and game design to digital culture and theory.

Matthew **Wysocki** is an associate professor of media studies. He is area co-chair for Game Studies with the Popular Culture Association. His research interests focus on "deviance" and technology, including computer hacker subculture, professional wrestling, and pornography. His research in the area of video games studies looks at issues of control and agency in games.

Index